I TRIED TO RUN REALLY FAR

The physical and emotional battle of running New Zealand's 3000-kilometre Te Araroa Trail.

Lewis Matthews

First edition

Illustrated by @insp.nuggs

NORTH ISLAND

NORTHLAND

PERSEVERANCE

'It doesn't matter how slowly you go so long as you do not stop'
-
Confucius

Day 1 - Baptism of Fire

Cape Reinga's pristine white lighthouse is New Zealand's most northern point. It stands confidently atop the cliffs, protruding out to sea under the beaming sunlight as if it knows its own beauty and significance. Gazing out beyond the famous lighthouse, you can see the lush turquoise Tasman Sea colliding with the deep blue of the Pacific Ocean, like an artist mixing paints to find the perfect blue on their pallet. There's something remarkable about standing on the safe and comfortable edge of land and looking out to the horizon, seeing nothing but the endless ocean until it touches the sky. It's humbling, providing perspective, letting us know how small we really are in this vast universe. Little do I know just how humbling this experience will soon be.

We arrive a little before midday, just like the hundreds of tourists around us. Such a massive event, something that means so much to me, something that I will consider to be one of the most outstanding achievements of my life is about to begin, and only Phil, Jill, and myself know about it. All these beautiful people, in awe of the fantastic scenery, have no idea about the extraordinary event which is about to begin. It's a reminder to me of how little we really know about what's happening in the minds of people around us.

We take a couple of pictures under the yellow sign that points to other famous cities and landmarks worldwide. Although, I must stick out from the crowd, with my bright orange backpack and vibrant blue running shoes. Not the normal tourist attire.

The classic pole points to this adventure's final destination: 'BLUFF - 1452km'. If only! The route I will be running is 3006km. Jez Bragg set the record for running it in 2013, when he completed the trail in an amazing 53 days. I'm hoping to better it, but I know it's a long shot. Jez was a much more experienced ultrarunner. I feel like a novice in comparison.

I look at my watch – 12.00.15.

"Bollocks! Fifteen seconds late already."

This is it, time to go. I'm about to begin the adventure which has consumed my life for the past fourteen months. This epic challenge will take me the length of beautiful but brutal Aotearoa – the land of the long white cloud – New Zealand.

'Ping!' The sound of my hand hitting the pole sends a shiver down my spine. I run off, dodging bemused tourists, to cheers from Jill and Phil.

I'm calm but only just containing my emotions. I glance back at Jill and Phil, who are hugging. It hits home; we're all in this together. They've both taken over two months leave from work and travelled to the other side of the world, leaving their families and friends behind for nine weeks, to support and care for a man who will have to become a feral running machine.

The beginning of the Te Araroa Trail is breathtaking. The route turns off the main tourist path along a fantastic ridgeline with panoramic views – endless sea ahead and gigantic dunes to the south. I gallop along the ridge before cascading down to a small, secluded beach set amongst the cliffs, pure bliss for any runner. Downhill sections have become a strong point in my running repertoire, and the ridgeline and descent are tempting me. I'm torn between going for it, and claiming a new 'Strava' crown, or slowing down, conserving my energy and taking in the vistas. Sense prevails. Foot off the gas. Remember, you have a long way to go.

This is just the beginning of the stunning scenery. Not even 15 minutes in, and I find myself alone on an immaculate beach that you'd struggle to create in your dreams. All I can see is the immense blue sea, the pristine sand and the beaming sun. Idyllic, immaculate as I say, apart from the footsteps of my next victim.

Don't worry; this isn't some murder confession. It's one of the many mental games played by a man who spends nearly all day inside his own head. The objective is to identify any footsteps crossing my path and set that person as the next unlucky 'victim'. With no idea who they are, how far away they might be, or if this person is even walking the trail, they are being hunted. If caught, we might exchange pleasantries or have a little conversation, maybe even eat together. Yet, more often than not, a polite nod will suffice and we both carry on with our day. I met some fantastic people along the way but, sadly, never got to spend much time with anyone. Time flies and, for me at least, this is a race against it.

In my excitement, I call home to Keily, my partner. It's midnight back in Cheddar, but I know she'll be up. Half asleep, she answers but can't get a word in edgeways.

"You should see how amazing this is! Oh wow, look at the cliffs! Bloody hell! Look how steep this is!" I cannot shut up. She just sits and listens, and that's all I need. We've been lucky to travel and enjoy together a lot of what the world has to offer – from a breathtaking road trip in Iceland to our first backpackers' holiday in New Zealand, and train journeys through beautiful Italy. I feel the need to share these early moments of joy with her.

We all need the support of others when facing any big challenge, and I'm lucky to not only have the help of Jill and Phil in a van, but several people ready on the end of the phone, if and when needed, day or night. One significant milestone will be Keily's arrival towards the end of February. That's six weeks away, and we should be well into the South Island by then, but it holds my focus. Be in the South Island when Keily arrives.

From Cape Reinga to 90 Mile Beach, I cross a couple of small bays between ascents up and over the ever-evolving landscape. One moment I'm in the energy-sapping dunes, my feet sinking into the sand with every step. Then, suddenly, I hit a short rocky patch. The colours change to a deep Mars red, otherworldly, before I'm back to charging descents on the soft white sand, between coastal shrubs and bushes. On these stretches, it feels like I'm skiing down to the bays and beaches.

After two hours of this draining but awesome trail running, I descend the boardwalk to the Tiriparepa headland, and the scale of the task ahead of me becomes clear. My eyes track along the coast to the horizon but the end is nowhere in sight. This is going to be a long couple of days. Because of a late start, the original plan to run the full 101 kilometres to Ahipara is out the window. Maybe we can make it to 80km?

Today will be a baptism of fire for all of us. We (me, Jill and Phil) planned for me to complete the first 20 kilometres and meet at the beginning of 90 Mile Beach. So, with confidence, I descend the steps, looking out for our old and battered Toyota HiAce who we've christened 'Gerty.' The name came about when one of us called the van a 'Gert Hog,' in a suitably West Country manner, and this got shortened to Gerty over time. She may have 450,000 kilometres on the clock but I'm sure she'll be waiting.

They're not there.

Now you might be thinking, you've been going for three hours – that's not long – you should be fine. But this is where I'm meant to replenish my supplies, rest if needed and, all importantly, top up the sun cream. With no phone signal, we can't make contact.

Now is not a time for panic. Yes, they're not here, but they can track me when they get a signal, and it's a beach; how hard can I be to find? Little do I know of the trouble Phil and Jill are going through. I decide quickly. Time to crack on. Hopefully once they reach the sand, they'll quickly find me.

Phil and Jill do make it to the access point, but one look at the submerged sandy track stops them abruptly; there's no chance our plucky HiAce can get through. They can't chance it, but they can't drive further south either. It'll take too long. They have to get on, now.

What happens next goes to show the extraordinary nature of some humans. In this case, the magnificent Māori community in the Northlands. Jill explains their situation to the parking attendant and a few phone calls later, a truck arrives. It's the same legend who was managing the Taputaputa campsite we stayed in the previous night. Jill jumps in the front and Phil hops in the back. Phil, who is documenting the trip, is rubbing his hands at the prospect of a fantastic filming opportunity – hanging off the back of a pickup truck, tanking it along the beach at 100 kilometres per hour.

Meanwhile, I'm shuffling along the beach. The unspoilt scenery is a feast for the eyes. The never-ending sea to the right, the ever-shifting patterns in the golden sand at my feet, and the giant dunes rising high to the left. In the distance out at sea I can see an intriguing rock formation, Matapia Island, a small patch of land with a giant hole in the middle. This is your next target. Get your head down, get to that island.

Now as beautiful as this scene is, it soon loses its allure. Whenever I look up to check the island, it never seems to get any closer. Every time I turn back, the cliffs never seem further away. Thirty minutes in, and it feels like I've made no progress. This afternoon will be long, very long and monotonous. Sea, beach, dunes, sun. Sea, beach, dunes, sun.

The unobstructed sun has beamed upon my back for four hours. Fears of dehydration grow. I'm desperate to see the van appear as I need water and respite from the sun. I have to keep faith that Jill and Phil won't let me down this early on. Do I drink all my water now or sip slowly as my thirst increases?

I was in my own exhausted world. When all you have to do is put one foot in front of the other, with no obstacles and nowhere to focus your concentration, you think about anything and everything. From friends and family to business ideas, even how The Villa are getting on. You name it, it probably ran through my thoughts. Often it takes something external to snap me from a daydream.

As I shuffle along in my disoriented state, I'm disrupted by a loud, "Caw". Just another seagull, I guess. It sounds again, but this time sounds like my name. Bemused, I turn to see Jill hanging out the side of a pickup and Phil at the back, camera ready.

It's all too confusing for me to be overly excited. My casual greeting,

"Oh, hi guys," is weirdly understated compared to Jill's manic mix of excitement and relief. She shoves water and a peanut butter and jam sarnie into my chest. Word of advice, the last thing you want to eat in 30-degree heat is a claggy brick of a sandwich. We won't be seeing them again.

The absolute legend who drove the team onto the beach points south to a bluff sticking out from the coast.

"That'll be the next chance for the van to get on," he suggests.

"How far?" I ask, hoping it won't be too much of a trek. None of us have quite mastered the art of judging distance yet.

"Ah, about 6 k's, I reckon," comes the response. He's a local man, he looks wise and full of knowledge, so I trust him.

16 kilometres later, I reach the bluff. He may well be extraordinarily helpful, but his judgement of distance is awful.

This adventure began 14 months ago, in 2018. My first run was a flat five kilometres that left me outrageously stiff and sore for the next two days. However, starting as a novice is a part of the challenge. It's not just about the trail itself, but the months of preparation beforehand and trusting the principles of self-improvement and physical development. The challenge is to go from non-runner to multi-day ultra-runner in less than 18 months. Looking back on this whole process, it's often the training that holds some of the fondest memories. Specifically going from someone at probably their worst level of fitness in their adult life to someone who can knock out a 50-kilometre run straight out their back door on any given Sunday. You have to love the process.

I bring up training because, before starting the Te Araroa, my longest completed run was 50 kilometres, a pretty decent distance but nowhere near what I would need to do. Progress through the early months was smooth and gradual, just as planned. However, with eight weeks to go, injury hit, just as peak week was about to begin. Back-to-back fifty-kilometre days were scheduled, but there I was, feet up on the sofa instead.

The injury occurred when running the roads from Cheddar to Bristol. Most of my training had been out on the Mendip Hills. I was conscious that I might not have enough road running experience to survive the gravel once out in New Zealand, hence running to Bristol. With under five kilometres to go, a grim twinge and catching feeling tweaked in my left knee, bringing me to a painful limp. To this day, I haven't completely figured out what the problem was, but this late into the training, all that I could do was rest, work on what could be worked on, and hope for the best.

I was fortunate to have the help of my friend and physiotherapist, Jo Burkinshaw. She was on hand as physio every week to reduce fatigue, iron out any knots, and help keep me in working condition. In fact, it was her eagle eye that noticed my left leg ran smooth, but my right knee would shoot out ever so slightly upon foot contact. 'BIG TOE' became the cue.

My foot just slapping the ground was causing the issue, possibly a side effect from a football injury the previous December. Thinking, and calling out "BIG TOE," made me concentrate, use my foot with more control, and, therefore, realign it to the correct position. It solved the problem, but with eight weeks to go, the pain reappeared, and there wasn't much time to fix it.

30 kilometres in, and my knee is stiffening up, catching with a severe and sharp shooting pain. How in this world am I going to do this? It's Day 1, and I'm already injured! People have put so much work into this, it cannot end on the first day. You have to keep going.

Run a little, hobble in gut-wrenching pain, walk, then try to run again. This goes on, hour after hour, along with all the worrisome woes. Yet, somehow, I'm still moving, and that's all I need to do. Put one foot in front of the other. Just run for 60 seconds. Just finish this kilometre. Just complete the next 10. Just get to the end of today.

The effects on the mind and body are strange when you test it to previously unexplored levels. Hikers often declare the first five days, along this beach, can be the hardest of the trail. It plays tricks, or more likely, a fatigued mind causes the havoc. A sense of time is lost as you float in a strange never-ending cycle. The ridiculous levels of fatigue, mixed with exhausting pain and blistering heat, lead you to a transcendent state, while still being fully aware of everything going on. Add in the white noise of constantly crashing waves, and a never-nearing horizon, and it's easy to see how your mind can drift to a seemingly parallel dimension.

"The van!" I shout with elation. Oh, the relief. The first thing other than sun, sea, and sand I've seen for hours, snapping me from my dehydrated trance. What a majestic sight it is to see Phil and Jill hurtling down 90 Mile Beach again. I've quickly become attached to this little home on wheels. Who knew it would elicit such strong feelings of safety and security?

Phil swings open the door. Shattered, I dive in to lay flat on my back.

"Shade!" I shout, gratefully. Lying there, staring at the ceiling, my only thought is, how in the hell am I going to do this? Even though these doubts run through my mind, deep down, I know that stopping can never be a consideration. I know I'll keep going, but the severity of the challenge is becoming clear, and we're not even 40 kilometres in.

The beach goes on as the hour's tick by, and the sun begins to fade then disappear, revealing the dark and mysterious beauty of this stunning beach at night. With a full moon, and not a cloud in sight, the sand is illuminated under the pale white light, shining like shards of metal. The sea and sky have a purple hue, with the whites of the crashing waves still visible. It's truly a stunning sight and, looking back, I can fully appreciate it. However, at the time, it was hard to take it all in.

The slight camber has been giving my left side a battering all day. You wouldn't think it would have such an effect but, after 80,000 steps, it takes its toll. My left hip has almost entirely seized, and I can barely run for ten meters at a time. I've broken down to a walk, which in itself is stupidly painful. Only 10 kilometres to go.

The van has pushed on to set up camp and can't return due to the high tide, so it's a solo effort to the end. With the wince of a beaten man across my face, I stumble on to Hukatere Campsite, finding Jill and Phil waiting by torchlight. Such a welcome sight. However, more welcome will be my bed.

There are no two ways about it, today has gone far from what we planned, leaving me battered and bruised. The pain shoots from hip to foot. My feet feel tender to the lightest touch, and my energy has been hit for six. Do you know what the scariest part is? I have to do it all again tomorrow, and the day after, and again after that. How in the world am I going to do this for another 50 odd days? Have I bitten off more than I can chew?

Distance: 70km
Elevation: 781m.

Day 2 – Mind Over Matter

Rule number one: we had decided I must get seven to nine hours of sleep. To run day in and day out for such a long time, proper rest for recovery is vital. If this was a shorter event, of a few days, we could make the sacrifice, but not on a challenge like this. Maybe towards the end, sleep can be spared, but not in the first days and weeks. That means I won't be off and running until about 10 a.m.

Anyway, I'm not the kind of person to jump straight out of bed and get my trainers on. I like to take my time in the morning and set up slowly, so I feel prepared for the day. It's valuable to get my head in the right place, let my body loosen up, and have some social time over a big, hearty breakfast. I love Gerty, but with only enough room in the van for one thing to happen at a time, our process is slow. Luckily, Phil quickly perfects the art of packing up, and we soon have ourselves operating like a well-oiled machine, but everything still takes over an hour.

The morning is further hindered by the severe aches and pains debilitating any movement. Half asleep, I stumble across the campsite for my morning pee and, although anticipating the torment, I almost crumble to the floor in a heap. I can barely walk without shards of pain shooting from my feet to my forehead. *How on earth am I going to run?*

The beach's last 30 kilometres lay ahead. Sounds like a nice easy stretch, right? But guess what? It looks exactly the same as yesterday. There's no hope of setting off at my usual pace so a walk it has to be, or should I say a stumble, to try and loosen up. My mind is bewildered at the prospect of making it to the end of the beach, let alone Kaitai or beyond.

Somehow the stumbling works and, through grit, pain, and determination, I eventually break into something resembling a slight jog. This remains my pace, with intermittent recovery walks, until finally, in a fatigued blur, the end of the bastard beach is in sight.

Fortunately, I'm joined by the lovely Cheryl for the last five kilometres. She's on a family holiday. Apparently, a Kiwi's idea of a holiday includes chucking your kid on a bodyboard, getting them to hold onto a rope attached to the back of your car, and proceeding to tank it up and down a beach until said child falls off. Character building, right?

Cheryl and her husband Dave are experienced ultra-runners who live down in Nelson on the South Island, with the beautiful but brutal Richmond Ranges in their back garden – perfect for their hobby of choice. What a difference it makes to have some company, and experienced running company at that. Miraculously, the charms of conversation distract me, my pace picks up, and the pain all but disappears.

My brain and body are being tricked again. The moment I'm out of my own head and not thinking about my poor feet and hips, the pain disappears. It's evidence of how powerful the mind can be.

It reminds me of a training day with Danny the Paratrooper from back home. I had joined Danny and his team on a trip to the Brecon Beacons, and he duly obliged. I was nervous. It was likely to be a real test of my fitness, both physically and mentally. *These guys will be fit*, I thought, *but more than that, they will have grit.*

I placed myself in the middle of the pack as we began our ascent. The Brecons aren't massive, but they are an excellent place for training – with steep climbs and ranging ridgelines. It soon became apparent to me that a few of the lads were blowing hard. One by one, I picked them off, keeping my head down, marching on towards our first peak. *Did they know something I didn't?*

When we had all finally ascended Pen Y Fan, Brecon's highest peak, Danny proceeded to take five kilograms of weight out of one trooper's bag and shove it straight in mine. He turned to the trooper,

"That isn't to speed you up. It's to slow him down!" he stated, pointing at me. A wave of confidence swept over me. Not only could I hang with these boys but push on ahead. This was back in August

2019 with six months to go before my trip. It's safe to say I was feeling fit, and my mind was strong.

Back in the present, the never-ending, hip-wrenching, quad-blasting, blister-inducing, relentless bitch of a beach finally comes to an end. Surely an achievement worth celebrating? But this is only the beginning, no time for that.

I remember that feeling of confidence from back on the Brecons. *Maybe I can push through the physical pain, after all.*

An afternoon break in the shade is a welcome relief from the unforgiving heat but, like any moment of pleasure out here, it doesn't last long. With the sun descending, I must press on. To stick to my predetermined daily average, I need to cover another 30 kilometres and, if I thought it was hot on the beach, as soon as I move inland away from the sea breeze, it goes to the next level. The beaming sun bounces back off the tarmac, roasting me from all angles, and sweat drips from every pore. *That's probably a good sign. If you're not sweating, you wouldn't be taking on enough water and minerals. Good job, Lewis,* I quietly congratulate myself.

Now, you'd think flat roads leading inland would be the perfect opportunity to gain some speed and distance. I feel so too, but how wrong I am. Heat, empty legs, and severe tiredness are a constant battle. But is it? Personally, I think it's more the monotony. Off-road, there's so much to concentrate on and occupy my mind, whereas hitting the tarmac is exceptionally repetitive. You don't really need to watch your step, and it often feels like you're getting nowhere.

From Ahipara, at the end of 90 Mile Beach, it's a pleasant 15 kilometres through quaint fruit farms to Kaitaia. On a typical day at home, 15 kilometres would take a gentle 90 minutes. Out here, on Day 2, it takes nearly two hours, and I just cannot see how my body will manage another 15 kilometres on top. I feel cooked.

I manage to stumble an extra five out of town, but soon ring Phil and Jill to call it a day. It's 8 p.m., 50 kilometres done. There's still another hour or so of sunlight, but I've simply had enough. Every step sends pain straight to my hip and, whenever I push off, my knee screams and complains.

Should I have carried on?

You have to be a harsh critic of yourself when trying to perform at an intense level. Yes, praise yourself when it's warranted, but also acknowledge when you've fallen short. That's the skill of self-analysis. Sometimes we hide or put the blinkers on because we don't want to deal with it, but we can't shy away from these flaws if they are going to hold us back.

To answer the question, yes, my body could have carried on but, at that moment, the level of fatigue and pain was new. It overwhelmed me. I'd never experienced anything like it. It just goes to show how my inexperience was affecting me.

Distance: 50km
Elevation: 267m.

Day 3 – Who am I kidding? I Can't Do This

It's 8 a.m. in the depressing scene of Kaitaia's McDonald's. My body is in pieces. I've never felt anything like it. My left hip radiates pain, and just walking brings a screaming agony from my feet through my legs. My body is not in a good place, and neither is my mind.

There's a little light on this darkest of mornings. It's my nephew's third birthday, and I'm calling him. There's Ned's cute face on the other end, not a clue what is really going on, shouting,

"Go Lewy, go!" It brings a lump to my throat.

How are we going to do this? We're all thinking it. Phil and Jill are looking at me, both feeling sympathy but also thinking, *Shit! Have we bitten off more than we can chew?*

"Lewis, how old is Ned?" asks Jill.

That's it, I'm broken. With my hood over my head and hands over my eyes, I sob. It's the morning of Day 3, and it starts with tears in the middle of a fast-food restaurant.

At this point you might reasonably be thinking, *Why in the world would someone put themself through this?* I think it's high time I explained. Throughout my life I've been inspired by thrilling adventure stories – from Sir Ranulph Fiennes to Ed Stafford, and further back to Shackleton and Scott – and a desire for my own adventure has long burned inside.

The achievements of these great people are inspiring, and what gives me the belief that I, too, can do something unique, is that they are, or were, precisely that – people – just like you and me. If they could do it, what's stopping me? Now, what I'm attempting is nothing like circumnavigating the earth, or being marooned alone on a desert island, but it is pretty damned hard.

On top of that, as a teenager I promised myself I would spend my twenties seeing as much of this beautiful planet as possible, and I like to think I've seen my fair share. Still, New Zealand has stayed at the forefront of my mind ever since my first visit, when I'd heard stories of this country-length walking trail.

In addition to these inspirations and travelling experiences, I had a childhood dominated by sport. My parents were a great, positive influence – almost daring me to live life on my own terms, win or lose. They've always been in full support of a mind that dares to dream, and sometimes thinks a little laterally to societal norms.

The final icing on the cake was watching Ross Edgley succeed in becoming the first man to swim around Great Britain. His achievements lit the paper for me to begin putting the Run Te Araroa adventure together. Hopefully you can see how this story has come to be.

So, now I find myself here in the middle of McDonald's, questioning my own dreams and judgement. *What the hell have I got myself into?*

After a quite frankly horrible 20 minutes, and an even worse coffee, it's time to hit the road. Strangely enough, it's as easy as that to get going. If I'm going to question myself, and deliberate on my ability, we might as well be on the move while I do so.

Once I've finished my sobbing and wiped away the tears, we look at one another. I apologise and give the nod. Logic has overcome emotion. We crack on with *Go Lewy go,* ringing in my ears. If I've learned one thing from the adventures that inspired me so much, it's that physical pain can be excruciating, but the most prominent challenges will be in my mind. *You must keep moving.*

Leaving from last night's pick-up point, I turn off State Highway 1 down the gravel roads to the entrance of Raetea Forest. I hadn't realised the problem gravel roads will soon become.

Now, I love my Vivobarefoot shoes. You get to feel everything, but that is a blessing and a curse. After wearing them all through training, my foot strike is a thing of beauty, biomechanically sound due to laboured hours building impeccable technique. Yet, the one place they fall short is on the bastard gravel. With my feet so tender, each step is filled with pain, as the small stones penetrate my soles. It's great to get feedback straight to your feet but, after more than 150,000 steps in two days, it can be a little too much, leading me to play hopscotch – trying to find elusive smooth spots.

The nasty gravel continues between the luscious fruit farms, heading towards the jungle-like Raetea Forest. The trail passes through the quaint Takahu, a lovely little village that looks as though it hasn't changed in 50 years, much like the next stretch of road. I'm navigating potholes, an ever-narrowing width and a precarious drop to the left. *Where the hell is the van? There is no way it can hack this kind of surface.*

Despite my throbbing feet, I still revel in this delightfully peaceful, rural setting. The sun shines high in a cloudless sky, illuminating the luscious jungle hills unfolding ahead. New Zealand's famous kauri trees have stood in this forest for over one thousand years. Sadly, the kauri is dying out due to the introduction of non-indigenous plants and animals, and some ignorant deforestation in the past. There's a vast conservation effort underway to protect these magnificent trees, and I dearly hope they succeed. I'm no tree hugger, but I do get a sense of connection when out in the wild, amongst giants that have stood for longer than we can even comprehend. They seem wise, full of knowledge and stories of times gone by.

"How the bloody hell did you get up here?" I exclaim in amazement whilst Phil and Jill stand proudly next to the van.

"A little bit of luck – a lot of skill," Phil tells me smugly. I've just run up this horrible winding track, barely wider than the van itself, with certain death dropping off to the left, yet here they stand. As much as this is an adventure for me, it's quickly turning into a Top Gear challenge for them. We have all developed a love for the van. She's definitely the fourth member of our crew. One day I will have my own version of the beautiful Gert Hog.

You might be wondering who Jill and Phil are and how they became a part of the team.

Jill is a personal training client of mine, but out here she's the road manager, chef, physio and a whole host of other jobs. She's a strong and principled woman, the kind of person who will tell it to you straight but is always there to confide in when you need it most. Yet, if you need a laugh, she often finds herself in an inappropriate fit of giggles in the worst moment possible. Also, how many sixty something grandmas do you know that can deadlift over 100 kilograms? Strong in mind and body – that's Jill. She's old enough to be my mother, but she's the first person I'll ask to accompany me on any adventure.

Then we have Phil, who was recommended to me in a chance conversation at the barbers, of all places. He was in after the first meeting, raring to get out and film this mad adventure. Phil's a creative and kind soul, a gentle giant. He throws himself into the deep end but you wouldn't ever think he can't swim, with his unflappable demeanour. He's calm, considered and a genuine listener. When he's so immersed in his craft, it becomes the centre of his focus, and organisation then seems to elude him, yet he somehow manages to come through with the goods. Phil provides the calm counterbalance to Jill's urgency.

We might be a mixed bag, but that's what it will take to make this happen. We need all types of qualities and characteristics but, most importantly, we all need to get along and look after one another – and we do.

So, 'they' say, *If you can get through the first two forests, then you can tackle anything the Te Araroa throws at you.* Assuming that 'they' are previous hikers, well-experienced in tackling this trail, I can hope to take their word for it. This is to be no picnic. Although peaceful and pretty to gaze at, once in, it will be a steep, dense and humid bush, sapping any energy and drenching me from head to toe in my own steaming sweat.

Initially, the path is decent, and the gradient gentle, a cushty start. However, this isn't all going to be plain sailing, not if the trail notes are anything to go by. Ahead lies an 18-kilometre route that should, supposedly, take a hiker nine and a half hours and, as it's after midday, I don't have nine and a half hours left to play with. *Five hours, Lewis. You can do 18 k's in five hours. Now come on.*

The challenge is set, the pack is kept light, and I set off at pace, until *Bam!* A hill. In New Zealand, if there's a hill, no matter how steep or how long it is, the path always goes in the straightest direction possible – point A to point B by the most direct route. I was no longer running but more scrambling and rock climbing.

This is precisely what I've trained for – these conditions, this terrain. Suddenly an energy, an air of confidence washes over me, snapping me into driven action. The incredible and debilitating pains of the past two days again disappear, and my overwhelmed, fatigued brain clears. I fly up this hill. Step after step is more lunge after lunge. Lactic acid builds and burns, and my legs throb with every heartbeat, but I'm a man possessed. Put me on a flat, tarmacked road and I struggle. Put me in front of the most horrible, thick and steep native bush, and I absolutely smash it. *I feel amazing.*

This uphill blitz, thrashing through thick brush and scaling giant root walls, continues for two and a half hours until, reaching the summit, I get my first real glimpse of the scale and the vastness of this mad adventure. From here, the views cascade in all directions, displaying bush-coated hills as far as I can see. A startling moment. The size of my task really hits home.

An unidentified feeling stirs in the back of my mind, but I can't put my finger on what it is. Am I scared? Am I in awe? There's no time to deliberate. *You have to be out of here in less than five hours. Keep moving.*

The descent is far quicker than the ascent, but I'm certainly not hurtling. When the track is runnable, it's incredibly technical. You can't just open your legs and go for it. You have to concentrate on every single foot placement. With roots and rocks everywhere, one misstep and it could mean adventure over. I am consumed by concentration, entering a strange state. My eyes track a few steps ahead, recognising viable foot placements. I'm not even thinking of the steps I'm taking as I take them.

Ninety minutes into this gnarly descent, with a couple of kilometres to go, my attention is broken by the sight of Phil nestled in the bushes. *Am I supposed to stop and have a chat? Should I say something? Am I supposed to carry on so he can get a brilliant action shot?* His furious arm-waving makes it clear it's the latter.

The trail breaks onto the lower bush and farmland and, with it, an intense sense of relief as the world opens back up. The thick forest had enclosed me beneath its canopy but, as I break out, the whole world seems to expand. The air feels fresh again in these open and rural spaces. How rural? Well, it's a strange sight to see the skull of a cow resting on the footpath at your feet, just another sign of how far off the beaten track I am. The only people who come through here are hikers and the landowner. No need to remove the ungainly and massive skull.

After gingerly manoeuvring past some live cows – yes, I'm scared of cows – and a farmhouse guarded by psychotic hounds, I'm relieved to see the van. This has to be my best output on a section so far, smashing our estimate by an hour.

There's no time to hang around. After a short break, it's time to hit the road. Another 20km of tarmac and gravel until the next forest. The sun is baking in the late afternoon, just as it has been since we left Cape Reinga. However, I've learnt my lesson, and I lather on sun cream. My neck is blistered and burnt, and occasionally warm liquid drips down my neck as the blister juice dribbles out. Nice!

From my first few steps, it's clear that the odds of reaching the next forest are slim. All energy and exuberance have been spent through Raetea. The pain reappears, and I can barely break into a jog for more than 200 meters. Run for 200, walk for 100, that is all I can manage. Any slight gradient on the road reduces me to a power walk. The gravel and the sun are winning.

Painstakingly, I reach Mangamuka at around 7 p.m. and call it a day. Although the day has had my favourite section in it, it was sandwiched by two of my worst performances, leaving me having completed only 42 kilometres. I should have carried on, but it was shocking just how fatigued I really was. Shocking because it was all so new.

My total distance each day is dropping fast. 60 kilometres is the required average, not falling 20 short. This is ridiculous. I need to step it up, but I don't know how I can give any more.

Each evening Jill and Phil pick out a spot for us to stay the night. Unfortunately, you can't just pitch up wherever you like, but there are freedom campsites. Whenever we can, we will find one and settle in. If only paid sites are at our disposal, Jill goes in to explain our charitable adventure and haggle on price.

Tonight, we settle at the most idyllic spot. We're deep in Mangamuka Gorge beside a beautiful little stream, with the dense bush ascending up and away from either side, and our superb little campervan sits in the centre. After a wash in the stream, and my evening treat of alcohol-free beer, we get stuck into barbecued steak and call it a night. It's been such a draining day. We'll just take tomorrow as it comes, and hope I can get through it.

Distance: 43km
Elevation: 1348m.

Day 4 – Discipline Trumps Motivation

Although last night was relaxing, I was kept awake with exhausting pain. I've been routinely taking two lots of painkillers every four hours and, whenever they can, Jill and Phil both act as physio. Fortunately, they've turned out to be pretty handy – with a little direction they're doing a great job, despite it often leaving me writhing in excruciating agony.

Still, it's better than the constant pain I still have down my whole left side. The left leg quadriceps is particularly bad due to the camber – and probably from compensating for the injured knee. My feet! How can I not mention my feet? After days of constant duress, all the muscles and tendons on the bottom are incredibly tender. A thumb to the sole of a foot is agony. These pains have been around since halfway through Day 1. How long will they go on for? Will they get better or worse? There's one way to find out.

Bloody gravel roads! They are becoming the bane of my life. Slowly, and I mean slowly, I work my way up the gentle gradient from Mangamuka to the next forest.

In truth, I'm struggling to get my head into gear, and both Phil and Jill know it. Initially, we decided they'd only intervene when I needed it most. Constant whooping and hollering 'you can do this', would quickly lose value. For me, discipline trumps motivation. Motivation might be the kindling that gets the fire going, but it's the discipline that keeps it roaring. Therefore, we prioritised thoughtful self-discipline and sparing interventions from Jill or Phil when required. The 'you can do it' conversation won't cut it either. Straight up truth – no fluff.

This was based on the method I worked on with sports psychologist, Marcus Nel. Firstly, I give myself a rating from 'one' to 'ten' on my rate of perceived arousal (RPA); with 'one' being extremely low, feeling distraught and on the verge of quitting, and 'ten' being elated, ecstatic, and on top of the world. We decided optimal performance was operating at 'five' or 'six'. This would mean feeling nondescript, leaning towards content. I can perform at a 'four' or a 'three' if I have to, but any lower and we agreed I would need to sort my thoughts and mental state out before continuing. If I'm above a 'seven,' I was to enjoy the moment but bring myself back down to earth before carrying on.

Right now, I'm clearly struggling, putting myself at a 'two', and it's mostly because I'm remarkably pissed off. My legs just will not work, and every step is painfully energy-sapping. Why the lack of energy? I've been struggling to eat through these first three days, as you can tell by looking at me. I've consumed nowhere near enough calories. My face reflects this. My cheeks have sunk to the bone, and my features look increasingly skeletal. We need to find a way for me to consume more calories and fast.

Cue Jill. She jumps out of the van and walks with me for a good 20 minutes, just talking at me as I keep my head down, staring at the floor, unable to speak for fear of bursting into tears. She speaks at me and gives me the truth – no fluff, no bullshit – precisely what is needed. She reminds me that I decided to do this, I want to know what this feels like, and it's me who has committed the last 14 months of my life to it, not anyone else.

"What did you expect?" Jill asks, letting me know how this is going to go.

She finishes up by building back my confidence, reminding me that what I've managed to do so far is extraordinary and, importantly, that she believes in me. She gives me the truth, builds me back up, and tells me to get on with it. Precisely what I need, but she hates doing it. She only told me how hard she found this after the adventure was over.

With renewed determination, we plough on along another gravel road, winding our way to the next forest. Run, walk, run, walk, do whatever can be done to keep moving. After the talking to from Jill, I tell myself, *You will not quit at any point.* I'd sooner fall short of the mark, having given it my all, than stop and leave. I want to finish this journey with my head held high, confident in my conduct and maintaining my character throughout.

As we range further along the 'road', it disintegrates into a dirt track, but still, the van ploughs on. After fording a couple of streams, we feel it may be time for the van to stop. When Jill and Phil turn back, they have a lucky escape making it back through. Otherwise, it would have been a long walk back to town for one of them. By 'town', I mean one dairy and a radio station. A dairy is the Kiwi name for a corner shop.

Here I go, into Forest Number 2 – Omahuta Forest. Almost instantly, my mood lifts as I run down the first hill into the belly of the beast. I cross paths with a lovely lady named Gertrude, an older Austrian woman who's hiking her way down to Auckland. Now let me tell you, she is a mighty impressive lady. She must be in her late 60's but is still out here getting it done, even with a massive backpack holding everything she needs almost twice over.

"Where are you hoping to stay tonight?" I ask.

"Wherever I am at 6 p.m. I will pitch my tent. I have my house on my back," she says simply.

The contrast between us couldn't be more evident. Here I am, a young man trying to race my way through the trail as quickly as possible, and there she is older, far more experienced and taking her time to take it all in – a reminder for me to do a bit of the same.

The trail descends to the stream floating through the centre of this gorgeous forest. Although I'm looking around for one of the trail's orange route markers, there aren't any to be seen. *Have I made a mistake?* Checking the map reveals the stream is the path. I can let go of the frustration and enjoy the perfect scenery. It's so peaceful amongst the thick bush – stunning trees, exotic birdsong, and sun glistening off the water. For the first time in days, I feel calm whilst on the move.

It's becoming more apparent that these fleeting moments of tranquillity are precisely that – rare and short-lived. Before I know it, I leave behind the gentle stream for a thrilling high bank track. I'm running a single trail, hopping fallen trees, jumping deep gullies and teetering high above the flowing river below. There's only one option in my mind – attack.

With the danger of a deathly ten-metre drop ever present to my left, concentration is intense, and my adrenaline pumps. The more trees I jump and gaps I leap, the more the excitement grows and, with it, my confidence. I'm flying along, and nothing is going to stop me. It seems the forests are where I come alive.

Of course, there are a few treacherous moments, the odd slip underfoot or hopeful leap but, with each successful step, I just want more. I don't want it end. Admittedly I should probably slow down, it's Day 4, and there are thousands of kilometres to go. The last thing we need is an injury. However, I also need to revel in these fleeting moments of exhilaration when I can.

I'm in the zone, experiencing the elusive runners' high. Yet, it only takes a split second to bring everything to a crashing halt. I jump a fallen tree, spotting the dreaded palm leaf on the other side all too late. I can see it, but there's nothing I can do. All I can do is hope to catch some grip. I land, I slip, and I'm now falling headfirst towards jagged boulders thirty feet below.

Thoughts of imminent death really do flash through my mind. I'm falling fast, but time has slowed down. Perhaps that's the adrenaline. I'm fully aware that if I do not grab hold of something, this will be it.

My brain is strangely calm, working with clarity to find a solution – urgently. Basic survival instincts have kicked in. Yet, with each millisecond passing, panic fights composure.

My hands scramble for anything. One root missed and then another.

"Shit Shit Shit!" I grab, I miss. I grab again. I continue falling but now not so calm. I'm bracing for impact.

"No, no, no!" *Is this it?*

My body tightens, eyes close, I hold my breath so tight. *Please no! Just grab anything!* I clasp at another root, praying it sticks. This is my last hope.

'Bam!' like a parachute snapping the air, I'm flipped the right way up, barely keeping a grip with my left hand, hanging just a few

metres above sharp, protruding rocks. Silence, but for my own thoughts. *You lucky bastard!*

The scale of the fall reveals itself on the climb back to the top. If I hadn't managed to grab that root, there weren't many to grasp after it. Lying on the trail, covered in dust and dirt, bruised and scratched all over, I cannot believe my stupidity. I cannot believe my luck. Lesson learnt: Don't step on dead palm leaves – and slow down!

Of course, I'm not going to tell anyone about this little trip. Firstly, I have to play it down – *this cannot affect me*. Secondly, I don't want to scare anyone. *They don't need to know about this.*

The trail continues from Omahuta Forest through Puketi Forest along the Pukatea Ridge. Ascending the ridgeline isn't too much trouble, along the well-maintained path, such a treat after the previously tumultuous terrains. However, despite this respite, I'm not out of the woods yet. Well, I am literally but, figuratively, it's a different story.

I'm welcomed by blistering heat, and any serenity gained is lost in an instant. With no clouds in the sky, and the sun at its peak, the heat is relentless, bouncing back off the 4x4 track. Not a patch of shade and, to make matters worse, my water supplies have run dry. Dehydration hits me. I stumble, now feeling stupidly weak, sick to my stomach and scarily dizzy, suddenly dangerously close to collapsing. *You can't keep this one quiet. You need help.*

With my panic increasing and mind scrambled, I continue but don't know if I can make the last kilometre. Everything has flipped so quickly, again. Luckily, I have one beautiful bar of signal and the whereabouts to make a hopeful call to Phil and Jill. They're on their way, water the priority. Without a phone signal, things could've quickly gone south. *Better planning required. Another lesson in quick succession.*

Strangely, despite nearly falling to a rocky death and collapsing from dehydration, I'm wearing a wry grin; I feel a little spark. I've gone to a dark place and found the mental fortitude to keep going. *Maybe I do have what it takes. Perhaps I can pull this off.* Despite my own naivety.

It's been an excellent start to the afternoon, already completing 36 kilometres. The last 20 to Kerikeri see a change in scenery, leaving behind the thick forest for the golden farms and rural back roads. Time is on my side and the pressure off. It's still tough to make a decent pace, but our destination is never too far out of reach. 56 kilometres complete.

The day's work leaves me with a sense of relief and a hint of self-belief. For once, we'd achieved the desired target. The past three days, we've fallen short of the mark, but not today. *Don't get ahead of yourself, but perhaps you're finding your feet. Just keep moving.*

Distance: 53km
Elevation: 1420m.

Day 5 – Time Waits for No One

As experienced over the last two days, the Te Araroa is full of contrast. Just yesterday the trail ran through wild forests, across golden farms, and then into civilisation at Kerikeri. Today promises to be no different.

It's a gentle run through town before heading southeast to Paihia, via Waitangi Forest. Instead of wise old Kauris and Towais tangling the land, Waitangi is full of young Pines shooting up in regimented fashion – for commercial use. Although not as rugged or natural as the previous sections, it's still satisfying to run between the towering giants. Only one thing upsets the apple cart – the logging tracks are peppered with my favourite gravel.

I'm hoping to run ten kilometres per hour with ease, just like during training, but that was when I was fresh. This is never going to be the case after days of torturous scrambling. It's just hard to come to terms with running six or seven kilometres per hour.

Now we all have to remember that this is a trail for hiking. What I'm attempting isn't really in sync with the true nature of the Te Araroa. I have to recognise that and embrace it when I can. Along the trail, there are several sections where you have to take to water and, often in these sections, there are uncontrollables to contend with.

Today, I'm required to get from Pahia across the bay to Waikare. The popular mode of transport is by kayak. One problem. The tide is currently on its way out, and you need an incoming tide to kayak this route. We have a decision to make. Just skipping the section and driving around, never to return again, is out of the question. We are left with two choices: stop for the day in Paihia and wait until the next morning's tide or, go around to Waikare, continue along the trail, return to kayak the following day, and then back to where we finished the previous night. We choose the latter.

Already at this early stage, we're feeling the pressure of our pre-booked flights home. We can't afford any waiting around, especially for a whole day in Paihia. We only have 58 days to complete the trail. Time waits for no one. Perhaps an open return would have been a better idea.

The drive to Waikare is my first experience of what Phil and Jill have to deal with daily. It's like a bloody rollercoaster. Sharp turns, steep cambers, dodging other cars coming straight at us – all on yet another gravel road. I don't know whether it's Phil's driving, or being sat in the back, but it feels like we're in the New Zealand Rally Championship. In front my two teammates sit impassively, as cool as cucumbers. It's just another day and another road to them.

With the sun seemingly getting hotter each day, it's a laboured run inland, away from the cool sea breeze. Crossing the first bridge gives cause for concern. *Am I seeing things? Am I dehydrated again?* Three, let's say, hefty blokes floating in the gentle stream below – tunes blaring and barbecue raging – the epitome of relaxed Kiwi style. There they are, cooling off and completely chilled, compared to the sweaty, sunburnt and frantic mess running overhead. I bet they took one look up and thought, *Nah, I'm good right here.*

Snaking upriver, more families are relaxing in this idyllic setting. It seems like a great holiday destination, but it's probably where they live. If anything, it's quite a poor part of the country, but they all seem more than happy. What more do you need? Living off the land with your family, in paradise, seems like a good deal to me.

It gets weird. The further inland the trail goes, the stranger things become. There are old, beat-up cars, ten to fifteen of them ditched and torched. *What the hell are they doing up here? Just ignore it.* The road continues, but now through the river. That's right, the 'road' goes through the river – no bridge or anything – just straight through to where, on the other side, it becomes a rutted, two-track dirt path. Checking the map, it says there's a road here. *Absolutely no chance.*

There are more old cars that look like they haven't moved for years, a home that looks like it hasn't been occupied in decades, and tat everywhere – as if the previous owner was a hoarder. Maybe I'm way off, and someone does live here. It all feels a little like a horror movie, with me the character to be murdered in the opening scene.

Ah, the old orange triangle. This one pointing past the house in the general direction of 'over there somewhere.' I have no idea where to go. That's how these signs sometimes feel, pointlessly pointing in no real direction. Or is it just me not seeing what's supposedly right in front of my eyes? That's often the case too.

The map notes say to take the Waikare Māori Roadway, but checking the GPS mirrors exactly what I'm thinking. *I'm standing directly on the highlighted trail line. Where's this roadway? There hasn't been a 'road' since crossing the river.*

Disoriented and confused, the next hour is spent trying to find some sort of path. I continue hacking my way in the general direction of the trail map for another 30 minutes. Sometimes a rogue route looks like the trail, but sure enough, it leads me straight to another dead end. Again and again, this happens, causing my blood to boil and mouth to spit scathing swear words at every mistake. But eventually, through blind luck and persistence, an orange arrow comes into view, hanging on a tree straight over the river, pointing right.

"Screw it, just walk in the stream," I shout to myself. I don't see another marker for an age, but the little blue circle on the screen lets me know I'm always near the map line, a win for technology. Occasionally, when the river is too deep, I hop out and cut across the bends but, other than that, it's quite easy-going. *How in the world is this a roadway?*

Later I realise that a Māori Roadway isn't always a road, it's just an access to Māori land. When I read them, the trail notes even say, 'from here, walk four kilometres upstream.' At least I went the right way.

Five kilometres upstream, I arrive at a deep corner. Climbing right isn't an option as the bank is now a small cliff. Neither is wading through. It gets far too deep way too quickly and there is also the pleasant surprise of a dead pig floating in the river. After five minutes of wondering what to do and a failed attempt to climb the bank, common sense kicks in and I backtrack and, of course, the missed trail is as clear as day. Let's just say it's a learning process.

I stomp up a path that's being maintained and find some young workers in a clearing at the top, having a well-deserved break, I'm sure. They'd been driven up from Auckland at 4 a.m., dropped in by a 4x4, and are now waiting for their ride back out and all the way home, only to do the same thing tomorrow and the next day. *That is one hell of a commute to work.*

Their route out of here is the same as mine, the Papakauri Track. However, they'll be bumping along in their truck, and I'll be grinding it out on foot. Watching them race past and disappear in a matter of seconds is demoralising, to say the least. They offer a lift. But no, I must persevere.

Now into the early evening and free from the depths of Russell Forest, the trail continues along the roads, through more steep coastal farmland to Oakura. With a drive all the way back to Paihia, and an early start for the sea kayak, we can't leave it too late to finish up.

Sitting in the back of the van, I do my best to hide another wry smile. *Yeh, you messed up today, but you know what? You didn't stop. You figured it out and kept pushing forward, just like yesterday.*

Distance: 50km
Elevation: 1043m.

Day 6 – Cows and Other Dangers

If you want a partner to kayak across a bay, how about a Kiwi serving in the military, hiking the trail himself, with a background in sea kayaking? Dave often spends his weekends going out for a four, five, even six-hour kayak trip around Nelson and Abel Tasman. I couldn't have picked a better person.

We set off around 8 a.m. the boys at Bay Beach Hire think it will take us around three hours to get over to Waikare. *Challenge accepted.* Little do they know of the secret weapon we have in Dave. We're told that we'll run out of phone signal two-thirds of the way across, so we are to send a message when halfway across, at Marriot Island. A phone call to Jill and she almost drops her coffee. I imagine the two of them about to finally sit down and relax for the first time in days, only for my name to flash up on their phones.

"Shit! Phil, we gotta go. They're almost there!" I hear her scream.

We reach Waikare in a little over two hours, arriving ten minutes before the van. A job well done. My turn to be smug. It must be said, without Dave, it would've taken me a good three hours if not more. The man is an absolute beast. My arms felt like they might fall off after an hour as the lactic acid burned deep. Luckily, I've already had some practice dealing with pain over the last five days. On the plus side, it was nice to give the legs a rest.

Despite blisters and burns, it was a beautiful journey – New Zealand delivering another picture postcard panorama. Crystal clear water reflected the bright blue sky. Boats bobbed in picturesque harbours, and the deep green forested islands provided a perfect backdrop to this painter's dream. It was a pleasure to experience this all with a top bloke and great man. Dave, thank you.

Leaving Dave behind with the kayaks, we rush off to last night's endpoint. The rest of the day's trail consists of a little main road running and cutting through coastal farms and forests, nothing too steep and nothing too high. The only challenge is my aching body.

It's Day 6 and, in all honesty, my body feels no better than it did after Day 1. Yet, each day, I find enough within me to keep moving. Dare I say I'm getting into a bit of a rhythm. This is life now. It's as simple as that.

The afternoon looks set to be a dull affair across the sloping farms. Breaking from the cover of a small forest, I ascend up a steep farm hill, only to reach its peak and discover a herd of cows. We are soon in a standoff. *Be brave; they're harmless. Just walk towards them, and make sure they can see and hear you.* I'm pretty sure that's the advice I'd once been given.

As I'm from Somerset, you'd assume I'd see cows as just part of the scenery. But the truth is they scare the hell out of me. They are giant bovine beasts, some with large, dangerous horns. At any moment they could run and mow you down, if they were so inclined. I believe I'm right when I say more people are trampled by cows than eaten by sharks each year.

The biggest beast mirrors my actions, proceeding to step forward. It's a game of chicken, but with a cow. *Don't back down and keep advancing.* Great, now all the other cows take an interest and proceed to follow their leader. They don't back down either – quite the opposite – they charge forward to within only a few meters.

"Oh shit!" That's my cue to run. I dart to the right, managing to dive under the electric fence. There was no time to check but, luckily, it turns out that no other aggressive farm animals are on the other side. *Harmless my arse.*

An hour later, things take another turn for the worse. The kiwi bush can suddenly get very thick, and the trail can quickly disappear. You do have the little orange triangles to guide you, but you can end up miles off course if you miss one. After choosing left instead of right around a tree a few hundred meters back, I've clearly taken a wrong turn, and find myself whacking through draping vines and giant ferns.

This can't be right. The map clearly shows the trail is a few hundred metres to the west. *Maybe I can just cut across*, I think. But when does 'cutting across' ever end well?

Sure enough, listening to my stupid voice, I descend into a deep valley. What an error this turns out to be. Very soon, I've lost my bearings and can't see the route I took to end up here. No matter which way I go, there's a dangerously steep climb ahead – and I mean 'climb'. One slip, or one loose root, and that could be it. *No time to think about it now, get in the zone and get a move on.*

Once again, I find myself grabbing roots and trusting trees to drag myself up. A few slips make my heart jump into my throat, and my palms a little sweatier. Looking down just isn't an option. I'm well in the bush, and the drop is anywhere up to a good 30 metres. *If I fall here, it will be some time before anyone finds me, if at all.*

Pushing scary thoughts of imminent death aside, I increase my focus and continue to haul myself up the valley wall. *There's no time to curse your stupidity.* Despite more perilous slips, the fight and crawl brings me from the depths and, to my good fortune, straight back onto the trail floor. Once again, covered in dirt, scrapes, and scratches, I lay back exhausted. *Lewis, you really are an idiot sometimes.*

Once more my stupidity has put me in another dangerous situation – one that could have ended in the worst possible way. *If you are unsure, just turn back.* Oh, and most infuriatingly, I lost my shiny new sunglasses in the process.

Descending from the ridgeline, I arrive at the stunning Whananaki Footbridge, the longest footbridge in the southern hemisphere. It connects North and South Whananaki and will be a brilliant opportunity for Phil to utilise the drone he's brought along, to document the adventure. He sets himself up to see me coming and get another brilliant shot.

Little does he know I've wimped out of running through the farmland and stuck to the road for the last 500 meters. Cows are a struggle, but if there are bulls to contend with, I'm not down for that.

The road runs around the back of where Phil is waiting, and I cross the footbridge to a hero's welcome on the other side. Jill is waiting with a group of tourists and it's a pleasant surprise, although I feel unworthy of such a lovely gesture. They are incredibly kind and so excited to hear from me. However, when you're struggling with horrible pains and haven't interacted with people in days, you can come across as moody and ungrateful. At least, I can.

Apologies if you were there and are reading this. I should have been much more conversational and taken more time. Sometimes, even though we are surrounded by all these beautiful views and fantastic people, all I can see is the foot in front of me and my bed at the end of the day. *You're not being present. You need to take in what's around you.*

"Where's Phil?" I ask.

"He was waiting for you. Did you not see him?" responds Jill, looking confused.

"Oops."

The evening sessions are always the slowest, a day full of pain and high levels of energy expenditure leaves me completely spent. The last five kilometres are often a sad-looking walk with nothing left to give. I try to run, and it lasts ten seconds before feeling absolutely shattered again.

Sorry to go on about it but words cannot do justice to what this level of pain and major fatigue feels like. Unless you've put yourself in a similar situation, it's hard to comprehend. Clearly, this was going to be hard, but I'd never experienced anything like it. I'd put myself through brutal workouts and cruel training runs, but nothing compared to this. You know it will be challenging, but you can't comprehend the pain until you experience it. I often have conversations with people about how my legs could barely move each morning, and how my feet would send pains through my body with every step. If I stopped for even 20 seconds, it would take an age to get back on the move again. However, it's clear they don't really get it. You can try to imagine how difficult this would be, I can tell you how hard it was, but you will never understand until you've felt it too.

Sandy Bay is in sight, one of the most beautiful and serene bays on this journey. It's only small, but it has perfect waves breaking onto a little golden beach, with just a handful of pristine houses settled in from the beach – the ideal spot to camp. However, these views are transcended by the gorgeous Gerty as she sits seductively in the car park. *Finally, the van, I can stop.*

Once in, I'm too shattered to get back out. Not even to wash, let alone take in the scenery. As bad as this sounds, I've seen beautiful sights all day, no more are required. Give me food and sleep.

For the first time, Jill starts to show cracks in her steadfast character. She's usually very talkative, laughing along whilst doing the cooking, often checking if I'm ok and doing another ten things all at the same time. This evening she's reticent, and heads off for a walk, alone. Usually, she might be gone for ten minutes, but tonight it's much longer. At times not much needs to be said and talking too much can often make things worse. On this occasion, Phil and I feel time and space is what Jill wants, and she is the kind of person to talk if she has to.

The next morning, she lets us know she felt sad and homesick, and it had just hit her out of nowhere. We'd all agreed that we need to look after one another on this trip. Of course, I'll need a lot of help, but this is also tough for Phil and Jill, so we need to be a team and look out for each other.

Distance: 51km
Elevation: 1434m.

Day 7 – Jill's Magic Porridge

For once, we awake to an overcast day. There's even some welcome drizzle in the air. Today we face a couple of estuaries. Much to my frustration, we have no choice but to drive around the first. The tide is in, and we aren't equipped to deal with it. It's only a few hundred metres, but there's nothing we can do about it. I feel like I'm cheating. Ironically, the drive round is much longer than it would take to cross at low tide.

Despite the respite of a cooler morning, it's the worst I've felt since Day 1. My demeanour has completely switched.

"I don't know how I'm going to do this", I confess to Jill as she walks alongside knowing I'm in a far from a positive place as it is. Yet, of course, she coerces me that little bit further, getting me through the last couple of kilometres to the van.

The pain is borderline unbearable, my mind is a mess, and my eyes feel like lead. The thought of running a further 45 kilometres just seems unfathomable. In my fragile mindset, I just cannot see how I'm going to pull this off. The moment my bum hits the seat, I'm fast asleep. I'm clearly running on fumes.

We arrive at the beginning of the next section and, still, my eyes struggle to prise themselves open. Perhaps it's not a lack of sleep, but a lack of calories. Every time we stop, my appetite is at zero, and the thought of ploughing down tuna pasta, rice and chicken, or sandwich after sandwich, makes my stomach shrink. Not only can Jill tell from my performance, but she can see it in my ghoulish face.

This is when, in a moment of inspiration, she throws together a high-calorie feast. Porridge hasn't been on the menu to date – because who wants to eat porridge in 30-degree sunshine? Yet it quickly becomes a lifesaver. Jill's Magic Porridge, a little bit of coffee, and miraculously I'm ready to go. The following hour is the fastest of the run so far. *Where the hell did that come from?* Jill's Magic Porridge, and a large coffee, are definitely staying on the menu.

The recipe: oats, soya milk, dark chocolate, banana, peanut butter, honey and protein powder. We estimate a bowl to be around the 800-kcal mark, maybe more. Easy to smash back and full of calories, what more could I want? We're on to a winner. Let's just hope it doesn't get boring and bland. Soon enough, I'll be knocking back nine bowls a day.

After a contrasting morning split by the World's Greatest Nap, the third section of the day begins up and over Kauri Mountain, providing spectacular views looking south along Ocean Beach to the majestic Te Whara.

It was on the drive north for the start of the adventure when we first caught a glimpse of the magnificent mounts of Te Whara. There they stood, shooting straight up from the depths of the big blue, dominating the scenery, dwarfing all around it, and filling me with nerves. It was the first imposing skyline we'd seen and a first glimpse of what I was letting myself in for. Everything seems larger now we are actually there. They certainly belittled the rolling hills from back home.

The trail descends onto Ocean Beach. A six-kilometre flashback to Day 1. Luckily the camber is on the other side. The kilometres topple slowly, and the mounts loom as they grow closer, before I'm eventually face-to-face with the vertical ascent.

The trail breaks up and away from Ocean Beach to the ridgeline track. Same recipe as every other ascent so far, straight up in the most direct route possible. Over the space of two kilometres, it climbs 476 metres. That's some tough going but, having already completed more than a marathon, I have to dig deep to find enough in the tank to make it up. Oh and, of course, the sun is now belting down. Imagine running a marathon before hopping straight on a Stairmill for 50 minutes – with a halogen lamp poised directly above your head. The sun in New Zealand is strangely intense. When you're in direct sunlight, it roasts your skin in seconds.

As the sweat drips off the end of my nose, I feel alive! I've been plodding away all day, and now it's exciting to feel my lungs burn and my legs build up with adrenaline-inducing lactic acid. The everyday struggles out here have been joint pain and muscle soreness, low energy levels, and battered feet. However, when the trail throws something different at you, it's energising; the pain and discomfort changes. Yes, old aches are still there, but the endorphins fly when your lungs and quads begin to burn. You might think it's a bit sick and twisted, but I love it!

The grassy climb soon turns into what can only be described as a tropical jungle. Tree roots tangle around the tall pillar-like rock formations. The terrain is not easy, but it's also fun to leap from rock to rock or tiptoe along and between roots. One misstep, and I'll go tumbling, but it has to be attacked with everything I've got.

This ridiculous trail is mesmerising enough, but it would be wrong not to mention the spectacular views on display. Rugged peaks rise out of the sea as if pulled up by Maui himself, their vastness demanding a moment of humility. I gaze back to bays farther North, and it's staggering to think I passed them just days ago. It truly is a spectacle, and gratitude overwhelms me.

I want to write 'I'm hurtling down the steps into Urquharts Bay,' but the truth would be, 'I'm slowly, shakily stepping down into Urquharts Bay.' My legs are knackered and full of lactic acid. The steps are steep, and all that force landing on each leg leaves them shaky.

As I wobble my way down, Phil appears out of the corner of my eye, sitting off the trail in the bushes with his camera. My ego kicks in. I step up the pace, only to stop around the corner to have a chat with Jill. They seem to pop up out of nowhere. Phil soon catches up, and we make our way down to the bay, but I run on ahead, desperate to finish over in Whangarei Heads. Firstly, because that's where the boat leaves tomorrow and, secondly, because Jill can't be arsed to cook. Fish and chips beckon me to the finish line.

I run the bay with the drone buzzing overhead, Phil taking the opportunity to film this incredible setting. The boats float silently on the still water as the sun sinks low beyond the bay. It's beautifully still, gentle and quiet – apart from Phil and his drone, of course. It would be wonderful if each day could finish in idyllic surroundings like this. *Embrace it whilst you have the chance*, I remind myself. I must have listened when I told myself to be more present.

I lay in bed, feeling proud. I try not to give into pride too often, purely as a means to keep my ego in check but, after the past week, might a little pride be warranted? I've been in pain since Day 1 but I'm still moving, still putting one foot in front of another. You know what? I think I can do this.

A challenging 53 kilometres completed, 385 in total.

Distance: 53km
Elevation:1850m.

Day 8 – Milestones

The two sides of the bay could hardly offer a greater contrast. We leave the beautiful and serene environs of Whangarei Heads and move to the grimly industrial Marsden Point. The gentle lapping of the waves against the pebble beach is replaced by the screams and screeches of thousands of seagulls circling a giant oil refinery.

I've never seen so many birds in one place at one time. I'd already had a couple of encounters with irate gulls and didn't fancy being lynched by a mob of them today. Luckily, I escape without even a drop of guano on my head.

The next day and a half will be spent hugging the blissful coastline, occasionally breaking inland to bring some respite from the monotony of sun, sea, and sand. How people go on holiday for two weeks to sit by a pool or on a beach all day is beyond me. Thirty minutes of sunbathing and I'd be bored and desperate for something to do.

Today is an opportunity to eat up some miles and maybe work my way closer to my 60-kilometre target. After struggling through the first three days, I'm almost a full day behind schedule. There's not a tremendous amount of elevation on this stretch, so maybe this is a chance to eat away at the deficit. I'm glad that I can even consider this an option – it shows I'm adjusting to the challenge.

I'm aiming for a 70-kilometre day. Getting up early to catch the 8 a.m. boat makes a real difference, and sets us up nicely. Alarms will be set for 6.00 or 6.30 a.m. from now on, depending on when we get to bed.

I'm meeting the van regularly. Seeing Jill and Phil breaks up the day, but I worry I'm becoming over-reliant on them. Don't get me wrong, the pain is still awful, and massages are certainly required, but these are clearly more than just physical breaks. At times I might only cover seven kilometres before scheduling to see them again, even if only for a couple of minutes.

The way I'm coping with the pain and discomfort is by using the van as a milestone and, the more I struggle, the shorter each milestone becomes. It breaks the day up – from 60-70 kilometres into more manageable chunks – and I crave the affirmation of achieving these bite-size pieces by having the team and van appear. It's just not the same to complete a chunk of the run and then carry on alone without seeing anyone. I can tell Jill and Phil are thinking the same as me, *I'm doing this too much.*

Out of the forests, and after another afternoon break, I join the Mangawhai Cliff Walk. Often when man mixes with nature, it doesn't go too well for nature, but here they have got it right. A beautiful path cuts into the cliffs, and you walk directly above birds dancing beneath your feet. Trees hang to the heights like daredevil rock climbers, and waves crash below. From this vantage point it feels as though we're part of nature, and not just intruding. Another magical moment provided by the all too generous Te Araroa Trail.

After this brief and beautiful interlude, the day finishes along yet another gravel road, this time with 4x4's and pick-up trucks screaming past and getting sideways around each corner. The dust kicks up, clouds my eyes, and is a nightmare to breathe in. I can't see when the next idiot is coming. It's dangerous and blood-boilingly frustrating. The combination of fatigue, dust and reckless drivers puts me in a rage. I've had enough.

Despite my feet getting battered by every stone and rut, I manage to continue, much like I have since setting off on Day 1. Each step from the beginning of 90 Mile Beach has been a challenge but still, through gritted teeth, I persevere. Despite every bone in my body willing me to stop, something keeps me moving. Something pushes me forward.

As I see it, a small flame flickers deep inside when every ounce of your body tries to put it out. It flickers just enough for you to continue putting one foot in front of the other, to continue day after day, to wake up and go again every single morning. Even when your mind tries to turn against you, when it throws every reason under the sun at you to stop, this small flame burns bright, and it knows why you must carry on. It knows the pain your body and mind feel yet, no matter how horrible that may be, it knows it would be no match for the turmoil caused by giving up. This flame is your reason, your why, and if it's powerful enough, it holds you steadfast through the toughest moments.

Completing the Northland feels like an immense milestone. It feels like an affirmation that we can persevere, and that my mind is winning the battle against the demons that demand it to stop.

447 kilometres completed, eight regions and 2,559 kilometres to go!

Distance: 64km
Elevation: 1021m.

AUCKLAND

PROCESS

'In short, the wise man looks to the purpose of all actions, not their consequences; beginnings are in our power but Fortune judges the outcome, and I do not grant her verdict upon me.'

-

Seneca

Day 9 – Breaking It Down

I wake up feeling nervous. Despite my attachments, it's all been quite comfortable the last few days – well, as comfortable as I imagine it can get. There haven't been many long stretches away from the van and the terrain has, for the most part, been kind. This is all about to change across Dome Valley.

The morning starts with yet another beach run. Luckily, 15 kilometres is just far enough before tedium sets in. *You shouldn't wish away these beaches. They're where you make the best progress.* Soon enough, as the trail works its way down the island's spine, the beaches will run out and I'll probably miss them.

At the beach's end lies a little taster of what's to come. The trail climbs into the giant tangled mess that is Dome Valley. I say a taster because, although the trail has headed inland before, the next 30 kilometres through the dense Omaha and Dome Forest will take it to a new level of elevation and difficulty.

After leaving the beach and running through the charming handful of houses which make up Pakiri village, the trail drives straight up harsh farming terrain – and I mean straight up. The coastal views become more spectacular with each and every burning step, and the familiar theme of 'having to earn it' is all too apparent. It's clear now, for whatever incredible and wonderful experience that comes my way, I'm going to have to earn it.

Intensity – that's the only way to approach such steep and rugged terrain. Dawdling and moaning is demoralising, and just as costly for energy. No, you must attack a hill like this. You must match its aggression.

Upon reaching the 500-metre peak, it becomes apparent there will not be a patch of flat running through this farm, and not in the following forest either. Not only does the trail constantly undulate, but the terrain underfoot has also become a runner's nightmare. My friends the cows have roamed these steep hills, leaving deep ruts to dry under the baking sun. Ankle rolling is a permanent threat. Every foot placement has to be well measured or it could be game over. Progress has to slow. *You're going to have to keep up this power to make any progress.*

The forests offer no respite. The ruts are replaced by a non-existent track with a thousand crisscrossing roots. It's more like a game of hopscotch than running, and it's going to continue for another 20 kilometres until reaching the road. Luckily, it's so dry that I can catch a grip on the roots. If it was a damp day, it would be even more challenging.

There's a plus side to this kind of terrain. While I often struggle to focus on the flat, what should be quicker, sections, I seem to thrive with being off the beaten track. My mind enters an ultra-focused state. On tracks like this, there's no time for daydreaming, just total focus on the task at hand. You envision every step, your mind is well ahead of the game. You feel full of energy, pains disappear, there are no distractions, and everything in your peripheral vision becomes a whizzing blur. You are in ultra-focused tunnel vision – in the zone! Four hours passes like 30 minutes.

I'm unsure of what a runner's high really is but I'd say it feels something like this. For 30 kilometres, I've been engrossed. It's only upon reaching the team that I snap from this possessed trance.

There's still time in the day to get a further 15 kilometres, and closer to the desirable 60-kilometre average. However, it quickly becomes apparent I can't match the focus of my afternoon stint. Yet, through hard graft and laborious fatigue, 54 kilometres are ticked off the total. Job well done. *You need to have more days like this.*

Although the terrain proved a challenge, and I had been taking far too many breaks, we seem to be settling into a pattern at last, and I'm now performing well. We've found our roles, a system is in place, and it should only take minor tweaks to keep it working smoothly and improving.

Part of the process is to break things down. If you get handed 60 kilometres, it seems like an awful lot. If you zoom out and look at how far you have to run, it feels unimaginable that you might reach your intended destination for that day. When you actually start to run, the day begins to break into sections – manageable chunks that add up to the sum total. That next ten kilometres doesn't feel too far, that next kilometre is even easier, the next 100 metres, and even the next step – easier again.

Put it this way, if I say to you,

"I want you to take 4,200,000 steps in the next 60 days," it sounds an impossible task. Yet, if I say, "take one step, then another, and again," eventually, you'll get there. Those individual steps don't seem so bad. At the brink of your limits, in severe pain and fainting with fatigue, if I ask you to take one more step, it wouldn't seem so terrible. You'd be able to do it. At times, the run is reduced to exactly that. Putting one foot in front of the other.

Distance: 54km
Elevation: a considerable 1,960m.

Day 10 – My Way or The Highway

Another day, another near-death experience. Again, from my own stupidity, but more about that later.

The morning starts with a 19-kilometre stint across farmland and well-graded forests. It's a straightforward run compared to the tangles of yesterday's woodlands, and a popular day hike for the locals. Although I only exchange brief greetings, it's a relief to be amongst people again.

Yesterday, because of the terrain, a lot of time was spent away from the van, and this morning is the same. When I'm forced to be alone for long periods, everything is fine. I feel I have been abusing the comfort of having the van there for me whenever I desired. From today, we've agreed, there should be no reason for me to see the van any sooner than every 15 kilometres – except in an emergency. I can't afford to be so reliant, as soon days will be spent alone in the wilderness, something that I've pushed to the back of my mind. *Do not get distracted by what is to come*, I remind myself, *focus on today.*

I meet the team in Puhoi, where the trail gets back to the water after its inland venture. A kayak section down the river to the coast is to follow. If walking, you'd wait to catch the high tide heading back out to sea. But of course, we time it terribly, arriving at low tide.

Puhoi is pretty, it reminds me of an old Western movie set, but no matter how attractive a place it is, there's no way we can wait the hours it'll take for the tide to turn. It's time to hit the road. With no riverside path, I have to join the main, winding roads from Puhoi, which, to begin with, aren't so bad.

But then I join State Highway 1.

With the traffic at a standstill, I luckily manage to cross the four lanes with ease, much to the confusion of drivers and passengers alike. *What in the world is this idiot doing?* Their faces seem to say.

I have no idea if this is legal. It's not quite the M5, but it's still pretty busy and pretty scary. I cross and head up the slip road to join the Hibiscus Coast Highway, which leads to a moment of madness.

Traffic is backed up to the crest of a hill. Unsuspecting cars hurtle over to find queuing cars at a complete standstill. Slogging my way up, I reach the crest, and a huge 4x4 comes shooting over, only to see the gridlock all too late. He swerves towards me, I dive down the bank, and the 4x4 skids down the road with the loudest *'screech!'* finally coming to a stop, the driver visibly shaken. We both take a deep breath and exhale. He's safe, I'm safe, and nobody is hurt – but that could have been the end – not just of this adventure. I come to my senses. *Running on the highway. What were you thinking? Just call the team.*

Phil and Jill give me a two-kilometre lift to Waiwera, where I'm met with more frustration. On this section, you need low tide but now it's making its way in. *Bloody tides.* For the next three kilometres, the trail skirts along the base of the cliffs, which is manageable in the right conditions. But, with the tide almost in, there's no chance, it would be immature and dangerous. Once again, I take another detour via the Hibiscus Coast Highway to Owera. Drowning or being hit by a car was not a choice I was expecting to have to make.

Have I just killed any chance of claiming this record? Not only have I gone off the trail, I have taken a lift. Although quite far off the pace, we maintain that we can still pull it back and break the record, but if we do, will it even stand? Let's face the facts, I've taken an alternative route, we're turning a blind eye to the fact I jumped in the van for two kilometres and, way back in the Bay of Island, I did two sections back to front. Surely these alterations will mean an incomplete trail? Maybe, subconsciously, I've already given up bettering Jez's achievement. However, out loud, I'm refusing to let myself and the team believe it.

With these thoughts and questions spinning in my mind, there's only one thing to do, carry on. The choices made and the actions taken are now in the past. What's happened has happened, and

I cannot change it. *But will it matter? Have I discredited myself?* Sometimes it's hard to move on, even if you do tell yourself to.

Although still by the coast, the ambience is set to become very different over the next few days. We've reached the Auckland region, the most populated part of the country. I'm trading hours of isolation on pristine beaches and in dense forests, for dodging through holidaymakers and weaving past shoppers in town. Rural traffic of cows and tractors has been swapped for town traffic of people and cars, and it feels bizarre to be among so many people. There they are relaxing, enjoying life, passing time with family and friends, eating, drinking, dancing, smiling, and having a great time. Then there's me, the one anomaly amongst it all. A sweaty, tired, sunburnt, slightly grumpy Brit plodding his way through the mass of enjoyment. I must admit, I briefly feel a pang of jealousy as I scamper past aromatic barbecues and laughing couples. Everyone seems so relaxed and happy. To them, I'm probably just some nutter going on a run in the heat of the day.

The day feels disjointed much like my conflicting thoughts. Yet, after working my way through the streets of Red Beach and Silverdale, somehow 40 kilometres have been chipped away, and there's still plenty of time left in the day.

I escape the masses down to the charming and stunning Stillwater. It feels like I've been thrust into a beautiful oil painting. Small boats gently sit atop the near-perfect water with the steep and luscious green headlands extending up to meet the lowering sun. There's a calmness, a slowness to the little harbourside town. It's a complete contrast to the previous hour, and to what comes next. It's incredible how much the surrounding scenery and atmosphere can impact how you think and feel. I've gone from feeling rushed and enclosed to free and calm. My thoughts have changed. *Head down and go,* has become, *look up and take it all in.*

The trail continues down the coastal track to Karepiro Bay to cross the Okura River. At low tide, it's quite a comfortable crossing at Darce Point, a one-kilometre wade with the water lapping at your shins. At high tide, it's advised to wait it out or advance further inland to find a safe point to cross. Of course, the way this trip has been going for us, we hit it at a high tide. Although a shorter crossing, it's anybody's guess as to how deep it's going to be. Phil and Jill are on the other side with the drone up in the air. There's no way Phil is passing on the opportunity to film me being swept out to sea.

The tide is heading out and at a rapid pace. I cautiously step into the river. Its force is immediately apparent and I fear losing my footing, so step straight back out. Fully aware that I might be heading for a swim, we think it wise to empty my water bladder and pack in the essentials.

"Don't forget to use a stick!" Jill shouts. She's adamant that I'll need it to help me across.

"Bloody stick," I curse to myself.

Step by step, the water creeps higher and higher, although refreshing in the searing heat, it takes your breath away upon reaching a particular region. Not even close to halfway, and the water is already above my belly button and getting higher... Chest height now, and I'm still going down. Arms up and on my tiptoes.

"This is it. I'm getting ready to swim," I shout.

Am I getting any help from the sidelines? No. All I can hear is laughter from Phil and Jill amongst their terrible advice.

"Use your stick!" Jill shouts again.

The bloody stick is useless! The water is now just under my chin so I lob the shitty stick away. I must look ridiculous. The only reason I'm not swimming is that I don't want to get dragged out and miss my landing spot, *tiptoe, tiptoe, tiptoe.* Eyes shut, breath held, I keep moving forward before finally, the level begins to drop. Despite it lapping at my chin, I'm on my way back up and out. *Slowly does it, it only takes one deep spot, and you're flying downstream. If only I had a stick to check ahead.*

Much to Jill's relief and amusement and Phil's disappointment, I'm soaked but safe. I think he wanted to see me swim. Standing there in nothing but my towel, wringing out my drenched T-shirt, would you believe a car pulls up with two kayaks on its roof? *Typical, why couldn't they have arrived ten minutes earlier?*

After a top-up and a complete change, you'd think that would be enough for the day, but there's still time and kilometres to cover. The route heads back into civilisation along Auckland's undulating North Shore, lined with town after town, all the way to the city.

This final session is an extremely painful 13 kilometres to Browns Bay, with the last five a drained and stiff stumble – proper grit required.

I arrive at that evening's camp, but we still have daylight and time on our side. Although feeling physically done, and I'm moving like a speed walker, there's no other choice. I have to continue. If this adventure is going to be a success, it's at times like these that I have to push past what I want to do and more. My mind is made up.

Jill schedules to meet me and my knackered body at Browns Bay. I'm absolutely spent so decide to starfish on the grass, quite possibly asleep. On the other hand, Jill is at the far end of the esplanade, expecting to see me bound around the corner at any minute. Instead, she watches me climb from the floor like a zombie, and hobble towards her, barefoot, stinking, and mumbling,

"Jill, I hope there's a shower."

My prayers are answered. It's time to have a wash, and a proper one at that. Tonight is a step up from my usual sponge down at the back of the van; we have access to the beachside shower. This is luxury now and, with what remains of my dignity, I hobble across camp looking like the hunchback of Notre Dame walking over hot coals – towel across my shoulders and nothing else but me in my nasty, sweaty pants. Every step sends pain through my poor bruised and battered feet. God only knows what the other beach dwellers must think of this creature desperately writhing in pain for a power wash. It's so cold it takes my breath away, but I don't care. I stink, I'm sticky with sweat, and it's the first wash I've had in days. Not counting the dip in the estuary, of course.

With my left quadriceps like a gravel road, it's time for another brutal massage at the hands of Phil and Jill. The routine goes as follows. Jill warms the muscles up and works on as many knots as possible. For any of the more challenging spots, we send in Phil to do the heavy work. The pain is excruciating, as I am sure many of you know. Each trigger point sends the leg into a frenzy with the muscle spasming and dancing away, eventually releasing the knot and therefore releasing the tightness in the hip. It's always painful, close to the point of tears at times, but it lets me run a little bit closer to pain-free.

Distance: 66km
Elevation: 1615m.

Day 11 – Hamstrung

The daily routine seems to be well in place. Eight hours of sleep, breakfast routine, morning session, lunch break, afternoon session, afternoon break, evening session, final recovery, wash, food, socialise and bed. This has been the schedule pretty much day in, day out. Occasionally it changes if I'm away from the van for extended periods, but we've settled into a pattern, and we're making good progress. We're slowly clawing back at the time lost in the first few days. We're in the process.

Today we're on for a 70-kilometre plus day. An early start means I'm up and at it in the pleasant morning sea breeze, while Auckland's North Shore sleeps. The streets undulate from town to town, in and out of one beautiful bay after another. As the hours tick by, I look on with jealousy as the North Shore slowly wakes up and people head for the beaches and coffee shops. One of my favourite things to do back home is for Keily and I to head over to our favourite coffee shop, in Wells (shout out to 'Strangers With Coffee'). Whenever we travel, the first thing we do is find the best independent coffee shop in the area. I will happily admit I am the coffee snob that a certain fast-food chain takes the piss out of in their adverts, but I prefer my coffee to taste spectacular, not of burnt tar!

After dodging sunbathers and morning walkers, I make the 20 kilometres to Devonport. Enough time for one last fuel stop and massage before boarding the ferry to Auckland's Central Business District (CBD). I've never been great on the water, I feel every movement, and my stomach tends to not agree with the motion. You know that feeling when your stomach leaps to your throat, everything gets a bit blurry, and the colour rushes from your skin? I just about manage to keep my porridge down on the fifteen-minute journey. By all accounts, this ferry crossing is a piece of cake compared to what's to come on the Cook Strait.

I've spoken about Te Araroa's contrasts, and here they are again on full display. A concrete jungle has replaced awe-inspiring and beautiful forests. I'm now walking shoulder to shoulder with businesspeople, tourists, and locals as we herd ourselves through the bustling streets of Auckland. It feels so bizarre to stand and wait for the green man to let me cross the road after the freedom of the forests.

The streets feel like a giant maze, leading me to take many frustrating wrong turns. Yet, instead of getting wound up about not being out in the 'real' New Zealand, it's far better to embrace the contrast. It's interesting to be surrounded by so many people, but it's much more palatable knowing I'm quickly heading back out.

The CBD soon turns to suburbs, but the pace remains slow. The streets drag me up and over Mount Eden – a hot, sweaty, and confusing inconvenience. Views are offered up back across the city, though not worth the effort. I express my annoyance to the team, back at the van.

"It's like they just put these stupid bits in the trail for the sake of it. It's just a waste of my time," I moan, forgetting that this is a hiking trail, not a running track. A single look from Jill is reproach enough. *Yes, yes, I know.*

I'm moody because I'm shattered, and consequently, I'm soon fast asleep. Jill will wake me in 15 minutes. Any longer, and it'll be a struggle to get me going. These power naps are becoming lifesavers, just when I feel my batteries are running empty a nap, some food, and coffee sort me out. *Maybe this can be a new addition to the process.*

I've felt fatigued before, but never like on this adventure. At times I have enough energy to enjoy some conversation. Others I sit vacantly, barely able to bring my arm up to feed myself, and just to move takes a monumental effort. It's our hope that these rests will work wonders, but getting going again is sometimes like starting up a steam train, struggling and stumbling until it loosens up.

Forty kilometres complete, and it's only mid-afternoon. *I'm flying. We might hit 80 kilometres today.*

Then, out of nowhere, a sharp pain shoots up my hamstring. A horrible stinging pain all too familiar. *Shit, shit, shit. No, this can't be happening.*

Hobbling across the Mangere Bridge and wincing with each step, I reach the team and try desperately to stretch out. Jill works away, doing her best to ease any tightness, but to no avail. I attempt to move off again but, after another sickening five kilometres, we have to call it a day; the searing pain is just unmanageable. It feels like I've pulled or torn a muscle. This might be game over. *After all the hard work, all the training, and the help from so many people – it can't end like this, not this early.*

My demeanour changes from optimistic to distraught in a matter of minutes. My emotions have already been on a rollercoaster of a day, but this tops it all. I lecture myself: *You cannot make a decision based on emotion. Listen to sound judgment and solid reason.* My stoic mindset kicks in.

We send an emergency message back home to Jo. Her response is encouraging. She suspects the hamstring is overworked, extremely tight, but not torn or pulled. A glimmer of hope, but I don't want to get carried away.

We spend the evening applying hot and cold to the affected area, to increase blood flow, alongside some light massage. On the outside I'm focused but, inside, deeply saddened. *This has to be more than just tight muscles. This looks like adventure over.* I've experienced pulled hamstrings and quadriceps a few times in a childhood spent playing any sport going. They can take six or more weeks to heal, and this injury feels exactly the same. *How can this possibly be just tight muscles?*

We find our campsite at Murphy's Law Irish Pub and decide to treat ourselves to a meal out. It'll be a chance to relax a little and break from our process. Phil and I devour a Mexican sharing platter as we discuss our options for the next day. I know what you're thinking, *Mexican food, in an Irish pub, in New Zealand?* Credit where credit's due – it's surprisingly delicious. In my mind, there's no way I'll be able to run tomorrow or even the day after that. I just cannot see how it'll be possible. I can barely walk from the pub to the van, let alone run 60 kilometres.

Although we laugh and joke, inside I'm desolate and barely able to hold back the tears. My friends and family, the local community, businesses, Phil and Jill have put so much into this, and it might be coming to an abrupt and dismal end. 18 months of my life have been invested in this adventure, and it's hanging by a thread, or should I say a hamstring? *Is this the end of the line?*

Distance: 45km
Elevation: 735m.

Day 12 – Dig Deep

I awake despondent, and probably the most negative I've felt on the adventure to date. It's going to take a miracle to make it 60 metres, let alone 60,000. *What can we do?* As a team, we must stick to our process. Many aspects of our plan work well, and we're making minor adjustments each day. This is in our control.

I set off, limping, hopping, and hobbling. *Just start gently, keep your body moving, and grit your goddamn teeth!* If the pain isn't enough, there's a horrific smell of ammonia to contend with. We only made it as far as Auckland's water treatment plant last night. Nothing says wild and beautiful like the stench of ammonia.

My hamstring feels like a guitar string wound almost to a snap. With every single step, I'm making sure not to apply too much tension. Every time my left leg begins its downward sweep, the hamstring groans and burns as it threatens the end of the line. Even with plenty of painkillers, the pain is unignorable.

Stopping at the van nearly every hour to rest and work through stretches is the only option. It's the only thing we can do to relieve the pain, just enough to loosen me up and continue shuffling along. The hamstring is on a knife-edge, but, somehow, our adjusted process is working. I'm still moving. The hamstring hasn't 'pinged' yet and, surprisingly, we're knocking off the kilometres. All fingers remain tightly-crossed.

Jill and I use Proprioceptive Neuromuscular Facilitation (PNF) to release tension and bring some mobility back to my ailing leg. It involves stretching, contracting, and relaxing the muscle to increase the range of movement. Oh, and it is excruciating! Frequently we find ourselves on the roadside, or in the middle of the park, Jill folding me up like a lawn chair as I scream and swear each and every time, much to Phil's amusement. There's no way I'll make it through without their help. *We are moving forward;* I dare to believe.

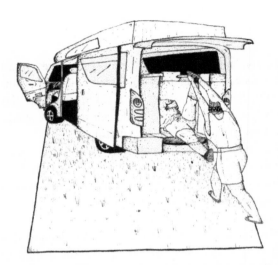

At home, I'd have had my feet up for the next three or four days but, out here, what choice do I have? *Your mind and body have got you this far. You're not going to fail now.* There's the gruelling determination we need!

I run angry, angry at the pain, producing an unmatched drive. My mind digs deep, going to very dark places to continuously get up, get out, and go again and again, all through the worst agony I've ever run in. This isn't just some low-level dull ache, but a sharp and searing burn cutting down the back of my leg with every step, sending a grimace back up to my face, and expelling grunts and expletives out of my mouth.

I spend ten hours in this constant battle, and it's undoubtedly the most challenging day's exercise, both physically and mentally, I've ever had to face. It is amazing what the mind and body can endure.

With the sun sinking over the horizon, we're well out of the city and into the rural Kiwi countryside. Something magical happens as the sun falls. Everything takes on a gentle and warming tone. Green and yellow hillsides are touched by a soft orange light, and the sky is illuminated by calming ambers and reds. It mirrors my relief at the end of the most trying day.

These hills look over our next region to conquer – Waikato. A mass of farmland split by the mighty Waikato River. The view is both inviting and intimidating, leaving me to wonder what stunning sights and harsh tests lie ahead. I'm excited to be getting back into the real New Zealand, strong and unyielding, but also wild and beautiful.

Despite the internal and external obstacles we've faced throughout Auckland, utilising our process has got us through. My injury could've easily thrown everything to the wayside, but with our strategy in place, we made the best of the factors still within our control.

A process isn't necessarily fixed. By definition it's the actions you can control, so it's therefore adaptable. Yet, these adaptations will only be optimal with applied objectivity. If we let our emotions get involved, they can blur the lines between absolute truth and those influenced by our thoughts and feelings – the subjective. Then it becomes difficult to decide what is the right thing to do.

What comes next is a real test of facing adversity. We will try to remain steadfast, with good judgement and sound reason, and not be influenced by what our emotions want us to hear.

664 kilometres completed, and two regions ticked off.

Distance: 57km
Elevation: 778m.

WAIKATO

OBJECTIVITY

'There is no good or bad without us, there is only perception. There is the event itself and the story we tell ourselves about what it means.'

-
Ryan Holiday

Day 13 – Unlucky For Some

I'm boiling, completely drenched in sweat. Frantically, I strip from my soaked sleeping bag and down to nothing but my pants. This is an all too familiar flush of heat, the kind you have when your body wants to empty itself out, but you're not sure which end. I scramble and stumble to find the zip. The last thing I want to do is let loose in such a confined area.

We're in Mercer, on the Waikato River, and there's not much to speak of – just a pub, petrol station, and a man desperately running across the forecourt in shorts and sliders.

I burst from the tent, hoping the petrol station is still open. It's touch and go as I shuffle along, praying that I can forestall a traumatic download. *The door's locked. What the hell am I going to do?* Darting back towards the van, it becomes apparent my efforts have been in vain as I projectile vomit across the car park. *Got to keep moving.* The puke's not my only problem.

Being typically British, I don't want to make a fuss by waking the others. Instead, I proceed down the verge towards the river. Still puking and almost filling my pants, I trip, stubbing my toe and slipping out of my sliders – falling flat on my arse. I hold on, just.

I can't hold it. Onto Plan C. I politely knock on the van with a contradictory assertiveness. Maintaining politeness whilst keeping a sense of urgency about the situation is another very typical British characteristic. Without his glasses, Phil can't see at the best of times. When half asleep, he barely opens his eyes, looking like a confused mole. In his dazed state he passes me our little portaloo that's the size of a suitcase, tosses me a loo roll and, before I know it, he's again catching flies in a deep slumber. A further five hours of sleeplessness proceeds, trying not to move for fear of a shart or worse. Occasionally I reach for the bucket to throw up, until there's nothing left to give. It's a great night!

In the morning I am severely dehydrated with zero calories left in me. We quickly concede that there's no chance I'll be up and running today. Every movement threatens the unpredictable, and I can barely stand up, let alone run. Phil isn't feeling too great this morning either, but that is his story to tell. All I will leave you with is an image of the petrol station bin and Phil's boxers.

It's in situations like this when you need a person of Jill's character. With our backs against the wall and our pants in the bin, we need help. Jill comes to the rescue, booking us into an Airbnb. Jill is one of the best organisers I've ever met, and the epitome of a doer. She's often said to me,

"If you want something done, ask a busy person." In this case, we didn't even have to ask.

With us being held up for the day, my mind isn't on the run, it's not really on anything, which is probably a good thing. As the day progresses, things slowly start to improve. Eventually, we're both able to hold down solid food. It reminds me of a top-level alcohol-poisoning hangover from my late teens. Was it Phil's cooking or just a bug? Was it dehydration? Was it exhaustion? We don't really know.

There's no way I'll be running tomorrow either. I haven't eaten or drunk anywhere near enough. It would be immature and reckless to attempt a run. In these moments, you have to put your emotions to one side and examine the facts.

I've been unwell, and my body is already under a tremendous amount of stress. I've not consumed enough food, and I'm still dehydrated, leaving me at risk of making things worse. Working through this with the team makes it easier to reach a decision. We all know it's the right thing to do.

The difficulty is dealing with the disappointment. We're two days behind schedule now, after spending the last week clawing our way back. Although the decision is clear, it's not a comfortable one to accept. But, even if I wanted to run tomorrow, there's no way Jill and Phil would let me. Slowly, our chances of breaking the record are dwindling, which at such an early stage is the first seed for a troubled mind.

Distance: 0km
Elevation: 0km.

Day 14 – Crazy Reset

After days on end of use and abuse, not to mention my body's exorcism the night before, the van needs a good spring clean. A reorganised van helps us settle ourselves and hit the reset button, returning us to our process.

After an afternoon of crazy golf – not what I was expecting on this adventure but a very welcome diversion – and a chill in the van with a film, we're back at the crime scene, Mercer. It's a word which will bring back awful memories every time I hear or see it, reminding me of a night I'd much rather forget.

Who won the crazy golf, I hear you ask? Come on.

Distance: 18 holes.

Day 15 – Seen Better Days

Thankfully an uneventful night passes, and we're all well-fed and watered. It's time to get back to the trail. Seeing as we're now two days behind, we've really got some distance to make up. There's no way this will be done quickly. We will have to chip away at the deficit over the next two, three or even four weeks. Each day we need to gain a few kilometres here and there, five or ten if feeling good.

The first session of the day throws a couple of unwanted challenges my way as if to ask, 'are you sure you're up for this?' I'm confronted with herds of malevolent cows, an unmaintained track, and long wet grass up to my hips and nips, as I whack my way from farm to farm. I navigate each obstacle successfully, but it wouldn't be the Te Araroa Trail if it gifted a flat and easy return.

With the first ten kilometres under my belt, and my body covered in grass seeds, I meet the team by the Waikato River for breakfast number two.

Today is set to be another scorcher, following the meandering Waikato as far south as we can go. The terrain looks to be relatively flat, running from farm to farm and down backcountry roads. I haven't mentioned them for a while but, of course, these backcountry roads are gravel. Sometimes I hit a smooth stretch for a few hundred metres but, more often than not, it's like standing barefoot on a floor of Lego pieces.

The hottest part of the day is always the late afternoon. The sun has been up for hours, warming both the earth and us. It is constant. With no shade to hide in, there's only one thing to do – suck it up and deal with it.

At times it gets too much, and I slow to a dizzy walk, even on easily runnable surfaces. At around 4.00 p.m. each day, we schedule breaks. After eight hours under the unrelenting sun, an extended rest just about gives me enough energy for the last stint, and respite from the belting rays. To counter the lost hour, I stay out longer in the evening and take advantage of the cooler temperatures.

Rocking up to the van, I find Phil fast asleep across the back seats and Jill lying on a patch of grass, sunbathing or reading – both activities are code for sleeping. To be fair, they work their socks off all day and, in heat like this, there's only one sensible thing to do. They never neglect their duties and always wake up to help me out, but the irony makes me chuckle. I laugh at the snapshot of an exhausted runner arriving at the van to find the support team catching a couple of recovery z's.

56 kilometres clocked up. Not quite the 60-kilometre target, but all things considered, it's an excellent return to the trail. We make it down to just past the Huntly Power Station and settle in at Ngaruawahia for the evening.

It seems like a charming town. The buildings are old and full of character, but you can feel the town's heyday has long gone. The main street is pretty much deserted, and the old hotel is rundown and empty. The railway runs right through the centre, but I don't think much stops here anymore.

After a quick wash in the river, and some delicious calorie-filled chicken chorizo pasta, one of my favourites, it's time to settle in for the night. Top bunk in the van for me. Jill is to spend her first night in the tent.

As with every other aspect of our adventure, we had discussed the sleeping arrangements in advance. I was given first choice, as my sleep was a priority for the team. I settled on the top bunk – it was the most comfortable for me. Phil and Jill slept on the bottom, next to each other. A development based on experience was that Jill would sleep in the tent, when possible, because we discovered she snores. I'm sure she doesn't mind me sharing that information! Sometimes I would go in the tent, to give Jill a break.

A car and a couple of questionable characters turn up just before we settle down and, unfortunately for us, they're up all night listening to music, drinking and no doubt, getting high.

I must be honest, I was oblivious to all of this whilst cocooned up in my little top bunk, conked out and oblivious to it all. I sleep so well up there, it's my own little space, my comfort, my safe and secure place on this trip. Why didn't Jill wake us to go and say something? I don't know, but I'm sure they were in no state to move on, let alone comprehend a word we might have said, let alone move on.

Distance: 56km
Elevation: 392m.

Day 16 – Coping Mechanisms

Jill is certain she was woken up during the night by someone using the outside of the tent as a urinal.

"Things often sound closer than they are when you're in a tent," I try to reassure her.

She's not wrong though, someone had pissed on the tent. How about that for her first night's camping? However, being the trooper that she is, Jill doesn't let it faze her.

By contrast, after a wonderful sleep in my little cocoon, I feel revived – rid of any remnants of the illness and ready to push on. The first session is up in the Hakarimata Scenic Reserve. Phil and Jill decide to drive ahead to get a short hike into the forest, and I think that's fair enough. Whenever an opportunity like this arises, they take it. Yes, they are here to help me run, but they're also here to experience a majestic country. They often hike in for 30 minutes or so before turning back and driving to the next meeting point. It gives a little taste of life on the trail, and Phil gets excellent opportunities to film. We anticipate this might be a slow stretch, so they head back to sort the van and enjoy a moment of peace.

I am crushing it, moving much faster than we'd anticipated. I skip across roots, duck under trees, and hurtle down steps the quickest I've done so far. The first 12 kilometres are completed in 2 hours 45 minute. That doesn't sound fast, but this far in and through challenging forest, it's a solid effort. I'm getting better and better in the bush, already my strong point on this adventure. *If only there were no flat, boring roads on this trail.*

From the Hakarimata summit, I hurtle down the near-vertical steps back into Ngaruawahia, dodging flushed faces on their way up. It's great to see people getting at it, but it's delightful to be the one heading down, as their heavy breathing suggests it's one hell of a climb.

I reach Gerty, just as Jill slams shut the side door, having finished sorting the van. She must have been just about to put her feet up before seeing my smiling face suddenly appear.

"I won't stop for long," I promise, sensing her understandable frustration.

I join the cycle path to Hamilton. However, as beautiful as running alongside the river is, it doesn't occupy much space in my brain. The monotony of slapping pavement gets to me again, so it's time to break into my bank of coping mechanisms. Music is an option, but that only works for about an hour – great when in need of a short boost. However, with hours left to chew away, it's time for a good old podcast, hours of engaging conversation that, for the most part, occupies the mind and takes the repetition out of pavement running. My favourites on this adventure are 'The Joe Rogan Experience' and '2 Bears, 1 Cave.' Both brilliant listens, if you haven't come across them.

The development of these coping mechanisms came from working with Marcus Nel. Depending on my RPA, I would use different mechanisms to bring me to an optimal performance level. Sometimes I go through the process and consciously pick the right tool. Other times it's more autonomous, which is most likely down to the practice and knowledge gained through months of preparation.

Self-talk and imagery are the two mechanisms I use the most. With the former, we spent time looking at whether I speak to myself or not, what type of language I might use, and what the responding actions might be. I often use self-talk to identify a problem, or for a burst of discipline and drive.

To identify a problem, I ask the question as if Marcus is there. *Why are you feeling like this? How can you make things better?* For the extra drive, I try to keep things positive. However, for me, it seems a mixture of positivity and self-inflicted insults work well. *I can do this all day! Stop being a little bitch!*

We would spend four weeks looking at a specific technique. The first week was an introduction to the method. The following two weeks would be development and further learning. The fourth would be a review of my understanding and application. Our process was planned and precise, a reflection of how we were to approach the adventure.

This wasn't the only mental preparation that helped develop me and my capacity for this run. In the two to three years prior, I had made significant changes in my life. We hear stories of 'aha!' moments, that change the course of someone's existence, and they often sound too good to be true but, for me, one such moment really did occur.

My time at university and in my early twenties was spent drinking too much and trying to be 'one of the lads.' as opposed to having any real focus on what to do with life. As a result, I soon found myself neglecting my well-being and the well-being of people around me.

One Sunday morning, I awoke on my parents' sofa with a splitting headache. I felt dizzy, fragile, and on the verge of puking. This wasn't my first rodeo; it was all too familiar a feeling. Dad was sitting exhausted on the sofa. He'd spent the night by my side after friends had carried me home. He and mum were distraught and undoubtedly worried. Keily was away, aware of what had happened and also worried sick, but angry too. My brother came over and did what all good brothers do – he laughed at the state of me.

After being told all this by my parents the next day, there was a sickening, sinking feeling in the pit of my stomach. It was nothing to do with the hangover, it was nothing other than shame. I'd been drunk and hungover many times before and had passed it off as being young and 'living my best life,' but this time disappointment cut through – disappointment in myself.

From that day, I started to get my act together. It was a year later when I finally acknowledged this turning point in my life. I was on a business course, and we were asked to find a story of change and development in our lives, and then take the time to figure it out. The premise was, 'the thing holding you back from development and progress is you.' It's true, we needed to dig into our own lives and find out what obscured views, misguided values, or egotistical morals were holding us back.

We worked through my story, helping me realise I'd spent my time in university and at home searching for significance and connections – basically wanting to be liked and be 'one of the lads'. At university, it was a fight to be accepted in such an alpha environment, a house of eight men in their early twenties. At home, I wanted to be an important part of the football team I played for, through performance but also socially. It sounds so stupid now to put such importance on these things, but it is amazing how lost you can get in a potentially toxic social environment, or more so, in a poisonous perception of it.

It was reflecting upon my 'aha!' moment that helped me to see I already had significance, love, and connections. My mum, dad, brother, and Keily were there for me in a true moment of need. The people I'd been neglecting, the people who had shown me love and held me dear to them all this time were right there, and this was how I was repaying them? It pains me to this day to think of my dad sat at the end of the sofa, disappointed and upset at his drunken mess of a son. It was at that moment that I made the decision to change. I quit my football team, spent more time with my closest family and friends, and stopped chasing significance – because I already had it.

It was also while on this course that Stoicism came into my life! George, one of the mentors on the course, had a book called 'The Daily Stoic,' by Ryan Holiday, a great author. George recommended I read Holiday's other book,' Ego is The Enemy'. This was my introduction to studying philosophy and my motivation to truly question how I look at the world and act within it. This led to a further and more in-depth study of Stoicism, which has played a significant role in my life ever since.

A lot of what you are reading in this book is heavily influenced by Stoicism, and I have no doubt you will spot such patterns as the following:

We can't control what happens to us, but we can react and respond.

How do we perceive the events that unfold? Do we see setbacks and problems? Or can we find an opportunity?

Do we get angry, frustrated, and upset and let our emotions cloud our judgment? Or do we identify the emotion, acknowledge it, then respond with logic?

Can we then take action on objective truth?

Can we act, not in anger and frustration, but with creativity and persistence?

And lastly, can we accept certain things are inevitable? Things will happen to us, but it is up to each of us, as individuals, to continue with courage and patience to do what is right by us, our friends, our neighbours, and the rest of the world.

This is a very brief summary of what is taught in Ryan Holiday's, 'The Obstacle is The Way'. It underpins most of my interactions and decision-making. How do I perceive this? PERCEPTION. How can I respond? ACTION. Can I accept what will happen and continue to fight the good fight? WILL.

I had to accept being ill, see it as an opportunity to bond with my teammates, plan moving forward, and practise patience. I had to accept waking up in pain, see the opportunity to help people, inspire people, and practise facing and dealing with adversity. I had to accept being alone, see it as an opportunity to spend time with my own thoughts, think about my friends, family, and home, and see it as a chance to think clearly and creatively. Notably, I had to take action on all of the above and accept what will happen as a result.

Three hours later, and the cycle path eventually leads me to Hamilton. It's strange to arrive in a city, only to be gone and out within the next couple of hours. Usually, you would find time to relax, eat, maybe grab a coffee and see the sights. Not us; we're in and out in a flash. Although I do spend twenty minutes running in the wrong direction. You'd think I'd get lost in the forests or the mountains but no, I got lost in the middle of suburban Hamilton.

I continue along the trail until the sun sets, and I'm spent. We're now well and truly back in the country, surrounded by farms and folding hills. Normally you might say 'rolling hills', but in New

Zealand, there is no such thing – only sharp, steep, and unforgiving mounds. You reach the top, immediately head straight back down before having to trudge steeply back up another. Luckily the roads cut between each mini valley, snaking along to their next destination.

The day is done, and Phil comes hurtling around the corner. It's a majestic sight to spot the silhouette of the mighty HiAce kicking up a sprawl of dust against the orange glow. Now, Phil loves Gerty but, at times, he forgets he's in a tall, unstable, and wobbly old machine with all our belongings in the back. Instead, he drives like Colin McRae on the New Zealand stage of the World Rally Championship.

Despite the aggressive driving, we do make it to Kaniwhaniwha Reserve. Another postcard pitch settled beneath the trees next to a beautiful babbling brook. The BBQ is on, and Jill's scrubbing the tent. Remember, someone had decided to urinate on it and so it stinks. Fair play to Jill; she's willing to give it another go.

It must be said, I do feel sorry for her. She got no sleep the previous night, and her bad luck continues. On this second night in the tent, she's disrupted by the late-night chatter of two girls in a tent across the field, who seem unaware that their synthetic home does little to stop the sounds of their laughter. Two nights in a tent, two terrible nights' sleep, not forgetting the tent smells like piss.

Things aren't much better in the van. It's now been three days without a wash for me. I often sponge down or use a water bladder as a shower, but it never cuts the mustard. By the time I finish running for the day, the sun would've dropped along with the temperature, and the last thing I feel like doing is jumping into a cold stream. All I want is food, a natter, and my bed. All day, I wish to jump in the beautiful waters, but whenever my opportunity arises, it's just too bloody cold.

Distance: 58km
Elevation: 1290m.

Day 17 – Up and Down

Today's run starts across the aggressive farmland – full of sharp ascents and steep descents. Yet, with such disruptive terrain comes spectacular, sprawling scenes across the heart of Waikato. It's an early start so the sun is still low, and dew sits settled above the vastness ahead. All the signs are there for a roasting day, but for now coolness lingers, allowing me to move quickly.

Am I getting used to this? I feel strong and swiftly settle into a rhythm. Distance runners would tell me something along the lines of *it will take around ten days to settle, and you'll be fine after that*, or, *I felt good after a week*. For me, it's not until Day 17 that I feel ok...ish. Maybe that's from falling ill, perhaps it was always going to take this long but, finally, the pain is no longer at the forefront of my mind, though I'm wary of indulging any early, unwarranted confidence.

You see, a sense of assuredness resides when you know you can go to 'that place' and come out the other side. Each time you push your body to new limits, and continue to make it through, a quiet confidence grows. After 17 ruthless days, I'm at a point where I genuinely believe I can take any mountain, river or rainforest the Te Araroa throws my way. *17 days and you're still marching on. You can do this.*

I fly through the morning session to our meeting point back at Kaniwhaniwha Reserve. Covering the 15 kilometres in just a couple of hours is quick by my standards – so quick that the van is nowhere to be seen. They'd ducked out to a nearby town to get supplies and, with no phone signal, there's no choice but to sit and wait.

Of course, it's never in doubt, and within 15 minutes, they arrive to the surprise of seeing my chirpy mug waiting for them. It would have been idiotic for me to push on without restocking supplies as what comes next will be the biggest ascent so far, a near 1000-metre climb through thick forest to the top of Pirongia Mountain.

After a quick start along a gentle track, the trail turns under the canopy and the action begins. With each kilometre, the route only gets steeper and the terrain more challenging, a combination of gnarly roots and stinking bogs to contend with. It's a daunting task but, luckily, I've managed to find 'the zone' again, and I'm soon blasting up the mountainside. It's unclear how fast I'm moving until I zoom past a group of three lads out for a day trip.

"What are you training for?" They shout, impressed but baffled by my pace up here.

"This," I reply, smiling through gritted teeth. I haven't passed anyone since Day 4 so this encounter puts into perspective that, even when hiking, I'm quick. What usually takes a hiker five hours I'm completing in two and a half.

Being in the zone is like nothing else, as all you think about is that single moment. You hike as fast as you can, and as soon as you get the chance to stretch into a run, you take it, even if for only five meters. Your breathing rate is up, your legs burn, and thankfully, the adrenaline is pumping. It doesn't come without its distractions though. At times your watch entices you to take a look, just to see how many kilometres you've covered. Yet you know, if you indulge only once, it will continue to draw you in for another. Soon enough, I'll be checking to find it's only been 100 metres since my last peek. This can quickly become demoralising, especially when just minutes earlier I had been flying – unstoppable. Luckily, now, the summit is in sight.

From this vantage point, my eyes follow the sloping forest off the mountainside which leads onto the expanse of farmland below, that seems to stretch into the distance forever. It's daunting to gaze South to the horizon, knowing that so far and beyond, lays my path for weeks to come. Despite the intimidating thought, I feel incredible, my spirits are high, and any pain is a secondary consideration. Plus, I have only six kilometres left to reach the van!

A boardwalk has been built on the heights of Pirongia, heaven for runners after such an intense climb. It's time to let loose. Flying along the narrow planks, with six-foot drops on either side and trees whizzing past your head, is reminiscent of sprinting down a corridor after a few too many drinks! I feel like the fastest man in the world. *You'll be at the van in no time.*

Yet, in keeping with the pattern of Te Araroa, the fun soon stops. The trail makes you work your ass off for these incredible moments and, when you finally get them, and you are at the peak of your enjoyment, it slaps you in the face screaming, *Enjoy this!* Steep descents, huge drops, massive bogs, and more tangled roots. *You've had your fun, now get back to work!*

For every incredible view, there are two, three, five, even ten hours of hard graft. If the track's flat and comfortable, the sun will be boiling your back. If you stop for too long, your body aches, and you suffer for abusing what it's given to you.

It takes me almost two hours to cover the six kilometres from peak to Gerty, *so much for being with the van in no time.* Rest and porridge is the order of the day, and maybe even a short nap? Supposedly, the 'hard' part of the day is done, but I'm not convinced. Just because it's not a massive mountain doesn't mean it's easy.

In the mid-afternoon sun, Phil, Jill and I sit for a good hour, sheltering from the incessant heat in the dust-coated van. It's here, in the stinking, sweaty, and tired old Toyota, that we share an earned confidence. It's in the way we talk, in the way we sit, it's even in the way we laugh and smile.

Now, it's important to note, this is confidence and not arrogance. Of course, we can look back on the last 35 kilometres and be content with our efforts, and look forward with assuredness. Yet, we must not forget that at any moment, this can all come tumbling down around us. *We are doing well, but we have to stay focused.*

The late afternoon is spent meandering along gravel roads through the foothills surrounding Pirongia. Despite its calming beauty, the monotony is inescapable, so much so, it slows me to intervals of stumbles and jogs. Upon reaching the van again, my eyes can barely stay open and yawns continuously pour out. It's a question of whether the next ten-kilometre forest will be a stretch too far.

Falling asleep in the back of the van, soon justifies our decision to stop.

As I mentioned, we can't just camp wherever we like, and unfortunately, the nearest site is a 45-minute drive. Yet it's oh, so worth it, the road winds down the forested foothills which sit high above gorgeous valleys abundant with native plant life. Even as the forest gives way to the familiar New Zealand farmland, turning back reveals a view which can be enjoyed from the van's welcome comfort. I think it is fair to say the price has been paid for this one.

It's strange, after such a confident and assured day, flashes of self-doubt start to surface. I lie in bed, questioning my decision to stop. *Am I being savage enough?* Maybe it's the fatigue talking, but perhaps the fatigue is right.

Distance: 50km
Elevation: 2072m.

Day 18 - Humongous Sets of...

The forest run that looked so dark and daunting just last night, now appeals to my running senses. Excited by the prospect of swift-flowing trails through the covering trees, I attack before eventually clearing and entering the heart of Waikato's farmland.

A runner's dream can swiftly change to a nightmare; with the last of Pirongia completed, ahead lie the folding hills of Waikato. Sharp ascents and equally tricky descents follow one after another with no reprieve. It's a question of which gives first, the body, the mind or this harsh country.

Hours are spent tackling these near-vertical fields, but lessons of perseverance still ring in my ears. It's no contest – *they might batter and beat me down, but I will conquer them!* Such perseverance pays off. The reward? A cascading run through the thick Waikato Forest. Even with knackered legs, I can't pass up an opportunity like this to pick up the pace, dodging and weaving through pine trees down to a cooling stream, the perfect stop for a refreshing dip of my cap. Restored and invigorated, I deal with the final climb to meet the van at 24 kilometres. A morning run as ever-changing as the terrain. Today is lining up to be gorgeous.

Contrast again. Following a solid start, things quickly turn sour. After wiggling my way past the explosion of tourism at Waitomo Caves, it's back into more folding farmland. A sign warns of 'Bull in Field.' *Shit, there's no way around this one.* There he is, high on his hill, keeping a watchful eye over his pasture. *Run along the bottom fence, and hopefully, he won't spot you.* He doesn't move an inch, but that doesn't put me at ease. *One farm done, three to go.*

Still on edge, with adrenaline high and eyes wide, I work my way from field to field, trying to identify any bulls within the cows. With only udders in sight, I make it across without an encounter. This may sound silly, but sound reason and judgement will only get you so far in the face of a (largely) irrational fear.

A quiet road would be perfect now, to calm my nerves, but what follows is a terribly maintained track, if you could even call it that. Easily one of the worst of the whole trail. It looks like no one has bothered to even trim back a shrub in years with overgrown gorse and thorns attacking from every angle.

Hacking through the mess, getting scratched and scraped to bits under the roasting sun, I start to lose my cool. With my adrenaline still piqued, my senses are beginning to get overwhelmed. I can't keep control of my breathing; a sense of panic starts to take over. An overpowering desire to burst into tears builds inside.

This blood boiling sensory overload continues, not letting me get a handle of myself, and I trip and tumble to the ground in a dizzying haze. Instinct kicks in as I sit with my head between my knees, fighting back the urge to burst into tears. *Just breathe, don't think of anything else, just breathe.* Whether that's a natural reaction or learned from training with Marcus, I'm not sure, but running through some breathing techniques brings me from such a heightened state back down to a manageable space. Slowly I gather myself and try to press on, desperate to reach the van.

I don't remember much of the last few kilometres, just the odd image of a despairing face under the melting sun, desperately running across arid fields, praying for the end to be in sight. Eventually I reach my friends and my home, and this releases me from the prison of such a toxic mental space.

After a restorative break, I have to press on across more jagged farmland. Often the trail is well marked and clear to follow, yet sometimes, like today, it's anyone's guess where the little orange triangle is trying to send me. Considering I've just had a mini-meltdown, I'm doing well not to lose it again as I spend twenty minutes pacing in a circle, trying to follow the confusing directions. With no clear path, 'as the crow flies' seems to be the best option.

Ahead stand three rather large looking cows. *They're harmless,* I tell myself unconvincingly. We know what happened the last time I took the advice of my cow whispering friends. Worried that at any minute, the bovine brutes will stampede, I march forward, and they stare back with their abnormally large heads. My eyes then drift to their undercarriage. *Yep, they're not udders.*

The three massive bulls now stare back, with their giant foreheads turned to point. Now they might not have been bulls. An old friend might be sitting there saying, *there is no way three bulls would be standing together in the same field*, in their best Somerset accent. Maybe that's true, but I saw three jacked-up bovines and what looked like three humongous sets of bollocks. I was not going to hang around to check. I turn, walk and creep into a run, taking my chances with the harmless sheep in the next field. The road seems a far better option to get me down into Te Kuiti – less threat of re-enacting Pamplona.

I arrive to meet the team on the High Street of the self-styled Sheep Shearing Capital of the World, Te Kuiti. Although this town feels and looks like a great place to post up for the night, emotions cannot dictate my next decision. The question that comes up each day is 'what is the right thing to do?' As always, we have to remain objective. So yes, I'm upset and angry, but the facts tell us we can't afford to start the next day 17 kilometres off schedule. It might well be 6.30 p.m., and I'm a little worried about not making it through before sundown, but I have to go on. *Better take a headlight, just in case.*

These last 17 kilometres run alongside the river through the forested cliffs, hills, and rugged farmland of Mangaokewa Gorge. Thankfully, the first five kilometres are a blissful jog under the canopy and I'm at ease again, settled by nature's beauty. The trail sweeps from tree to tree, occasionally dipping down to the stream, revealing views of the towering cliffs, stained orange by the evening sun. The temperature drops fast as the last bird songs ring out.

My calm wears off as quickly as it appears. There's a sudden decline in temperature as the sun disappears and, with 12 kilometres to go, it's clear I'll have to make fair use of the headlight. My enthusiasm for the trail drops as quickly as the sun. That didn't last very long!

I cross the last bridge to the river's true left side and, the further upstream I go, the more enclosed the cliffs become and the trail deteriorates. Even in good light, the route would be almost unidentifiable, through the long grass and horrid shrubs. It's getting so dark in the forests that I can barely see, even with the torch. I would've been better off holding a candle to my head.

If I thought matters couldn't get any worse, the trail runs through the triple threat of gorse, thorns, and thistles. There is no other choice but to put my head down and blast through. I'm covered in cuts and scrapes and my clothes are being torn to pieces.

The thin moonlight does little to illuminate my path. Drifting back to the forested banks, the trail soon has me tentatively picking a route high above the stream, with a deathly drop threatening to the left, reminding me of my fall back in the Northland. In this darkness, I take to crawling on my hands and knees.

The trail then disappears altogether. In the low light, it's next to impossible to see any path or directions. The track has switched between cliff edge, forest and farm since the first kilometre, and I could have easily missed an orange marker. *You need to crawl up and away from the river, and regroup out in the open.*

Wrestling away from the riverbank, I break from the trees and head to the top of a hill, to try and get a signal – but I can't. It's time to assess my options. The route is lost, I can barely see, and there's still six kilometres to go. The map suggests the trail is just next to me. It then dawns on me; there's been a stile at every fence, each with a beautiful orange marker. *I have a plan.*

I follow the nearest fence down towards the river until reaching a stile and, sure enough, there's a little orange beauty. It points into the darkness, leaving me to guess where the next one might be. I'm barely able to see two metres ahead. Tentatively I move forward, wary of hidden drops, checking the map for detailed topography, and searching for the next glorious fence and hopefully another orange triangle pointing into the frightful nothingness.

This blind scramble is set to an eerie backdrop of disturbed cows and their unsettling calls. There's no way to know what field they've settled in and, of course, no clue whether I've unknowingly jumped into another bull's paddock. From their point of view, all they can see is a light floating across their field.

Soon enough, with a mix of persistence and luck, I find myself back at the bank on what looks like a trail underfoot, following a series of orange triangles and moving fast. Yet, as I continue, the path dwindles, and once again I'm facing in all directions, unable to see anything resembling the way forward. I must have missed another marker, and who knows how far back?

In a situation like this, backtracking is the obvious thing to do, but trying to be innovative, I attempt to sweep right and cut across to where I hope the trail will be. In a heightened, ultra-focused state, this sounds like a brilliant idea. However, all I find are more thorns, thistle, and gorse to battle with.

Now crawling on my hands and knees through bushes and dense forest, possibly going in circles, I'm getting nowhere but surprisingly I feel very calm. You might think I'd panic, or at least be worried, but I tell myself, *Lewis, whether it's in the next two hours, or the early hours of the morning, eventually, you will get out.*

Recognising my idiocy, backtracking to something resembling a trail is the obvious thing to do and, despite going round in circles for the last thirty minutes, I at least know which direction I came from. Low and behold, there's a little orange triangle pointing to the right, and not to the left route I'd taken.

The shocking conditions continue but, after hacking away at the bastard bushes for what feels like an eternity, they begin to thin, and the trail actually becomes identifiable. As it widens some more, it turns into a beautiful two-track dirt road. *This is it. I must be close. I bloody hope the van is here. Oh, please let them be here.*

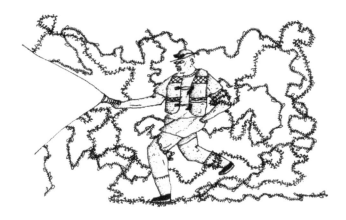

Running along, each and every corner promises salvation, only to reveal nothing around its bend. More corners and more minutes pass. *Surely, I must be close.* Doubts surface. *What if they couldn't get here?* It's entirely possible on some of these so-called roads. Then I see a small flicker of light shining in the distance.

"Hello!" I yell, but get no response. "Hello!" I frantically exclaim. This time I'm greeted by a great cheer. "Get the fuck in there!" I scream, my go-to response when pulling something out of the bag. What a weight that is off of a man's shoulders.

After my ordeal in the undergrowth, my body is covered in scrapes and scratches, and my feet are bloodied and blistered. Jill and Phil help sponge me down and cover my legs and arms in all the antiseptic cream we can find. I've quite literally dragged myself through a hedge

– forwards and backwards. However, I'm now right where I need and want to be, back in the safety of this little home on wheels, finally able to laugh at the state we're all in. There's no chance we'll find a campsite tonight, but who cares? The day hasn't gone anything like we anticipated, but at least it did get done. I lay in that top bunk with a great sense of accomplishment. *I managed to stay calm in the face of adversity and got the job done.* Feeling strong, feeling assured, I finally feel like the savage I probably need to be!

After settling into a process through the Auckland region, we felt we were operating smoothly and making significant progress. What followed in Waikato immediately tested our resolve and how we would respond when that process became unsettled. In this adventure, as in life, there will always be external events and occurrences beyond our control. Some may act in our favour and others to our detriment, but it's how we respond is most important.

Whether the external is acting for or against, there is a simple question to ask ourselves; What is the right thing to do? To get the correct answer and, therefore, the right reaction, it needs to be answered objectively. This is the difficult part. We have to answer not with our emotions but with sound judgment and reason based on the facts we have at hand. We may not like it now, but deep down, we know what the right thing to do is. The events of the Waikato region exposed us to this.

On the face of it, the unfortunate events that occurred – illness, hamstring – may have been a setback to our progress, but in our internal response, can we find the positive? Maybe not in terms of progress towards setting a new record, but perhaps I can discover it in a more personal way. Through this shared setback with Jill and Phil, have I developed greater bonds and deeper friendships that surpass the setbacks? Have I confirmed within myself an ability and strength to remain steadfast in the face of adversity?

891 kilometres. Northland, Auckland, and Waikato complete.

Distance: 68km
Elevation: 2016m.

MANAWATU/WHANGANUI

AT NATURE'S MERCY

'The chief task in life is simply this: to identify and separate matters so that I can say clearly to myself which are externals not under my control, and which have to do with the choices I actually control.'

-

Epictetus

Day 19 - Glowing In All Her Glory

We don't bother setting the alarm. I'm knackered, Phil and Jill are shattered, and we all need a good night's rest.

The morning light reveals a vast and hazy valley with no soul in sight, just a few young bullocks sounding off to let us know this is their patch.

We're still up at a decent time and, as we don't have to drive anywhere, I'm quickly out the door and on my way. The next meeting point will be back at the main road some 16 kilometres away. A reasonable distance to start the day.

I keep myself moving along the winding gravel paths. The incline becomes gentler and the hills look more like home as they roll into the distance. It's pleasant and uneventful – exactly what's needed after last night.

However, I'm close to 16 kilometres, and the main road is nowhere to be seen. *Have I taken another wrong turning?* A second check of the map reveals, to my horror, that the road isn't 16 kilometres away, it's 26. Not only is my body beginning to struggle, but I also can't seem to do basic maths anymore. To be fair, it's a happy mistake with no other choice but to push on. The team even drive in to find me, but I wave them off, determined to reach the road before I even think of stopping. This morning's effort will sustain my confidence for tackling longer stints moving forward.

A little side note which brings a smile to my face. As Phil flew the drone across the beautiful rolling expanse, he captured a Jurassic scene with giant dinosaurs marauding over the land. Ok, they were turkeys in the foreground, but the angle made them look like prehistoric giants.

No dramas. I reach the meeting point in good time. Next up, 11 kilometres along State Highway 30. It's never pleasant to run the main roads. However, in this case, it's necessary to reach the Timber Trail, an 80-kilometre walking and mountain bike route through, up and over Pureora Forest.

It's a little after 3 p.m. so completing the full 80 kilometres this evening isn't on the cards, but the next campsite is 37 kilometres away. There's no other choice but to get there. To add to the challenge, we don't know if the van can reach the site. Some roads do lead to the camp, but with the state they've been in so far, we have no idea if Gerty can actually make it.

We don't know the terrain, we don't know the area, and we can't load our maps because there's no signal. The decision is made to play it safe and for me to take an overnight bag containing food, a small stove and a bivvy bag. If the van doesn't make it, I'm sleeping on the ground with 40 kilometres still to cover the next day.

Last night I had found a way to be a savage, getting done what needed to be done no matter what. It's time again to turn on savage mode! It's become a phrase, a trigger to get me focused and ready to push my limits. Ahead, 37 kilometres across a 1275-metre-high mountain with an overstuffed backpack.

However, as I fly out the blocks, it's clear the bag is way too heavy. It bounces with each step, tugs at my shoulders and grinds into my hips, but I'm now in savage mode. I've started, and I'd sooner run 37 kilometres as is than turn back to faff and repack it all again. I'm too busy blindly being a savage.

In my savagery, I climb the trail's gentle gradient to the summit. Yes, gentle. Until today, all ascents have been on the most direct and steepest route possible, yet I now find myself snaking up the slopes over fine, smooth gravel and through what could have been sets for Western films. I'm half expecting bales of tumbleweed to blow past me. It's all a little too interesting and, dare I say, comfortable? At this rate, I might make camp before nightfall – the Te Araroa is never this accommodating!

After the summit, the day's elevation is done. From here on, it's a swift descent to camp – some 25 kilometres away. With confidence at a high and the challenge laid out, I attack.

Yet, of course, my aggression can only last so long before the physical stress becomes too much. You'd usually associate pain and anguish with an endless ascent, yet running downhill for hours on end zaps my energy and each pounding step overloads my muscles. *There it is. I knew the trail couldn't be all pleasant views and easy going. The TA strikes again.*

It's 7.pm., and I've been at this for nearly two hours, with only 12 kilometres to show for it. *So much for getting to camp by nightfall.* 13 kilometres and likely two more hours of relentless, hellish pounding still to go.

Although a grind, there's some joy to be found. Spectacular footbridges connect over lush, cavernous valleys, revealing stunning views below. A smile cracks on my face. Despite the trail's immense beauty, my energy levels continue to drop, as daylight fades. Darkness descends, and similarly I have to dig into my own dark place to push forward. No thoughts, no focus, just moving – trying to ignore the discomfort in my seizing legs.

The hours tick away, and so do the kilometres. Just like the previous evening, I know I'll get there. I just don't know when. However, getting closer only brings with it increased anxiety. *Will the van be there or is it the bivvy for me tonight?* Dread sneaks forward. *Please let them be there.*

It's now past 8.30 p.m. with only five kilometres to go. The switchbacks have been dispatched, and I've joined the worn roads. They look like the kind of surface our beast can handle, giving me hope that Jill and Phill will be there. I must sound like a mad man. I'm wishing and hoping out loud as I scan for any sight of Jill's or Bigfoot's footprint. I'm desperate, desperate because the van is my safe place, and the top bunk my little home.

The last five kilometres are agonising, and to pour salt into the wound, I rush past a luxury lodge. I fantasize a comfortable king-size bed, a power shower, a toilet with a flush. *If that's all the way out here, Phil and Jill must be too.*

I reach camp but there's no sight of Gerty. I run from field to field, getting increasingly desperate. They're nowhere to be seen. With fading hopes, I search the final meadow.

"Get the fuck in there!" I scream.

In the centre of the field stands the majestic sight of our beautiful van glowing in all her glory. Dread is instantly removed and replaced with the greatest grin I've had in weeks.

"Wow, am I happy to see you two!"

Our shower might be a bag hanging from a tree, my bed a shoddy mattress with no room to sit up, but they are a luxury compared to a sweaty bivvy bag on the ground. At least I would have been warm and dry and my belly full of food. There's nothing wrong with striving for more, so long as we remember to appreciate what we already have. And I have all I want and need tonight!

Distance: 75km
Elevation:1373m.

Day 20 - A Tin of Coconut Milk Can't Even Save Us

After two big days in a row, I feel unbeatable. My confidence is high, and I'm raring to go.

It's to be another long stint away from the van, with over 40 kilometres of the Timber Trail still to complete. Hopefully this will be much quicker than yesterday with no overnight backpack and no mountain to contend with. We set a target of 5 hours and 30 minutes to reach the end. This is new. Previously, I'd given rough estimates to the team and it was just about one foot in front of the other. Now, we're setting challenges. Savage mode has ignited some competitiveness in me.

At home, I could complete a ten-kilometre race quite comfortably in 45 minutes, and maybe get closer to 40 minutes on a very good day. Fresh, during training, I could do ten kilometres per hour on repeat, whether for three, four, or five hours. Out here, my average pace for ten kilometres is around 1 hour 20 minutes. Much slower than anticipated but, if that pace is consistent, I'm happy to keep moving. My first ten kilometre run that morning was spot on, hitting the 1-hour 20-minute mark, the next a little quicker at 1 hour 10 minutes. Things are pushing along nicely.

However, fatigue can sneak up and hit you out of nowhere. All of a sudden, I cannot stop yawning. My energy levels drop dramatically, and my legs feel like lead. The bench overlooking the forest below is just too enticing. Reasoning with myself that I've worked very hard over the last two days and haven't slept enough, both my body and my brain reach an agreement. I'm flat out, cap over face, counting the sheep. I'm wise enough to set a 20-minute alarm. To this day, it's the best nap ever taken!

Slightly refreshed and revitalised, it's easy to settle back into the good old 1.20 pace. With no severe changes in elevation, I work my way to the forest's edge and finally off the mountain.

However, upon reaching the van at the 42-kilometre mark, I'm back to feeling shattered again. It's 2 p.m. with plenty of time left in the day, so the decision is made to take another nap – this time a 45-minute snooze – and I'm out like a light in seconds. Actually, we're all shattered. Jill goes off to read which, as we know, is code for sleep. How she ever finishes a book, I'll never know. Five minutes in, and the kindle is whacking her in the face. Phil soon follows suit, starfishing on the grass in the open for all to see.

We're all exhausted, not only from the long days but let's just say sleeping in the van is an experience. Although there's enough room to sleep four, you'd all need to get on very well to make it work. The top bunk is cramped, and if you sit up at night, you'll likely knock yourself out on the van roof. The bottom bunk isn't the most spacious for two fully grown adults, occasionally you might wake up cramped against the sliding door or with a seatbelt halfway up your arse. If you want to get out, it's likely everyone will have to wake up as you climb across and out the side door. Of course, we have our tent and, whenever we can pitch it, either Jill or I have to be in it. To be honest; it's more often occupied by Jill. I feel selfish to claim my lovely top bunk but she insists, as my sleep is a priority.

Some nights, if there's no room to camp, we all have to be in the van. Now I don't want to say who, but one of us snores. I don't want to say who because she will kill me if I do. Hence putting up the tent at any opportunity, and why me and the snorer have to be separated. The snorer did warn me beforehand, and it must be said, it is some of the most prolific snoring ever heard. I'm no angel sleeper myself with the occasional violent snore and breath-hold, causing people to wonder if I was ever going to breathe again. These are just some of the challenges we didn't really anticipate or give any thought to. Occasionally it does affect us negatively, but it's all part of the challenge and fun.

It's important to point out that, as hard, horrible, and gruelling as this adventure can be, it's also fun. And for all the fantastic memories of outstanding views and beautiful nature, my fondest memories of this part of the trip are the times shared with Phil and Jill – sitting in the van, eating dinner and chatting. Going into this adventure, I didn't expect this to be the case, but it goes to show how we cherish beautiful moments of genuine social interaction.

It's the combination of a shared goal, the struggles, and the pain that strengthens the bonds between us. It is the connection between the event and the people involved that makes it so epic. Without this event, there wouldn't be true friendship and connections. Without these social links, the event would be empty and soulless. I can put my hand on my heart and tell you that Phil and Jill are two of the most important people in my life, and we will always share our memories of this adventure. I have many beautiful and amusing recollections from this trip, but the most dearly held always involve someone else there with me.

For example, after completing a further very tiring 25 kilometres, I reach Taramaranui to the news that there's a change in the menu. Phil gets us back to our supposed campsite for the night, where Jill has got her signature curry on the go.
We've been using an app to find our freedom sites, and Jill discovered an idyllic spot on the river, or so we thought. We arrive to find a sheepish and shocked Jill. The owner of a neighbouring campsite had been out to give her a rollicking. It turns out this isn't a freedom site, and the campsite owner certainly let Jill know it. We pack and move on.

Finally, we're settled on the other side of town, and our dinner is ready. One mouthful of curry, and Phil and I are both dripping with sweat. It's so hot that our tears burn our faces as they fall. My lips are on fire. The more my mouth salivates, in an attempt to cool down, the spicier things get. A tin of coconut milk can't even save us. Neither of us minds a bit of spice, but this is ridiculous.

I manage to finish mine because, well, what other choice is there? Phil manages a couple more mouthfuls but has to tap out. Jill can barely suppress the giggles, laughing at our expense as we scramble to cool our mouths any way we can. She wolfs it down with no apparent side effects. This is either an impressive and elaborate prank, or she has taste buds of steel.

So, we go from the promise of an idyllic, restful evening by the river to a mad dash and burning backsides. This is far from an ideal preparation before more big miles tomorrow, but we keep calm and carry on. Let us not forget, Jill is now banned from making curries and finding campsites. I think she just wants to get out of the cooking.

Distance: 67km
Elevation: 739m.

Day 21 - Nothing But Pants and a Towel

Up and at it, on the move again. It's odd to be constantly on the go. We haven't stayed in the same place for more than one night and, although it's a great way to see this wonderful country, we miss a certain familiarity, never feeling entirely at ease. It can be draining. It's not as if we're looking to rest, but for a chance to stop, more mentally than physically. I think that's why we all love Gerty. We could be in a car park behind a supermarket or on the riverside below the mountains. It never really matters because once we're in, we have everything we need to make it feel like our little home. A lovely view is a bonus.

It's the first day I've felt nervous for some time. The running will be split; a road section weaving through the valleys and farms from Taumarunui to Owhango, and an off-road segment – from Owhango through the Tongariro Forest and onto the alpine Tongariro National Park. It's the forest that brews the most nerves because I don't know what to expect. It'll be a long stint, with plenty of aggressive changes in elevation. We don't know if it's going to be easy-going or scrapping and scraping through brush and mud. With all the uncertainty comes nervousness. Add the threatening weather into the mix, and we have a recipe for an anxious start to the day.

I tentatively set off from Taumarunui into the valleys, and the heavens look poised for a downpour. *We're much too used to sunshine*. It's another tiring start. Clearly, I'm drained. We're twenty days into this, and the workload is catching up. My legs are used to the miles, and the pain feels manageable, but the tiredness is growing, reducing my energy, and making my eyelids like lead. Yet, I still struggle on, somehow managing to keep the now average slug pace.

The valley is another example of New Zealand's spectacular rough country – a lush green feast for the eyes as the road meanders from farm to farm between the towering slopes. It's surreal to trot past the town tennis court and swimming pool. A court that looks like it hasn't seen a ball and racket for 30 years, and a pool that's more like a large paddling pool. And town? I've seen three bulls, a thousand sheep, and a herd of deer, but no people to speak of. Very strange, but if you have the time and space, why not build a pool and tennis club for yourself and two neighbours?

The first 27 kilometres take a good four hours but, as we'd set out before 8 a.m., there's still plenty of time for Tongariro Forest. All seems well, yet the skies are still threatening. The air feels thick and muggy, it's an uncomfortable and sticky heat, and you just know it's going to pelt it down at any moment. Yet, we cannot wait.

Waterproofs on, there's no time to see what happens. There's still 34 kilometres and a mountainous forest to navigate. Nerves, anxiety – none of that matters. I'm here, my path runs that way and it must be followed. I know how far I have to go, time is on my side, and I've become consumed by focus and drive.

The trail notes read that the first 22 kilometres along the 42 Traverse follow a 4x4 track, leaving us all uncertain of what conditions await. Sharp gravel? Stinking mud and bogs? My worries ease at the sight of mud and loose gravel. Quad bikes have left deep ruts, but they've compacted the surface enough to make it runnable. It's more a playground for 4x4's and mountain bikes than a runner, but again, like the Timber Trail, it's able to capture the area's natural beauty whilst making it accessible.

The scenery has changed entirely. Both the previous evening and this morning were spent crossing jagged farmland. Now we're heading through sub-alpine conditions and beyond to the North Island's centrepiece – Tongariro. Large ferns line the canyon tracks. With such an array of vibrant and deep greens, you wouldn't be a fool to think you're in a South American jungle. I'm half expecting to see an Anaconda slither across my path or a Sloth hanging from the branches.

Even with suitable conditions underfoot, it's still harsh, hard work. The jungle humidity leaves me in a constant sweat, and the air is thick and warm to breathe. Yet, such trying conditions are balanced by a reward. From each ridgeline, views reveal the jungle range – a sea of trees, low dancing clouds, and unforgiving crags and cliff faces. In the depths of each canyon run chilled waters cascading from the mountains hidden in the clouded distance. A reminder of the volcanic beasts ahead – still to be conquered.

With ten kilometres to go, the Te Araroa turns off the somewhat comfortable 42 Traverse onto Waione-Cockers Track. Blink, and you'll miss it. It's only a small break in the trees, but it's enough to let me know things are about to get interesting.

A tight, overgrown track, a battle through bush and, of course, the heavens have now opened. The deep ruts quickly turn into water slides, and the crossings suddenly gain a daunting depth, with strong currents trying to drag me under. It feels like someone has grabbed the dial and turned the difficulty up to nine.

Now fighting my way through, and soaked from head to toe with a combination of rain and sweat dripping from my nose, I'm both exhilarated and beaten up. Every third step is a slip, and every opening soon closes. The worst part is trying to climb from each stream up the mud-splattered waterslides. With head-height walls of mud and enormous tyre ruts, it's a battle to find any sort of grip.

After battling for a torturous ninety minutes, things begin to level out. Although, there's no respite, the track is filled with bogs and puddles, and it's now pointless to try and dance around them. *Head down, straight through.* There it is, that flick of the switch to savage mode again. I'm eating up the miles with a grimace on my face. *Nothing is going to stop me.*

With just a few kilometres to go, I sense the van is close. I run with anticipation, with my head high, almost shaking with excitement to have this section dealt with. *It has to be there.* I smash through the overgrowth and there he is, Phil, looking as though he's entered a wet t-shirt competition. He's got his priorities right, using his waterproof coat as a cover for the camera. Jill is huddled under a tree, raring to get back to the van.

Another fantastic effort from the pair of them. There I am thinking *fair play, marching in this far to give their support, film, and help me over the last couple of kilometres.* Yet, little do I know it wasn't raining when they left. I'm not so sure they would have ventured out otherwise (I'm sure they would have).

Back in my youth, if I'd been out playing in the soaking rain and got covered head to toe in mud, Mum would make me strip down to my pants before even thinking of stepping foot in the house. It must now be an innate reaction, so now, before getting in the van, I'm down to my boxers – having chucked my wet clothes into the back.

Sitting in the front seat, still soaked and freezing cold, and with nothing but pants and a towel around me, we decide we're done for the day. Up next is a road run to the Tongariro National Park and, as it's getting late and the weather isn't great, we decide it's a good day's work in the bag, another 60 kilometres. *Save the road and volcanoes for tomorrow.*

"Do you want to know the good news or the bad news?" Jill questions.

"Let's start with the good news," I respond hesitantly. Jill replies with the familiar tone that everyone answers the good and bad news question with.

"I've managed to save us some money and get a deal at the campsite."

"Nice, and th..."

"But, tomorrow, there's pretty much no chance of you going up those mountains." Jill continues. "There's a severe weather warning. The Department of Conservation has deemed it unsafe. To let you know how unsafe, the shuttle busses that take tourists will not be running as they're not covered by their insurance if anything were to happen to a customer. The weather here changes very rapidly, so by the morning, the story may be completely different, but as it stands…"

Numb, soaked, and to be honest, a little sad, we can only look at what we can do right now.

"Let's get to camp, get showered, dried and fed, and then we can make a decision," I declare with confidence, in an attempt to hide my dejection.

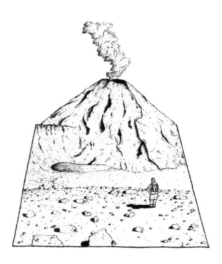

Over a dinner of bangers and mash, perfect in such wintery weather, we consider our options. If the weather is too severe to go up in the morning, we can sit and wait – although it's forecast to last for another two days, and we're already behind. Or we can skip this section altogether.

Our schedule is tight. With Jill and Phil taking time away from work to be here, they have specific dates to return. The attempt has to be all or nothing. A tight schedule is in place which only allows for an eight-day buffer, and we've already eaten four days into it.

We make a decision that we know will affect the rest of the adventure. If the weather is still severe in the morning, we will skip this section and gain a day back on our schedule. However, if we do this, any record attempt or full completion of the trail will be lost. Huge stakes and a decision we hoped we'd never have to make.

In all honesty, although we're slowly making back the lost time, I feel we are too far behind as it is. If all goes well with the weather, I will continue pushing to gain back time. But if the weather is terrible, I can't see us coming back from five or even six days behind.

The burning question is always, 'What is the right thing to do?' I've learned the answer is rarely black and white. What is right for one person may not be so for another. Some of you may think we should wait for the weather to change and stay true to the trail one hundred percent. Others may agree with our decision to move on if we have to. A decision like this is multifaceted; there is more than just me to consider. We must take into account this journey's aims, the people involved, and their lives beyond our immediate timeframe.

Distance: 61km
Elevation: 569m.

Day 22 - Blue Duck's and Cowboys

The next day we awake to see that the clouds are bunched, the rain still menacingly strong, and this shocking weather will likely continue all day. We come to a quick decision. We're skipping this section. It hurts to do so, I feel a little empty inside, but it's a relief to know Jill and Phil agree.

With our flights already booked, and considering we have already lost two days to illness, we just don't have the time to sit out the storm. It's also too dangerous to go up into Tongariro in these conditions. People die from getting lost in the fog on such a perilous track. The edge of a volcano is no place to be alone in the clouds, except for torrential rain and savage winds.

Coming to terms with a choice like this is hard, but we have to understand and accept that the weather is out of our control, and it's how we respond that is most important. Sometimes what to do is clear, easy to define by what is right and wrong, but other times, those lines are blurred. We've made our choice based on what we believe to be sound judgement and reason. We must press on.

Stepping up from the farms below into the Tongariro National Park is like moving onto another planet. From abundant green spaces and lush forests to the jagged rocks and harsh terrain. With the clouds low and a reddish tinge to the dirt, it feels like we've been transported to Mars. Unfortunately, the clouds are so dense there's no chance of catching a glimpse of any mountains. Still, you know they're out there. You can feel their presence.

There's no thrilling Tongariro Crossing across baron volcanic lands with bubbling pearlescent pools for us today. No, we're heading for the Whanganui River. Our next stop, Whakahoro and the Blue Duck Lodge.

I leave the National Park along New Zealand's spectacular Mountain to Sea Cycle-Path, another gem on this wondrous trail. From the summit of the lush valley walls, I'm welcomed by views cascading into the hazy distance, as the low clouds dance and linger in the depths below. It feels as though I've been released from the near lifeless high plains and thrust into bustling rainforests, so vibrant and full of life. The birds flutter and chirp, as their flashes of colour dance between the trees, and deer bound along the trail, guiding me along my path as they effortlessly jump and dive between the ferns.

The change is almost unfathomable. The lower the trail descends, and the further from the dark mountains I run, the warmer and sunnier my world becomes. It's bizarre to look back at the thick, aggressive clouds and think that, on the same day, I've gone from skipping a section due to severe weather to scorching sunshine where the only hindrance is the heat and flies. It does make me question our decision.

I join the Whanganui Road and catch my first sign declaring 'Blue Duck Station', although it teases me much too early. The last ten kilometres feel like a marathon, actually worse. Eventually, the lodge manifests itself, almost as if in answer to my fervent prayers.

The stunning Blue Duck Station is set amongst deep, tree-coated canyons, far inland along the Whanganui River. The nearest neighbours are fifty kilometres away, and the only way to get there is by boat. This is deep 'in country,' and feels like New Zealand's own version of the Wild West. Sheep farming and cowboys. I absolutely love it, Country living at its finest.

That evening Phil shot one of the most spectacular photographs I've ever seen, one that captured the paradise I'm trying to describe. A stunning black horse stands with mesmerizing power and beauty in front of the giant forested valley walls beneath a cloudless sky. Some people just have a gift, an eye for a picture, and it's safe to say Phil is such a person. Not only is the skill in capturing the image, but also in how he brings it to life in post-production. The colours I capture never quite match what I see in person. For Phil, the colours seem to pop just as they did in that single frame of time.

Tomorrow promises to be a big day, a 42-kilometre run across the Whanganui National Park to the Bridge to Nowhere. No roads lead here, hence the name, and the only other access is by water. The team will catch a boat from Pipiriki, the next town south along the river, and tow a canoe. However, if I'm not there before 1 p.m., they'll be gone without me and will not be leaving me the canoe. The game is on!

Distance: 54km
Elevation: 569m.

Day 23 - "Paddle!"

We need a canoe, not a kayak, because I've asked Jill if she wants to join me. As surprised as she is, her answer is an emphatic, *yes*.

Understandably, she has trouble sleeping due to the excitement, but she needs to keep her cool. Many people doubt her, they don't think a sixty-something-year-old woman will be able to canoe 32 kilometres before nightfall, but they don't know Jill like I do. I have total faith in her. I know what she's capable of.

Before canoeing, there's the matter of a marathon to deal with. 42 kilometres through the Whanganui National Park's thick jungle and bush-clad mountains. This is real wilderness country now, forests barely touched by humanity, save for the tight trails.

To leave enough time, we set a slightly early alarm, waking us at a dark and dreary 5.30 a.m. This will get me on the trail as the sun rises, leaving me six and a half hours to reach the Bridge to Nowhere – our rendezvous point.

Aren't early mornings just exceptional? Especially if you're up and at it just before the sun. Dew coats the ground, fog hangs in the deep gorge, and there's just enough light to illuminate the path. Then the birdsong starts, reverberating off the gloriously green walls enveloping the river.

The early hour, the weather, and the task at hand all combine to give a sense of real adventure. I feel like a genuine explorer of this wild land. My hamstring seems to have sorted itself out. So with the bit between my teeth, and plenty of energy to boot, it's exhilarating to be running right from the off, as opposed to my customary shuffle.

Each time I leave the team behind, a sense of pride grows within me at our growing achievements. Every morning now, my chest is held high and my confidence well intact. I'm now at the point where I fully believe I can get through anything this trail throws at me.

One of the standout features of this area, much like the rest of the Te Araroa, is the contrast. The first ten kilometres are deep in amongst the trees at the feet of the colossal gorge walls. Everything is so enclosed as you skip between the trees, everything rushes past in a blur. The trail then breaks from the foot of the hills and winds up the cliffs. Things really open up at the 600-metre summit. The earth's surface ripples and folds into the distance, showcasing a network of deep channels covered in pristine Kiwi bush and split by a rush of water.

Staring down from the summit, my mind begins to consider. *I was just down there. It felt never-ending, so tight, so enclosed.* Now I can see why after such a significant change in only a matter of hours.

The descent is just as epic. I gain momentum, skirting along hillside tracks, catching the last of the outstanding views, before diving deep again into the belly of the jungle. One moment I can see creases of hill after hill. Twenty minutes later, I'm immersed amongst them.

My focus is sustained, and so is my pace. With ten kilometres to go, and three hours left to spare, I'm delighted to realise I've managed to cover the first 30 kilometres in four hours, giving me time to slow down a while, to appreciate my surroundings that little bit more. *Now just a 32-kilometre canoe trip to contend with.*

I arrive at Bridge To Nowhere just as a tour is heading up the trail from the river. A few tourists look bewildered to see a hot, dishevelled man emerge from the forest, yet one kind lady does ask: "Are you the runner?" Jill must have been talking to them.

It's a challenge to remain chatty when you've just run a marathon through a forest, but I always remind myself to be patient. Although never really being in the mood to talk, it's still worth the time because the conversations are usually full of encouragement and admiration. *Remember, this adventure is meant to inspire others; being grumpy will never serve that purpose.*

I've arrived just after the boats have landed. twenty minutes sooner, and we could have left with plenty of time to get the job done. However, the boat has landed, the tour is underway, and we don't have access to the canoe. We have to wait. They ask me to join, but the covered seating area in the shade looks much more appealing at this point. *So much for not coming across grumpy.*

Phil and I decide to head down to the river. My jaw drops again. We're enclosed by enormous gorge walls draped in giant ferns which stretch way up into the sky. The slightest ripple folds through the water as the sun glistens off its surface, and the birds still sing uninterrupted at the top of their little lungs.

The change in climate and geography is, again, astonishing. Yesterday, we were up in the clouds atop a mountain plane in a scene dominated by the bronzes, greys, and dry yellows of the rocky and shrub-filled lands. It felt baron and harsh. Compare that to today, we've plummeted into what feels like a tropical rainforest. A wealth of greens from the variety of trees flood the senses beneath a beautiful bright blue sky. It feels rich and abundant with life. The two worlds can't feel further apart, yet we've got here in less than a day.

We relax on a huge boulder that seems to act as a river bus stop, as kayaks and canoes come and go. A couple of guides pull up with their tours, and we learn the rather unsettling news that most of their tours will complete the trip to Pipiriki over the next two days. It's safe to say they're surprised to hear we'll be trying to get there before sunset. I'm still confident but decide not to tell Jill this new-found information.

It's time. Jill's nervous, and everything feels a little anxious as we're about to set off. It feels like all the tour members have their eyes on us as Joe, the guide, talks us through the safety procedures. We don't fill him with much confidence. I get the impression that he doesn't think we're going to make it!

However, we remain confident, and, as I've got some experience with paddling canoes, I'll sit at the back. From here, I'm in charge of steering and matching the stroke of Jill in front. She's going to be the engine room and the lookout. She'll have to paddle, paddle and paddle, and keep her eyes peeled for logs, turns, and currents up ahead. She has to do the donkey work, but we feel it's the right setup, as she doesn't have much experience of steering.

It's 2.30 p.m., and we need to be off the water by 8, 8.30 p.m.— latest. Officially, the boats are meant to be off the water at 6.30 p.m., but we have no intentions of stopping.

I will admit, it's been a few years, and I'm a little rusty. We zigzag the first 50 meters, much to the amusement of the onlookers, and you can almost hear Joe thinking we have no hope. It's advised that if a jet boat flies past, you need to turn nose first to the wake. If you're side-on, it will rock and potentially tip you in, or worse, smash you against the cliffs. The next jet boat tour sets off next to us, and Joe is kind enough to slow right down. We manage to turn nose on, successfully achieving our first task, not capsizing in the first 100 meters. They all wish us luck and then they're gone. We're on our own. We'll next meet Phil down in Pipiriki. It's now down to Jill and I to get us there. A feeling I'm all too familiar with, but one entirely new for Jill.

We make a good team. We both have a similar character – stubborn to prove any non-believers wrong. Of course, no one has actually voiced doubts aloud, we're making this story up, but it adds to our determination anyway! I'd been Jill's fitness coach for three years by now and I know her character will not let her quit. Her arms may feel like they're going to fall off, but her mind will keep her strong.

I love the psychology behind teamwork. I can sense Jill's nerves and excitement, so I smother mine and try to project an air of calm and confidence, hopefully assuring her that we have this in the bag. Jill reflects the calmness and positivity from the off and believes we can do it. After the first 30 minutes it's clear that our positive approach is paying off.

Paddling along this calm and resting giant, you can sense its size and power. The cliffs tower high, and the sheer faces dive straight into the depths below, leaving you to wonder just how deep this river might be. You peer over the canoe's edge to see if you can catch a glimpse of the bottom, but all you see is the scenery reflecting off its eerily still surface. Although the river is gentle today, you just know it can be awakened from a downpour further upstream or off in the mountains. Even the conditions we'd left behind in Tongariro aren't enough to wake this sleeping serpent.

Luckily for us, the conditions are perfect, helping us to settle into a rhythm. We paddle and paddle, ticking off the kilometres, and soon arrive at Joe's Place, a gorgeous lodge sitting up from the river. Many kayakers and canoeists stay here for the night as they pass through but we're just here for a short break.

What an amazing life 'Joe' and his family must live. Their only access to anything is on the river. Nipping out to the shops? Hop in the boat. Got to go get some milk? Hop in the boat.

I chuckle to myself as we sit sharing a bar of Whittaker's Chocolate.

"Who would have thought us two would be here? Who would have put us two together as good mates?" I say to Jill. We laugh, but it's true. There are some 35 years between us, but we laugh, joke, and share similar philosophies and approaches to life. I never expected that one of my dearest friends would be a woman in her sixties, but I'm happy she is, and I'm grateful we get to share this part of the adventure together. It proves you can find a friend in anyone.

With daylight starting to fade, we can't spend too much time relaxing on the riverside. If this was a tourist trip with friends, it would be the perfect place to pitch a tent and get a barbecue on the go. But for us, it's back to the reality of four more hours in the canoe.

Luckily, the views continue to distract us, and the time just flies by. We manoeuvre around one corner, and the river flows into another dramatic gorge. Around the next, it surprisingly opens up into steep farmland. It feels more likely that we'd bump into crocs and piranhas rather than cows and goats but, as I'm learning, New Zealand is full of surprises. I don't mind the cows so much from a safe distance. Jill must think I've gone a bit mad in my usual solitude as she watches my attempt to converse with the cattle on the riverbanks.

Two hours later, heading into the last third of the river, we pull onto a small bank set below the cliffs to have some food and rehydrate. Jill is first to get out, but much to my amusement, she's frozen in her seat. After sitting for so long, she's seized up, and once she finally does heave herself up onto dry land, she can't get her river legs together, falling flat on her arse. Oh, but how I laugh too early. Similarly, I can barely move at the first attempt of standing and have to fight my way to my feet. I limp from the boat like a 90-year-old man.

Once the laughing finally stops and our legs have come back to life, we nail the flapjacks and some delicious elite-level, boysenberry cream sweets, and get ourselves ready to go again.

Now, being in a boat and surrounded by water for this long, you will inevitably need to relieve yourself. Jill at one end of our 20-foot island and myself at the other, making sure to face away. All I can imagine is Joe hurtling around the corner to find Jill asquat one end and myself piddling at the other. A second fit of the giggles ensue, we decide to keep the break short and clamber back in the boat.

We have developed our own unique technique for dispatching our vessel from the riverbanks. Common sense would say one of us should walk the canoe out and hop in when clear of the riverbed, but neither of us trusts ourselves to be able to jump back in the canoe safely without causing us to capsize. Instead, we walk it out far enough, so we're still supported to get in, and then, in unison, and I can't think of any better way to describe this, hump the canoe clear. It's safe to say, another fit of the giggles ensues.

Along the river are several rapids to manoeuvre. They're not white-water class, but get them wrong, and we could quickly be flipped out or smashed up against the cliffside. Joe had described the most challenging rapids to Jill but it's safe to say that her memory isn't great for specific things. She always says,

"I remember what needs to be remembered." However, now, when she needs to remember such vital information, she doesn't have a clue. "It's this one!" Jill shouts with certainty. The rapids are timid and easy. "It's definitely this one!" Wrong again. Time after time, we approach the rapids thinking, *this is the one*, and every time we get through, usually with ease. After clearing two or three, I'm starting to feel confident. I think I've got the hang of this. We line ourselves up and thrust our way in.

"Paddle!" we shout to each other, as if we know what we're doing.

"This has to be the one!" Jill declares. Looking at it, she could be right. She suddenly recalls the exact instructions. 'Hang right and cut across the white-water, and you might make it,' she confidently quotes.

Might make it? Joe estimated a ninety per cent chance that we'd be heading for the drink.

We line ourselves up.

"Paddle!" we shout, and paddle we do. We're getting smashed by the waves and thrown all over the place. In a situation like this, there is only one thing to do – laugh. I place my arms in the air to enjoy the ride as I'm certain it's curtains for us. Somehow, by sheer luck and a little bit of savvy, we make it through. *ninety percent chance? My arse.*

We relax. Our beautiful van is in sight, with Phil standing at its side. The drone buzzes overhead to catch our arrival in Pipiriki, and we wave, scream, and shout, absolutely delighted that we've made it – and in just over five hours. What an effort, particularly from Jill, as she didn't stop paddling and kept a watchful eye all the way. Well, when I say all the way, all the way except the last 100 meters.

I look over Jill's shoulder to see a huge rapid ahead.

"Jill!" I scream, "Paddle!" I try to steer us right of the white-water, but we have no chance. It's dragging us in at pace. I brace myself for capsize, keeping one hand on my oar and the other on the boat, and we almost hang on but finally we're dumped out the side. Luckily for me, I can see it all happening, and I manage to fall out, keeping hold of everything, and keeping my head above the water. I can't say the same for Jill. She paddles and paddles with everything she has, desperate to make it through, but of course, she's launched from her seat.

She emerges from under the boat with oar in hand, just as she had been told to. I can see the shock on her face, yet all I can do is laugh. I watched the whole episode unfold, and poor Jill just didn't see it coming. Maybe we could have made it if I'd kept on paddling, but I doubt it. Plus, it was worth it just for the laughs.

However, the joke's now on me as I have to drag the boat up the slippy, muddy, steep bankside to turn all the water out. The canoe nearly sank as we swam it to shore so, instead of bailing, we have to turn it over. Finally, we manage to hurl ourselves back on board. Only 100 meters to go, let's not fall in again.

Upon arriving at Pipiriki and tying up the canoe, we can do nothing else but see the funny side. We were pretty much there. Surely, we had made it. The end was in sight, but true to the Te Araroa, we couldn't have it all without a small price to pay. Mother Nature capsizing us much to her amusement, I'm sure. And to top it all off, a third pair of sunglasses were lost in the process. At least this time, they're not mine.

The day is done, 67 kilometres completed by foot, canoe and a little bit of swimming.

Distance: 74km
Elevation: 824m.

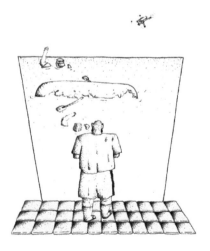

Day 24 - Fire and Vomit!

Just to make clear how glamorous this long-distance running can be, today's breakfast consisted of three bowls of Jill's Magic Porridge, three boiled eggs, three pieces of toast, a banana, a coffee, and plenty of vitamins to wash it all down. So most sessions begin with a belly and oesophagus full of food – it's like filling the car before a long journey.

As a result of this bingeing, I usually throw up a little bit to start each run. Initially, it was a bit of a shock to my sensibilities, but I've become so feral that puking whilst running has become the norm. I'm already uncomfortable, I already stink, so what's a little puke as you run along?

Today we have a choice between river or road. We choose to run. As delightful as it would be to continue downriver, it's time to get back to slapping pavement and I'm sure the views will still be stunning.

Although the road runs beside the river, it's by no means easy-going – just easier than jungle – or gorse and bramble. The first ten kilometres see the most undulation, revealing more fantastic vistas in the spectacular National Park. I remind myself to stop once in a while to take it all in. The steep valley walls begin to give way to farmland and more rural villages pop up. I pass through, ticking them off as my checkpoints.

Upon arriving in the little town of Ranana, I spot an enormous tree in front of the primary school and decide to take a break, under the shady canopy, and take in my surroundings. Someone's front gate acts as the corner shop. A cute wooden board declares 'Ice Creams \$2', but to my slight disappointment, another sign says 'CLOSED'. Yet, it only makes me chuckle. The calmness of this lovely little village is infectious.

The day's more relaxed feel is notable. No rapids, no trails to get lost on, no undergrowth to battle. All we have is a road to run and all day to do it. With few obstacles ahead, I'm eyeing up a hefty

75 kilometres and decide to break it down into manageable chunks. *Get the first 25 kilometres done.*

'COFFEE', a random road sign promises.

"Coffee!" I cry with delight. *A cafe? Out here? Is the heat getting to me? Am I seeing things? Oh god, I haven't had a good coffee in weeks. Lord knows I love a good coffee.*

I'm not seeing things. A few kilometres later and we find the welcoming Matahiwi Cafe. A sit-down and chat, with some surprisingly decent brown nectar, and I'm relaxed and happy. I could stay all day but unfortunately that's not possible. It's time to get back to it. Reluctantly I get myself sorted – another trip to the toilet, another glass of water, but I can't postpone things much longer. It's soon time for the afternoon session.

It's always difficult to get started after a nice break, especially at the hottest point of the day. It affects my outlook too. That which was spectacular and mesmerising now feels monotonous. It's a strange sensation to see beauty, acknowledge it, but not be able to appreciate it. When boredom strikes and discomfort kicks in, time seems to slow down. Or is it the other way round? Does time speed up during wonderment and excitement? Who knows? Maybe both, but I'm in the dreaded place of doing anything and everything to occupy my mind, and fighting the urge to constantly check my progress.

On the road continues, and my prolonged battle with the wristwatch paradox is finally broken by my second break, where I find Jill and Phil sunning themselves roadside, like the two Brits abroad they truly are. They're certainly chilled and, even though I'm bored, we're confident about getting the last 27 kilometres done.

We crack on, scheduled to meet again 15 kilometres downriver. The team sets off, and I'm back on it. However, only a couple of kilometres in, before even hitting something resembling a stride, a car pulls over.

"Looks like your day is done, fella." says the driver in his strong kiwi accent. "The police have shut the road. There's been a fire, and no one will be getting through here tonight." I'm confused,

Phil and Jill have gone ahead, but then he tells me, "Your mum and dad are waiting for you at the blockade." Instead of correcting him, I go along with it, just about holding in a giggle.

"How far away are they?" I ask.

"About 3K?" he guesses. Turns out this guy is another awful judge of distance. Seven kilometres later, I arrive at the van.

I can't quite believe my eyes. Plumes of smoke rise from the hills. Helicopters circle in the distance. They swoop to fill their giant buckets and loop back to dump water on the flames. It's a mad scene, and incredible to watch the pilots, police, and fire and rescue do their work.

Josh, an attending police officer, informs us that they're slowly getting control of the flames, but he has no idea if the road will be open tonight. Most cars have turned back and abandoned their journeys. It all feels a little too routine. No one seems fazed, surprising considering the alternative route is a long four-hour detour.

We decide to sit and see what happens. We have nowhere else to go and, if we have to, we'll just stay the night right here. I'm pretty sure Josh won't send us packing or give us a fine. What else can we do? There's no way we'll be going for a 4-hour drive, and we certainly won't be travelling on a road on fire.

Shouldn't we be feeling angry or upset? Well, no. This is an event well out of our control. We can't do anything about the fire, or the road being closed; we can only choose our response. Disappointed? Yes, but we can't let that influence our decision-making. There's no chance of continuing, so why get annoyed? Once again, we're at nature's mercy.

A couple of hours later, and much to our surprise, we're given a police escort through to the other side. They've managed to get the fire under enough control to take cars through. It's like a dramatic scene from a blockbuster movie. Helicopters buzz just above our heads and swoop to the river below. A layer of smoke clouds the air, and we can feel the heat blasting from where the fire once roared. Lines of emergency vehicles are ready and waiting, and we catch a proper glimpse of the massive buckets, each one almost the size of two fire engines, side by side. Trees are burnt to a crisp, electricity poles droop across the melted roads, and we trundle through in both amazement and, to be honest, a little fear.

People often say, 'You can't prepare for the unknown', but I'm not sure I agree. Perhaps the phrase should be changed. 'You can't completely prepare for the unknown, but you can be ready to respond to whatever happens.' We couldn't have prepared for a forest fire to halt our progress, but we could certainly be prepared to make decisions with good judgment and reason when faced with an unexpected event.

Our response is calm. We decided that if not for the fire, I would have made the target kilometres. Therefore, we call it and will continue tomorrow from where we would have finished.

Now, I didn't completely openly express my thoughts and feelings to the team. There's a little question in my head asking if we made the right choice. Did we take the easy option? Now that 100% completion is out the window, has it become too easy to miss sections?

There's heavy pressure on each decision, stemming from our own perceptions, of course. Let's not forget, when a decision is to be made, there will be implications – both good and bad – no matter what route is chosen. All I wanted to do was 'the right thing', and it wasn't until writing this that I realised doing 'the right thing' is subjective.

Distance: 55km
Elevation: 709m.

Day 25 - Bulls, a New Word For...

I set off walking with Jill along the river. She likes to keep as active as possible, and as the first couple of kilometres are through Whanganui, we decide to walk them together. I'm probably a little quieter than usual. I'm shattered and still wondering if we did the right thing yesterday.

As soon as it's time for Jill to turn back, it's a struggle to break into stride. Try as I might, my body just will not allow it. I feel broken. My legs are like lead, energy at a new-found low, and it shows. The riverside here is a running hotspot. Half the town goes whizzing past, looking confused at the sight of this athletic, youngish man running like he's shit himself. Yet, 25 days in, what could be expected?

They don't know how far you've run. I don't expect they will be running to Bulls today, whispers my ego, something I usually manage to suppress.

Fatigue is getting in the way of logic, and the jealous, childish ego is shining through. Bulls is the name of our final destination today, not athlete's terminology for running stupidly far, very slowly, for a really long time, although maybe it should be. Just what you need when you haven't quite got up to speed is a giant set of steep stairs to contend with. There I am, hobbling my way up, being passed by a young couple doing their morning sprints. Up and down, they race, looking like fine-tuned athletes. I feel and look awful, as if it's my first ever attempt at running. *Oh, the contrast.*

Yet, I make it. Now up and away from the town, the road runs inland for the next 15 kilometres before turning back towards the coast – and straight into a savage headwind. If I was struggling to move already, this headwind brings me to almost a complete standstill. If I stop moving, it feels as though I'll be carried back on the wind to Whanganui.

On the wind tunnel goes, with the HiAce acting as a beacon at the end of the deceptively long and tragically straight road. Each time I look up, it feels like I've gone backwards, and the van has driven further away. Yet, as every challenging section has done so far, it ends, this time with a coffee as a reward for my troubles.

Next up, the black iron sand of Turakina Beach. It's like a negative image of what most of us see when we think of 'beach paradise,' but I love it. Adding to this gritty scene is the colossal amount of driftwood, deposited by big sea swells and high rivers, which makes traversing the ever-shifting dunes and sand traps a challenge. Overcast clouds emphasise the darkness. It's harsh, dark and rugged, but still striking and elegant.

The tide is ranging in with not a patch of hard sand in sight. I slog away, zigzagging up and over masses of driftwood, but I can't find any traction anywhere. I just have to keep slogging it out for the next 20 kilometres. *This is going to take forever*.

If the treacherous conditions underfoot aren't enough, the river is up.

"Where do you cross?" I shout across to the gentleman riding his motorcycle up and down, trying to find his own safe spot to get over. He signals back, raising his hand to his chin to suggest its depth.

My mind flashes back to the last estuary crossing, yet I'm faced with a much faster current this time. I whip off my shoes, pack all my items in the water bladder, step into the river, and it almost takes me clean off my feet. *Stop, reassess*.

Getting across will leave me soaked from head to toe, if the man's predictions are right. A further 15 kilometres wet running would be a nightmare. Imagine the chaff on the feet – and anywhere else the sand might get.

Now, the map does display a forestry road running parallel, and I fancy my chances that, on a Sunday, there won't be much tree-felling going on. And I'll be on this beach all bloody day otherwise.

Fortunately, the river isn't anywhere near as deep as the man had suggested, although there's no way he'll be getting his bike through. It only comes up to waist height but is still a bit of a battle to get across. As Jill's on her way, I might as well take the change of clothes and head inland. *The soft sand can piss off.*

I lumber through the gravel infested forest and join the roads again. All around me is flat and empty land. It's like 90 Mile Beach all over again. I pick a landmark like a tall tree off in the distance, but it never seems to get closer. I listen to an hour-long podcast but I'm still on the same sodding road. I end up picking off telephone poles one by one just to keep myself moving. You'd think a flat open road would be perfect for picking up some pace, but I just can't do it. I hold a huge mental block for this type of scenario, and my mood is deteriorating to the point of screaming and swearing out loud.

Slow mile after slow mile, telephone pole after telephone pole, finally the little white tic tac becomes visible. Typically, upon seeing the van, I think, *I'll be there in a couple of minutes.* For 35 minutes, it remains in my sights. For 35 minutes, it sits there, testing my patience. It's happening again. Every time I look up, I swear it's never any closer.

Knackered and pissed off, I finally get close. Still, there's no movement. *Where have they gone?* Usually, there would be some activity – Phil might be out and about filming, Jill is usually out the back prepping some food – but nothing. *Maybe they're being Brits abroad again. It's so quiet.*

I peek through the window to see Jill absolutely zonked in the front seat, head back, catching flies – and Phil spread out in the back, snoring his head off.

It's too good an opportunity, I have to get them for this! I get my phone out and start filming. I knock and shout,

"I'll tell you what! It's hard work for these two, innit? There's me, doing all this running, and here they are having a nap!" All I get in response is laughter from Jill and the middle finger from Phil. This cheers me up immensely.

The last five kilometres are completed in my socks, my feet so sore and swollen they can't fit in my shoes. It's a good job I have plenty of barefoot running miles in the tank. Finally, I reach the day's end.

Distance: 66km
Elevation: 463m.

Day 26 - A Dark Turn

Pleasant is definitely the word to describe the morning run, both in feeling and scenery. Farms as far as the eyes can see and the sun shining overhead.

It's a bright morning made even brighter by a call home to Mum and Dad. We haven't spoken for a few weeks, leaving much to discuss. They could likely tell I hadn't spoken to many people, as I chew their ears off for about an hour and a half. But they don't mind, they're just eager to listen to the stories, as soon they'll be joining us. Neither of them has been on a long-haul flight for years, let alone to New Zealand, so I'm delighted for them to come and see this beautiful country and be a part of this fantastic adventure.

As if to prove that Te Araroa is ever changing, a stretch of mysterious and angry looking mountains loom on the horizon, casting a shadow not only on the land but also my mind. Their presence ominous, especially as we know that tomorrow I will be in amongst them. *Everything may be comfortable and calm now, but soon this will all change.*

Apart from the terrible conditions in Tongariro, we'd been pretty lucky with the weather, if you can count 30 degrees as lucky. By the time we reach the town of Fielding, smack bang in the middle of farm country, it is absolutely baking again. We schedule a decent rest stop to hide from the sun before heading on to Palmerston North.

However, the bright morning suddenly takes a dark turn. In my first steps from the van, my mind goes blank. I struggle to see, and my legs give out from underneath me. An overwhelming rush of heat shudders through my body, and the whole world spins as nausea overcomes me. It's as if someone has pulled the plug. Phil and Jill drag me back into the van, and I'm out like a light.

Forty-five minutes later I awake, confused and shattered. Heat exhaustion? Dehydration? I have no idea. I've been feeling pretty good through the morning session and have consumed plenty of water and electrolytes – maybe not as much as I thought. It's difficult to judge need accurately in such energy-sapping conditions.

It's at moments like this that you have to ask yourself, *how far are you willing to go?* To me, there's no doubt about it. I must get back on the move. I would've been kidding myself to think there weren't going to be dark moments, I expected to feel like this at some point and, equally, I expected to carry on. To be honest, this is what I'm here for, to test my limits. I want to see if I can go to those dark places and keep going. I've made it through the injuries and now have to make it through exhaustion and heat. Maybe it's foolishness or perhaps it's strength. The line between is often thin, but this is the test I'm after – to see my response to adversity.

Jill walks the first few kilometres with me to make sure I've got it in me to carry on. Despite nausea and an intense headache, I give her the thumbs up and, somewhat reluctantly, she leaves me to it. That must be a horrible position to be in. Clearly, Jill trusts my ability, but she can't be sure that I'll make it to the end of the road, let alone to Palmerston North.

The run along these busy roads is slow and taxing. My body is all over the place, but it's really a battle of the mind to make it through. With cars flying just inches past me, the continued worry that someone overtaking won't see me on the other side, and the heat – my stress levels are rising fast.

One of the most significant psychological elements Marcus and I worked on was awareness and, in this scenario, I'm stressed but not aware enough to deal with it. My mind is stuck on playing the game hard and not smart. It's not until making it past the bulk of speeding traffic that I eventually calm down and get some perspective on my situation. These were far from my finest hours, but we made it through.

Tonight, we are to be joined by Louis, a great running friend from home who has just moved to New Zealand with his fiancée. After just moving into their new house In Wellington, he is to leave and join us. Luckily his fiancée, Rosie, is very understanding. We will be running together from Palmerston North, over the eagerly anticipated Tararua Ranges, and back down to their Wellington home. It's safe to say I'm delighted to have him on board, as those ranges are a scary prospect for both of us. I can't imagine taking them on alone.

This all came about because months before the start of the adventure, we'd figured out that Louis would be arriving in New Zealand around the same time as us, and so he offered his help. The Tararua Ranges had long been in the back of my mind as my first real experience of tricky mountain terrain. The route demands a night away from the van and, more than likely, unpredictable weather. What better time to have a good friend alongside you? Upon showing him images of the extraordinary mountain range, he signed up there and then. Initially, he was going to do the ranges and head home, but he then decided if he was going to do that, he might as well keep running all the way. Result!

The Manawatu/Wanganui region has well and truly been a test of physical and mental fortitude against both internal and external influences. From the weather on Tongariro to the forest fire on the Whanganui, Mother Nature flexed her muscles, showing just a glimpse of her power.

We had our plan, I'd trained tirelessly for over a year, we'd put time, money and extreme effort into the adventure to get to this point. We have poured our hearts and souls into the past four weeks and prepared the best we could. Yet, there are forces at play that we cannot control.

Throughout anything we face, from adventures to all of life's challenges, we are likely to be at nature's mercy. At any moment, an external influence can cause an adverse or even detrimental impact upon our endeavours, and there isn't much we can do about it. We can prepare to react with creativity and perseverance, but we cannot always dictate the outcome. Although you and I know this, it is still hard to accept. Yesterday, I believe we responded correctly considering our circumstances, but the questions still chip away at me. Should we have waited out the bad weather? Should we have gone back on ourselves to redo the section?

Although frustrated as I lay in bed that night, I brush the questions aside, or at least attempt to put them to the back of my mind. *We have bigger fish to fry.* The Tararua Ranges loom, and Wellington is in sight. The end of the North Island is near, but it will not be an easy path to get there.

Four North Island regions completed leaving just Wellington to go. Starting from the 1477-kilometre mark.

Distance: 46km
Elevation: 385m.

WELLINGTON

SUPPORT

'Individual commitment to a group effort--that is what makes a team work, a company work, a society work, a civilization work.'

-

Vince Lombardi

Day 27 - Louis

I awake, knowing that today will be different. Many questions run through my head. *Will Louis be fit enough? Will he be able to cope? Will we be able to conquer these mountains?*

The dynamic has shifted within the group. Yet, this change is currently both good and bad because nothing has happened yet. The cat is both dead and alive whilst the box is still closed!

Louis and I have run together a handful of times. In fact, one of my first training runs was with Louis up the south side of Cheddar Gorge and before I knew it, he was merely a dot in the distance. By the time we met at the top gate, he was fresh-faced, smiling and barely out of breath. There I was blowing out my arse, trying to get the air in any way possible.

Fast forward six months, and we ran the West Mendip Way together, a 50-kilometre trail run from Uphill across the Mendip Hills to Wells. It was safe to say he was shocked by the transformation in me. I'd gone from gasping for air on a one-kilometre climb to smashing a challenging 50-kilometre run in five hours.

Louis has to find a way to pace himself. He's used to short races, from five or ten kilometres to half marathons, so the distances and pace we'll be running are totally different for him. We know he will start fresh and full of energy on the first day, whereas I feel like I'm at death's door.

We haven't seen each other for a while, so we chat away the miles and before we know it, we've chewed away most of the day's kilometres in just four hours. I can't believe the difference having a fresh partner, raring to go, makes. In hindsight, I wish I'd found more running partners.

The first 30 kilometres break us away from the town and into the foothills, giving us a glimpse of what's to follow in the imminent Tararua Ranges. We gradually work our way through the more familiar farmlands and forestry fire roads, and before we know it, we reach 600 meters above sea level.

What follows is one of my fondest running memories. Atop this summit, we are greeted by some of the gnarliest downhill trails I've ever come across. It's as if we've been transported back home – steep single tracks through woods, dodging roots, catching grips and slides, and using the trees to propel around corners. It's too good to turn down, what other choice do we have but to go for it? You can tell we're both in the zone. You can feel and hear the smiles on our faces, we don't need to see them, it's pure running joy, a runner's high. To top things off, the trail finishes at a glistening stream with the sun breaking through the canopy Just bliss.

The dust settles from the magical run, and we settle back into the reality of just plodding along. The track follows a map of streams for the next ten kilometres before we eventually reach the van at the 40-kilometre mark. As much as I loved that descent, it has absolutely zapped me, and my pace comes crashing back down. I swiftly settle back into my Te Araroa Trail shuffle, and it's perhaps just a little too slow for Louis.

I'm quite a competitive person, so I must be honest that competitive games are being played in my head. *He might be quick now, but will he last all day? How will he be coping three days from now? He hasn't been doing this for four weeks straight. Lewis, you're doing ok.* I do my best to not let my competitive nature spoil anything, but it gives me a little extra drive and grit when I need it.

What happens next is most unfortunate and comes out of nowhere, as many of you, I am sure, can appreciate. Suddenly, Louis' stomach doesn't feel so fabulous, and quite quickly, it wants to empty itself, and not from the good end – if there is a good end. He pulls aside just a half a kilometre from the van and does what needs to be done. Some 20 minutes later, he trundles in, looking paler than his usual ginger self. Yes, I left him behind, but how was I going to help? Plus, I need to eat and certainly don't want to ruin my appetite.

We rest, eat, and drink, but all to no avail. Louis clearly has half a mind on the much tougher days to come and so, rightly pulls out of the last section. We'd both drunk from the stream, so we don't think it's that. Could it have been his greasy veggie burger from the night before?

It's now gone 4 p.m., with 20 kilometres to go up over an 800-metre mountain. In my mind, I need to show what it's going to take in the days to come. Rightly so Louis stopped, but in my mind, I'm winning in the little competition I've created.

If the first two sessions of the day are giving us glimpses of what's to come, this evening session feels as though it's asking, *Are you really ready for this?* The ascent is higher, the terrain far more challenging, and the heavens are threatening to unleash.

Fortunately, right when it's needed most, I manage to go to 'that place,' get myself into 'the zone', and pound away at the hill, marching and charging at each and every step. I have to be quick because the clouds linger with intimidation, the sky has transformed from bright blue to grey to black in a matter of minutes, and rain feels imminent. The higher I climb, the darker the sky grows, but the rain is yet to fall.

Higher again I go, and still, it continues to hold. Yet, as soon as I reach the summit, the heavens finally let loose, soaking me from head to toe in a matter of seconds. You might think it would dampen my spirits, but quite the opposite occurs. The downpour charges me forward, and I keep ploughing on despite the torrent. The more adversity thrown at me, the better.

I charge through the seven-kilometre tricky forest onto the farmland below. Phil is the van master, and he times his arrival perfectly. Just as I hop the gate, he comes flying around the corner, parking right at my feet as I land. The back door flies open, and I dive straight in. Soaked head to toe but with 60 kilometres in the bag, we've made it to the start of the Tararua Ranges. A big tick in the box.

Distance: 58km
Elevation: 1920m.

Day 28 - Room With a View

Thankfully, Louis wakes feeling recovered. I'm relieved as today is a big one. We head into the Tararua Ranges, renowned for being some of the wettest and most challenging trail in New Zealand. The plan is simple: get as far as possible. The next viable meeting point is 53 kilometres away, which is doable. Unless you have three peaks standing over 1000 meters above sea level, persistent rain, slippery rocks, and stinking bogs in your path.

Despite some nerves, our confidence is high, and we set off across the lowland farmland, which we quickly discover is much more of a challenge with an overnight bag weighing each of us down. Although confident we can make it through, we know it would be silly to try without the safety of overnight gear. Some stories we've heard suggest it may not be a straightforward run and, on cue, a 'Never Travel Alone' signpost reminds us how lucky we are to be tackling this together.

It's not long before we start gaining elevation through the mountain forests and ascend into the low clouds. When you break into the fogs, you enter a new world, a damp and cold world full of bogs that swallow your shoes, trees covered in a thick coat of moss, and roots slithering below like a pit of snakes. We're both struck by its beauty and filled with awe at its darkness.

We cover the first five kilometres at a half-decent pace in 45 minutes, respectable considering the conditions. The second five, with an 800m ascent, take us 90 minutes. There's no way we could have gone any faster, we've pushed our limits to get some early elevation, but after almost two and a half hours, we still haven't reached the day's first summit. I've never been in conditions like it. With the bags on our back and the relentless climbing, it's already looking like we'll be staying the night.

Even when reaching an open ridgeline or decent descent, we can't find any speed. The terrain underfoot is just too challenging; one misstep, and we're knee-deep in a bog, one mis-calculated root, and we're slipping flat on our backs. We're averaging under four kilometres per hour – at times less than two. Every step takes concentration and enormous effort. We're either marching uphill, climbing up slips, or tiptoeing from slimy roots to trusty tree trunks, trying to avoid the bogs below. More often than not, we have to gamble that a branch will hold, or a root won't slip. There are no simple steps.

Hour after hour, we plug away. We're damp, our energy is being zapped, and our legs are getting sluggish and heavy, but our spirits never shut down, our desire never dwindles, and our concentration never collapses. We have a job to do, and we are both determined. This is why we teamed up – to face this adversity together.

Eventually, after five hours of non-stop toil, we break out above the treeline and on to the tussock mountainsides. We're quickly disabused of our dream of breaking through to unparalleled vistas. All we see is tussock grass and a grey abyss enveloping us. The Te Araroa is not giving us the goods after a mere five-hour slog. No way. If we want to catch a glimpse of these astonishing mountains, we will have to earn it.

Although it is disappointing, we get a sense of intensifying excitement – a feeling I believe everyone should experience in their lifetime. We've battled your way high up into the clouds only to be greeted by a veil of grey, adding an extra element to the adventure. We're climbing the mountainside, not knowing how far we might fall if we slipped over the edge. Equally, we can't see how far we have to go – the summit is never in sight. It begins to torment us. We feel like we are stuck repeating the same patch of trail over and over.

There is something to be said about the silent bond between two people striving through shared adversity. We'd spent the previous day covering 60 kilometres to get to the foot of these mountains and, today, we're a part of each other's experience as we toil our way up. We know one another's pain, we know one another's struggle, and we know that, despite this, we will both carry on. Conversation filled our day yesterday, but today it's not required. Just a nod or grunt will do.

When we do speak, there's a contrast in how we encourage ourselves. It might sound a little crazy but, if you've ever physically and mentally pushed your limits, you'll know that your self-talk doesn't just stay in your head. We laugh at our different approaches.

Louis gives himself positive self-talk, "You're an endurance machine!" he shouts or, "You're a beast, you've got this!"

For the most part, the things I say to myself are positive and encouraging but, when I really need to dig deep, I find more aggressive language works perfectly. I'll tell myself, "Stop being a little bitch!" or shout, "Come on, you little fucker!" It's heavily self-deprecating, but it does the trick for me!

After our first peak, we switch across the valley and up the other side to hit our highest summit for the day at 1466 metres. *How did we ever think we'd make 53 kilometres in one day?* It's been 11 hours since we left the van with only 30 kilometres to our name. This is, indeed, the Te Araroa showing we are at her mercy and, even in perfect conditions, I still don't think we could've made it through. It's as if she heard our confidence and thought, *'try this on for size.'*

At 7.30 p.m., we eventually reach our day's end. Our prize awaits us just off the ridgeline, down a steep and tumultuous descent. We spot its red roof amongst the clouds as it nestles modestly into the mountainside. Nichols Hut.

Up until now, the adventure has been mostly dry and hot, but today has been a complete contrast. With our fingers creaking and our feet frozen from being soaked, we cannot wait to get in. Fire on, food in our bellies, and a warm sleeping bag – our rewards for a hard day's work.

Typically, our elation is soon quashed. We've arrived on the back end of hiking season, and the scraps of firewood left behind are damp. We scavenge some dry bits, and Louis gets a little flame to light. It raises the temperature just a few degrees, but we know it won't last. We will be going without fire for the night. *At least we have a decent shelter.*

Just as we tuck into our freeze-dried meals, Louis takes one last glimpse out of the window. His stunned silence is enough to pique my interest.

I hop, or rather stumble, from my seat to join him, and we're treated to one of the most remarkable views a window has ever been a frame to. The clouds open to reveal the majestic Tararua Ranges in all their glory. Folds of giant mountains cascade into the mysterious valley ahead, lined by the trailing clouds. This brief moment, this fleeting reveal, is the true reward for all our efforts. 11 hours of grinding 30 kilometres to a total of 2,800 metres elevation – all worth it for that room with a view.

Distance: 30km
Elevation: 2806m.

Day 29 The Unwritten Sleeping Bag Rule

I spend the night fully enclosed in my sleeping bag with just the smallest gap left open to breathe. There was no escaping it; we were in for a cold night. We'd erected a fortress made of mattresses to insulate ourselves, but its effectiveness was only going to be slight.

The moment you open your eyes and peer out of the small breathing gap, you dare not move. You know it's going to be cold. You lie there waiting, waiting for someone else to make the first move, knowing that they're likely doing the same thing as you. It's a conflicting feeling when you do finally pull the bag from above your head and feel that first chill. The freezing air fills your lungs, and the hair stands on the back of your neck, but you dare not break from the warmth and comfort of the synthetic cocoon. You lie there comfortable and renewed from a good night's sleep, but you dread the moment you must break from the comfort and fully embrace the chill. Who will be the first to do it?

To increase the dread, you know that putting your clothes on isn't going to make things any better. Undoubtedly, nothing will have dried, your socks will still be sopping, and your shoes will still be wet. Everything will be cold, damp and disgusting. *Why bother leaving this lovely warm sleeping bag just to go back out there again?*

One of us has to make the first move. Louis sits up, and this is my cue to kick down the mattress wall. We're both bitten by a sharp intake of breath as the cold whooshes in. Our eyebrows raise, and goosebumps cover our skin. Jesus, it's cold! Next, we must perform an essential part of the unwritten rules of 'what to do when waking up in a sleeping bag'. Of course, we keep our sleeping bags on but lower them just enough to allow the use of our arms. We shuffle around the hut like two kids in a sports day sack race, scrambling for our bits for breakfast. We cook, eat, and prep our kit, all whilst staying in the bag. *Stay as warm as you can for as long as you can.* The moment you drop that cocoon that's it, there's no getting back in, and all you can do is embrace the clammy chill of sodden undershorts.

With our teeth chattering and faces grimacing, we pack our bags, fill our water, tidy the hut, and have a final trip to the long drop. We are ready. Damp, cold, and hurting – but ready.

After a decent sleep and plenty of freeze-dried calories, we're both feeling pretty fresh to get a move on. If it's flat, we run. If it's a shallow descent, we run. If uphill, we speed hike. We covered most of the elevation yesterday, one bonus to staying in a cold and damp hut 1200 metres above sea level.

On we go into the wind, and we know we're near our Tararua summit. With a 200-metre climb ahead and our spirits high, we charge on up the ridgeline. The next 20 minutes are 20 minutes of my life I will remember for the rest of my days. As we reach the peak, the clouds disperse to reveal the Tararua Ranges in all their glory. It's as if someone has removed the whiteout blindfold from over our eyes to reveal the astonishing landscape.

Simply breathtaking. The clouds create a spectacle as they dance between the channels, allowing the giant green mountains to belatedly breathe and bask in the sunshine. For miles, you can see peak after peak as the Tararua Ranges reveal their size and beauty. We hunker down and sit below the swirling winds to take this all in. Yesterday's outstanding efforts, a damp and cold night, and another great effort this morning have been well-rewarded by this astonishing view on this fantastic trail.

A sense of shared pride fills my emotion. We're nowhere near finished for the day, we're nowhere near completing our stint to Wellington but, through grit and determination, we've conquered this summit. Having experienced the shared challenges, we get to share the joy and pride of achievement. Don't get me wrong, it's incredible to achieve something hugely difficult on your own, but when you get to share this with someone else, it feels different. The other person understands it.

If you look at an image of the Tararua Ranges, they might look like any other mountain range, but a photograph cannot capture all the senses. We were shivering and soaked, the rain battered the sides of our faces, and the wind howled as the clouds rushed overhead. We could feel our hearts pumping, taste the salty sweat dripping from the end of our noses and we stank from all the hard work. The memory of these senses adds to how I remember the moment. They make it so much more than just a picture. They add up to affect what I see and feel. If we were both to look at the same image, it will have more of an effect on me. I have emotion attached to it, I've seen it with my own eyes; it is authentic to me.

Before heading into the Tararuas, I'd seen the elevation plot and the colossal drop on the other side of the summit. It looked both exciting and intimidating at the same time. I'd hoped and wished it was to be a runnable section, but after spending a day climbing up through bogs and roots, I quickly realised there wasn't much chance of us running back down.

The dream is of a section that we can bound down, one with sharp turns, a few steep drops, and terrain to keep our eye on but still enjoy. What we get are massive drops, huge bogs and the snake pit roots. The moment we pick up any pace, we either have to abruptly stop and slowly pick our path, or try to hop, skip and jump through the bogs or slide down a steep drop without falling and bashing our heads. It's a downhill nightmare.

This absolutely zaps my energy and kills my mood. It's kind of fun for the first 10 minutes, but this goes on for well over an hour. The sheer drops batter our legs, and every misstep punishes us with a slip or a crash onto our arse. I'm going as fast as I can, but Louis shows great prowess, often finding himself a good 50 meters ahead, but he kindly waits. As much as I'm happy for him to push on, it's not exactly the safest place to be hurtling downhill alone.

The first ten kilometres take us 3 hours and 20 minutes, an absolute age, although I'm pretty sure Louis could have got through at least half an hour before me. Despite the slug pace, we reach the immaculate Waitewaewae Hut or 'lodge,' as I believe it should be called. 'Hut' doesn't do it justice. It's enormous and in better condition than some hostels I've stayed in. It would be perfect for a long weekend. The setting is idyllic, deep in the forests with a wonderfully clear river running just away from the lodge. What more could you ask for?

'TRAIL CLOSED! FOLLOW DIVERSION!' Just our luck. There's been a slip on the regular route, making it unsafe to use, so somehow, someone has forged a new path slightly up in the valley on what is not such a well-kept trail, if you can even call it that.

Dreams of a steady jog down to Otaki are long gone, and our reality of hacking through the forest hits hard. We're jumping from root to tree trunk, trying our best to avoid the bogs. We climb and crawl the fallen trees that teeter above terrifying slips. One false move, and we could be dropping a long way to a very uncomfortable landing. The van is only ten kilometres away. *We'll be there in an hour and a half,* I think, foolishly.

With three kilometres to go, we break from New Zealand's very own Amazon jungle, and the path becomes much more manageable. With a lovely well-graded trail underfoot, we can't resist the urge to put our foot down. However, no matter how hard I try, I just cannot keep pace with Louis. It's time to let him push on. *If I get lost now, I deserve to not make it back.*

Kindly, Louis waits just before the swing bridge, the final obstacle into Otaki Forks. The team is scheduled to be on the other side, so it's right for us to both arrive together. Absolute relief floods in as we finally cross the long-awaited Otaki swing bridge to find Jill and Phil chilling in the sun and the van standing proud in the background. Safety, comfort and support are ready and waiting, right when we need them most. Just as Louis had been with me through the mountains, and just as Jill and Phill had been with me throughout this journey, they are here when we need them, ready to help and prepared to keep us going.

This monumental effort through the Tararua Ranges was a truly special experience within such an amazing adventure. It took us both to physical and mental depths that maybe we'd never been before, but you leave knowing that you can go there again if you have to. It wasn't necessarily the trail itself that was the most challenging aspect, although it was extremely tough going. It was a combination of our circumstances. We weren't out there to leisurely go for a three or four-day hike; we meant business, we were there to get through as quickly as possible, and that means as light as possible. Combine that with the cold and wet conditions, and you have got one challenging situation to overcome. But overcome it, we did.

Without Jill and Phil being there the moment we arrived, I don't know how we would have fended for ourselves. To be honest, this is true for the adventure as a whole. When I need them most, they somehow arrive – even in the most remote and strangest of places. It's not just their ability to get to you, but how they respond when they do. If you need space, you get space, if you need a shoulder, you get a shoulder, and if you need instructing, you get that too. They are the rock, the rolling hub, and the home on wheels. Yes, Gerty gets them around and acts as our shelter, but Jill and Phil make it the safe place – it's them that make it our home.

A long two-hour break serves us well. Sixteen hours of determination and concentration has taken its toll. Nevertheless, our day is not done. We've been on our feet for six and a half hours but must get at it again. As the challenge and trail continues, so must we.

Ahead stands Pukeatua Mountain. We have an opportunity to topple its 800+ metre summit, get ourselves away from the Ranges, and out towards the sea. With a good four hours of daylight left, we estimate we can comfortably make the 14 kilometres with time to spare. Although if I've learned anything so far, it's not to take anything for granted.

It's incredible the difference this break makes. With the physical recovery comes a similar switch in mentality. Being faced with a 650-metre climb over the next seven kilometres is no threat, and luckily for us, the trail is perfect; a runnable path clear of bogs and roots and nothing too steep to deal with. Our spirits are lifted, we feel great, and we've got the tunes blaring to get us up the mountain.

What goes up must come down, and our day is topped off with a gentle seven kilometres along the farm roads just inland from Reikorangi. As the sun begins to set, calmness descends upon the valley. The day is nearly done.

Although, we do have to check that neither of us is hallucinating. Out on these remote roads, you don't really anticipate bumping into anyone, but with one kilometre to go, an Adonis of a man comes running around the corner with his two dalmatians abreast. He looks like he's been carved from marble, with the sun glistening off his sweaty muscles, and his dogs run with the utmost precision. We look at one another to check; *did we just see that?*

Immediately after this, we're followed by a lovely German Shepherd, just jogging alongside us. We have no idea whose dog he is. Still, he's more than happy to saunter alongside without causing a fuss, again, we look at one another, confused. To top things off, we turn the corner to find a man walking with his stallion and mare down the middle of the road. He's placed himself in the centre to stop the stallion mounting the mare. Safe to say he has his hands full.

"Whose dog is that?" he asks us, before proceeding to tell us exactly whose dog it is. He both asked and answered his question, all in the same sentence.

Out of nowhere, a young lad, no older than 12 years old, trundles along on his pit bike and, without saying a word, whistles at his dog, smiles and rides off into the distance – the dog following. All this happens in the space of two minutes.

"Did you just see…?"

"Yes"

"Was that a…?"

"Yes"

"Did we just imagine...?"

"I have no idea."

I must give a special mention to the fantastic not-for-profit, El Rancho campsite. They had put Jill and Phil up the night before and would host us all again that evening – all for no fee. Once they heard what we were up to, and that we were raising money for our charity, they kindly helped us out.

"Charities look after charities," Bok, the manager, had declared. For that, we are hugely grateful. If you find yourself in that part of the world, please support them generously.

Distance: 38km
Elevation: 1937m.

Day 30 - The Old Man Shuffle

Louis is just about getting used to the mass of food we need to consume. When he first joined us, he struggled to get down even one bowl of Jill's Magic Porridge. Now he's slamming back the customary three bowls at breakfast. Although, this inevitably leaves us both a little too full and often struggling to keep it down. He's also become accustomed to the run's animalistic nature, burping and puking a little whenever we leave the van.

We complete the inland road before heading back past El Rancho and onto Paraparaumu Beach. It's here where I catch my first glimpse of the ominous South Island – a reminder that Wellington is by no means the end of this adventure.

It would be nice to make it to the North Island finish today, but with 95 kilometres still to go, we know it's not realistic. We've also timed things terribly and are to arrive in Wellington on a holiday weekend. Therefore, trying to book a ferry is proving difficult. We couldn't pre-book our tickets because we didn't know exactly when we would arrive. Now, just a day away, all our options have been booked up. This isn't going to be as simple as turning up and jumping on a boat.

We decide to run as far as we can, to try and leave a short run for tomorrow. This will either allow us half a day's rest or enable us to, hopefully, jump on a ferry and be ready to start the South Island as soon as possible.

Fortunately, there's not much elevation on our southward journey. However, that does mean our challenge will be the familiar foes of blistering temperatures and monotony. I can't speak for Louis, but I feel shattered and, once again, that's probably linked to the boredom of long, straight, flat running. Louis is definitely running better than me, and that's no surprise because he has been for the last three days. Yet, you can tell we've both had enough; our conversation has dwindled, and we're just plodding along. To me, it feels like Louis might be getting frustrated that I'm moving so slowly. If he is, he's doing a great job of not letting it show.

There is a break from the monotony, the astonishing Paekakariki Escarpment Track, another gem offered up by this beautiful country. Set high in the cliffs, stretching to the sky straight from the sea. From the summit we capture more fantastic views of the majestic South Island, and the sea reflects back a glorious mix of vibrant turquoise and intense blues.

The track sharply ascends for hundreds of steps, but they are, oh, so worth it. At these exposed heights, I can't resist the urge to run. It's like a switch, with the addition of elevation, an undulating path and certain death to my right, you'd think it might be time to slow down, but it makes me feel intensely alive. Instead of plodding up the unrelenting steps, it's head down and drive forward. When it comes to the steep steps back down, we throw ourselves at them in another rush of adrenaline. The drone buzzing overhead adds to the drama; Phil's not missing this opportunity.

Ten kilometres of purely fun running but, as soon as the trail ends and we're back to the roadside, the joy swiftly disappears, and similarly, our energy. Maybe we shouldn't have pushed it so hard, but I've learnt, *if it is there, take it.*

In addition to our energy lull, we're now seriously feeling the heat. I must admit I'm feeling pretty lucky, I'm accustomed to the sun, but for Louis, it's a different story. He's a man of very fair skin and a ginger noggin. Therefore, he has a decision to make. A T-shirt and shorts will keep him keep cool, but he runs the risk of sunburn. Or, wearing an undertop and leggings will give protection from the rays, but will be potentially too hot. He chose the latter and is beginning to pay the price. We call for an unscheduled stop for an all-important item: ice cream. Boysenberry Ripple, no contest.

Back to the heat, back to slapping pavement, and back to pain. Louis and I are running along the Mana Marina, and we spot an elderly gentleman some 100 metres ahead, out for what we guess is his daily jog, or should I say shuffle. He's doing the classic old man jog, basically walking but making it look like a run. *We'll pick him off in no time.* A minute passes, and he's not getting any closer. If anything, he's getting further away. We try to increase our pace, but we're moving like knights in rusty armour. *There he goes, the old man in his bright green vest, shuffling further and further off into the distance.* We genuinely can't catch him, a stark notice of just how spent we are.

After scuttling through the centre of Porirua, we arrive at the van with 42 kilometres left of the North Island. We're also greeted with very frustrating news that there are no ferries available tomorrow, or the following day. It's Friday but we won't be leaving Wellington until the early hours of Monday morning. We are short on time as it is and really can't afford a forced rest day like this, but what can we do? *Remember, it's out of your control. How can you respond?*

You can see it on Louis' face, he's had enough for the day, and the thought of a 400-metre climb just isn't appealing to him. His usual positivity has started to dwindle, and we can all feel the change. This isn't any slight on him. I'm surprised it has taken until now for him to show signs of being fed up.

It's bizarre to drive through Wellington to Island Bay, where Louis and Rosie live, just a stone's throw away from the North Island's finish line. As I look out of his living room window, I can see the end. Yet tomorrow we have to drive back out to this spot again. At least the North Island will be in our back pocket. The end is close, and a rest day beckons, but I can't rest or settle wondering what lies ahead on the next stage of our adventure.

Distance: 54km
Elevation 860m.

Day 31 - It's All About People

Wellington is bloody hilly. If we're hoping for an easy jog into Island Bay, we can hope again.

Tired and despondent, we get up and at it. I can't imagine how Louis must feel, having to leave the comfort of his own bed just to do this all again. At least it's the last time, for him anyway. Begrudgingly we hop into the van and get carted off to the day's start point. *42 kilometres to go, let's just get this done.*

Yesterday, the first hill was a step too far for us but, this morning, the fresh air and swaying trees help us to focus, and settle our mood. Any anxieties or stresses seem to have been soothed by a good night's sleep and getting back out in nature.

We break onto windswept farms where we are treated to another special view. Gold and green hills stretch south, one after another, before dramatically dropping towards the sea. It's as though Maui took what was once flat farmland and scrunched it up like a piece of paper, creating a mass of giant mounts and valleys, folding one after another. To the West, we catch another glimpse of the breathtaking Marlborough Sounds, so picturesque it's a question of their reality. It cannot be forgotten; I'll soon be traversing their ridgelines. To the East sits Wellington. A city settled in a natural harbour. The huge bay is engulfed by the surrounding mountains, protecting it from the violent and unpredictable Cook Strait. A low sun reflects off the harbour's still waters, creating an early morning haze across the horizon.

We revel in similarly striking scenery, as the beauty of this marvellous country carries us forward. The ideal start to our day continues as we dart back into the forest and find a blissful, zigzagging trail. With a little spike in adrenaline, it's the perfect opportunity to open up our legs and enjoy the running. Although brief, it rounds off a spectacular morning. However, inevitably with the Te Araroa, the 'amiable' start can only last so long.

The second hill will be the highest of the day, another 300 plus meter climb. With Louis chomping at the bit to attack, I try for all of ten meters to keep up but, in the end, I wave him off. "Meet you at the top," I shout and, before I know it, he's gone and I'm stuck, trundling in a knackered world of pain. I can't really say it's because he's fresh. After all, he's been through the same as me for the past three days. To be honest, as I'd previously told him, 'It probably should be you doing this run, not me!"

I should declare at this point that I don't really consider myself a runner. I can run, and run well, but I would never say that's what I am or what I do. As I mentioned, I gave myself 14 months to get ready from pretty much zero, and many of the people I ran with are much better runners than me.

I had this conversation with my running coach, Stuart Leaney.

"There are so many runners that are way better than me. They would absolutely smash this. It's something they should be doing, not me," I moaned.

His response was perfect.

"But that's exactly it, Lewis, they're not doing it. That's the difference, and that's why you are the right person for this – because you are the one who has made it happen and put yourself forward. There might be better runners out there, but they're not doing it. You are," Stuart replied with vigour and certainty.

Stuart's words filled me with confidence. Maybe it wouldn't take being the best runner to do this. Perhaps I need to be an adventurer on a run, rather than a runner on an adventure. *Many people in this world could do this better than me, but that's exactly the point – they're not doing it.*

On and on the undulations continue. First, we're up and down across the hills and now weaving through the Wellington suburbs. It's just impossible to find any rhythm – crossing roads, steep streets and dodging people – it's far from fun. By the time we reach the Botanical Gardens, we're just plain fed up. Frustration almost boils over as we find the trail goes through the maze-like gardens. *It just feels like the path is going through just for the sake of it. How many hikers actually continue on this exact path that seems to zigzag all through the city?* After a short and frustrating rest, we just want to get this done. Wellington is a beautiful city, but it's tough to appreciate its quirky hipster nature when feeling like we both do. We're running along the harbour amongst the relaxed city dwellers but struggling to adopt their chilled and happy demeanour.

Then a man jumps from the crowds.

"Hi Lewis!" he shouts. I look at him blankly, unable to place his face. *Louis is the only bloke I know in Wellington.*

"It's George!" he explains. A few seconds pass before the bemused look on my face turns to surprise as I realise it's George Henderson!

George had finished running the Te Araroa trail himself just two weeks prior, in a bonkers 49 days, demolishing the previous record by four days. He'd tracked us down by following our handy SPOT tracker and knew we would be passing by. It's an absolute pleasure to have George join us.

What a difference his arrival makes. The energy changes from sour and sombre to positive and energised in seconds. With our legs suddenly feeling light, we work our way across the city to Houghton Bay, and the time flies by on what was previously viewed as a dreaded last ten kilometres.

We round the last corner into Island Bay, to find the team ready to welcome us in. Louis and George let me run on alone to have this special little moment to myself. I've been trying to keep my emotions in check, aware as I am that there are plenty of unknown challenges ahead, but I can't repress a smile of pure joy when I see the beaming faces of Phil and Jill. In all honesty, a few tears do swell at the sight of their genuine happiness. I couldn't have got this far without them. The realisation hits. *Bloody hell! We've completed the North Island!*

Pictures are taken, and laughter shared. I have fond memories of this little moment of accomplishment. Two images really stand out in my mind. One hangs on the wall in Jill's living room – the three of us, Jill, Phil and I standing together, arm in arm, with huge grins on our faces. The second, Louis and I sharing an embrace. You really can see joy and relief, accompanied by an appreciation for one another. What an adventure we've all had together. What an adventure it has been so far.

Support has been the word most on my mind in recent days. The constant physical, mental and emotional support from Phil and Jill since Day 1, and then Louis joined the adventure during what was one of the most challenging sections so far. Not forgetting that he and Rosie kindly opened their home to us.

In truth, when we talk about support, we're talking about people, and it is the people involved that makes this so important to me. As I sit here now, writing these last few paragraphs, more names cross my mind with each passing sentence. It is an astonishing number of people that have played their part. From the business owners sponsoring t-shirts to those donating to charity. From friends and family believing in me, to colleagues urging me forward. From running partners at home, to Stuart coaching me. From Marcus' psychological preparation to Jo's constant physical help. Finally, Mum, Dad and Keily supported me with love, care and encouragement. You can see how this is more than just one person running alone. This run involves hundreds.

Even if I could have done this alone, I wouldn't have wanted to, and even if you tried, you would never truly be unsupported or alone. It is the human interaction, the shared adversity and shared achievement that makes this adventure whole. The reason for doing this is for people, the reason it works is because of people, and the reason it means so much to me is because of people.

When I drift off into a daydream and look back upon this incredible adventure, seldom do I have visions of the beautiful scenery or of individual achievement. Instead, it's the beautiful moments involving other people which come to mind. Instead of dreams of endless pristine coastline, I remember tears of laughter in the van at Phil not being able to handle his curry. Instead of remembering the view from Nicholls Hut, I remember Louis' excitement about it first. It's these moments with other people that I cherish the most, and that is why we cannot, and should not, ignore their importance.

North island complete. 1695 kilometres.

Distance: 45km
Elevation: 1653m.

SOUTH ISLAND

MARLBOROUGH AND NELSON

OWNERSHIP

'Waste no more time arguing what a good man should be. Be One.'

-

Marcus Aurelius

Day 32 - Day of Rest – And So Much Food!

Unfortunately, crossing the Cook Strait turns out to be a logistical nightmare. The only ferry available is Monday morning at 1.30 a.m.

So, Sunday turns into a rest day, allowing us to relax, and in my case, go on a food tour of Wellington's best eating spots. Pancakes for breakfast on Cuba Street, Cambodian for lunch at the food market, and pizza from Welly's Number 1 pizza joint for dinner. Let's call it a recovery day!

With our night to be spent out at sea, I'm not hopeful of catching any sleep so I try to get a couple of hours kip in the ferry car park.

Distance: 0km
Elevation: 0m.

Day 33 - Have I Found Heaven on Earth?

Once aboard, it quickly becomes clear that the odds of us getting a wink of sleep are extremely low. We're faced with the tactical challenge of finding the best spot to hunker down. It doesn't look promising. People lie on the floor, using their backpacks as a pillow. Others snag a row of seats to spread over. Personally, no matter what I try, it's hopeless.

Jill finds herself curled in a ball, teetering on the edge of a two-seater. I sit crumpled up, with my feet on my bag, trying, and subsequently failing not to get a crick in my neck. Each time my eyes open, Phil has changed position from lying on the floor at my feet, to sitting up against the wall, before he finally gives up and goes to the café.

All this happens as the boat rocks and rolls with the waves. If I open my eyes for more than ten seconds, seasickness kicks in, leaving me to worry if last night's pizza is going to make a second appearance.

We arrive in Picton and grab an hour's kip before catching the water taxi out to Ship Cove. It's a mad dash, and we're lucky to wake up and make it on time. But, once aboard, we can finally relax. What a contrast this second journey will be compared to that horrid Cook Strait.

There are two parts of the day that seem to have that little something extra about them. They bring out the very best of the surroundings but in very different ways. In the evening, as the sun closes in on the horizon, and the day is coming to a close, the golden hour truly comes into effect. The sky projects a range of colours from ambers and golds to purples and reds whilst the world is touched by a calmness; you feel the breeze, hear the last of the birds, and the golden hue settles upon the earth.

Similarly, at the beginning of the day, this world's beauty is captured, but in a very different way. Light gradually descends upon the earth as the sun begins to rise, just peeking over the horizon. There is an awakening freshness in the air as the sunlight lifts the settled moisture, and you catch its first warming rays on your cheek. Still, a touch of wind can send a shiver down your spine, waking you up to the fresh smells and sounds of the natural world, birds chirp, and the first signs of life begin to appear. It feels like the world is waking up.

Mornings are always beautiful, no matter where you are in the world. But a morning like this, in a place like Marlborough Sounds, really can't be matched. The sun has risen just enough to warm us up and send sparkles off the rippling sea, which glistens like a thousand diamonds. My jaw drops around every corner in this maze of sea-drowned valleys. It truly is breathtaking.

Jill and Phil are gulping in the fresh air up top. I decide to stay below deck, enjoying the scenery from the window, but also to spend some time alone with my thoughts.

The views are spectacular, and they allow me to find a sense of gratitude, contentment and calmness. I need to be in this clear headspace to be both present in this beautiful part of the world and to mentally prepare for the second leg of this huge adventure. With the Southern Alps in my way, and days away from the van at a time to contend with, now is not a time for panic. Now is a time for preparedness and clarity.

As we cruise through this blissful scene, I'm sitting with a grinning Austrian, Helga. Her enthusiasm shines through. She adores being out in nature and loves this trail so much that she comes back every year, to wander along the beautiful ridgelines on the Queen Charlotte Track. Her smile is infectious, leaving me to ponder just how special this part of the journey is going to be.

The boat pulls in, and the thirty or so other travellers rush off in a burst of excitement. We decide to wait and really soak in this beautiful cove. It's slightly unreal – like a CGI movie landscape. It feels like we've arrived in Motunui, and I'm half expecting to see Moana and her tribe come out of the trees singing and dancing to greet us.

Phil's drone buzzes overhead while Jill and I stand dumbstruck, staring around in amazement. At this moment I just want to be a tourist and casually walk this trail, swim in the sea and soak in the views, but we've got a job to do. This is it, the beginning of the South Island. 1300 kilometres to go.

Invigorated by my surroundings, I burst down the pontoon and straight into the dense forest. I'm surprised that I'm moving really well. I thought I'd struggle after such a lack of sleep, but perhaps the rest day is now paying dividends. I know this won't last forever, so I'm going to milk it for all its worth. The only thing slowing me down are the frequent stops to take in the views, which are equally mesmerising from high on the ridgelines. Each opening showcases idyllic bays and inlets. Small beaches are shaded by tropical trees, and yachts glide on the placid sea. If there's such a place as heaven on earth, surely, it's here.

I run in a dream-like state for the first four hours. For the next four, I'm not so lucky. Under a blazing sun, every hill is suddenly steep and each step draining. We'd set a target on 60 kilometres today but 50 is my limit – still a brilliant day, considering the lack of sleep, and this is hands down the most scenic and beautiful run of the adventure so far.

Distance: 49km
Elevation: 1710m.

Day 34 - Nervous – Not Fearful

I wake up feeling nervous. To let you all in on a secret, I've never spent multiple days away alone in a mountain range before. My first experience of this will be through the mighty Richmond Ranges. It will be a fantastic experience, but at the same time, the potential hazards need to be understood and respected. I won't lie, I'm scared, but until then I have the perfect thing to occupy my mind, another day of running the Queen Charlotte Track.

With a good night's sleep, and my senses suitably occupied, the first twenty kilometres fly by all the way into Anakiwa, another picturesque paradise. If you've ever been to Marlborough Sounds, you'll agree 'paradise' is no exaggeration. I sit myself down on a little bench on the beach with my feet crossed over, arms stretched out, and a smile on my face – content, and happy to wait for Phil and Jill, who are stuck in traffic. I really should carry on but sitting here is more compelling. It's clearly the wrong thing to do, but I do it anyway, and I am delighted with my decision. What a happy memory I have of sitting on that bench, breathing in the fresh air and smiling in amazement at the view.

You should have moved on. The next twenty kilometres are much harder. I'm now running roadside, and my views of the surreal Sounds have been replaced by dodging cars and slapping tarmac. With my mind momentarily distracted by Joe Rogan, and The White Stripes, I wander into Havelock. This is last spot of civilisation to get any last-minute provisions before heading into the Richmond Ranges. We're now well clear of the Sounds, and the mountains ahead provide a majestic but intimidating backdrop.

After an L&P - 'Lemon & Paeroa', a classic Kiwi soft drink - and a giant ice cream, it's time for one last push to Pelorus Bridge. I'm faced with my old foe. Gravel roads haven't been a hindrance for quite some time, but now every step feels like my foot is being repeatedly bashed by a hammer. Farmers barely bat an eyelid as a strange man shout and runs through their fields, suggesting it's nothing they haven't seen before. In case you're wondering why I didn't take a change of footwear to cope with different surfaces, it was simply a matter of economics – we were running really low on cash. Plus, I did worry that I might risk injury by changing.

All the pain is worth it for the sighting of a gorgeous stag. The sun sits low, emitting its golden haze across the rugged farmland. The stag stands proud, casting the most amazing entangled shadow with its splaying antlers. So assured, he doesn't even flinch when I amble on by, a stunning beast reminding me to puff up my chest and get on with the job at hand. Jill awaits at Pelorus Bridge, ready for a quick exit back to camp. 62 kilometres completed.

Tonight, everyone feels a bit subdued. We sit staring into the mountains where the clouds roll through, creating a menacing view. *This is what you are here for, to put yourself out of your comfort zone. It's ok to be scared. It's ok to be nervous. It's how you deal with it that counts.* This is by far the most nervous I've felt in a long time. That's not to say that's a bad thing. It means I'm excited but also aware of the potential dangers – such as sudden changes in the weather, swollen, rivers, precipitous drops, getting lost, and injury due to any of the above! Yes, I've got my SPOT Tracker, but it might take hours, or longer, if ever, for anyone to reach me out there. How often do we put ourselves in such a situation in modern life?

What I cannot do is let this nervousness turn into irrational fear. If nervous but in control of my thoughts, I can think clearly and make logical decisions. If fear and emotions take over, poor decision-making comes to the fore, and that's when the danger increases. The main threat in these mountains will be me.

Distance: 62km
Elevation: 1069m.

Day 35 - Sandflies and Chatter

Before the mountains, there's a 15-kilometre road run to put away. I don't know if it's nerves or fatigue, but energy and rhythm elude me, killing any chance of picking up speed.

After painstakingly repacking several times the previous night, we eventually settled on what I needed to take into the Ranges. It's the classic hiker's dilemma – is it better to pack light for or include as many provisions as possible? I think we overpacked by at least five kilograms, maybe more. We all know it's too heavy as I throw it over my shoulders, trying my best to hide the grimace, but the moment has arrived, and it's time to press on.

It feels like a flashback to 90 Mile Beach on Day 1. There I am about to head off on what felt like a completely new adventure whilst Phil and Jill look on.

"See you in a few days", I shout, trying to mask the fact I'm absolutely shitting myself. It's down to me to complete the 150 kilometres through this incredible mountain range and meet the team on the other side, in just three or four days. *You can do this.* I tell myself, whilst shaking with nerves.

My first charge is high alongside the Pelorus River on what would be considered a tricky path in normal conditions, one of those thin and gnarly trails that at times has you staring down at the rushing river below. With the weight on my back throwing me around, it's even more of a challenge.

I'm determined to attack any flat or downhill sections, breaking into a run at any opportunity. Still, the backpack's weight feels utterly unnatural, and my legs soon let me know. Previously they moaned and groaned from the sheer number of miles being covered. Now they're complaining about the weight being carried, tiring but in a completely different way. It feels more like weight training.

All the heat is contained beneath the forest canopy, creating quite the sweatbox, but I love it. I find it exhilarating when sweat drips off my nose; it's confirmation that I'm getting the job done. All my attention is on driving forward. *Get as far into these ranges as possible,* my only thought. Yet, despite the determination, my underlying anxiety cannot be suppressed. This mixture of emotions makes my breathing rate jump, my adrenaline pump, and my body shake with all the excitement I've created in my own little world.

Three hours of hard graft along the undulating 13-kilometre trail leads me to my first bit of real South Island elevation, a 750-meter climb over five kilometres to Rocks Hut. Because of the intense gradient, hard work, and harsh conditions, it's easy to fall back into the zone. The more challenging it gets, the deeper my little world closes around, creating that singular focus and pushing me forward.

I've spoken about being present in the moment and how, at times, getting lost in the zone can distract you from your wonderful surroundings, leading you to miss the bigger picture. However, in a time like this, being in the zone is precisely where I need to be. Today, being present is being so singularly focused.

1 hour and 30 minutes later, and Rocks Hut is in sight. It perches high in the mountains, looking down at the forest below and all the way out to the sea and Sounds, a superb location. If this was to be my final destination for the night, I would be delighted. Sadly, it's only 1 p.m., and there's still plenty of time and ground to cover. I'll have to move on. *Be present,* I remind myself. *You might as well stop for some lunch and enjoy the view.*

I barge through the doors to discover an older gentleman. He's set himself up quite nicely and is more than ready to call it a day, and you can't blame him. He's in no rush, so why leave here for a slightly less desirable situation further along? We sit and chat and he sounds both bemused and impressed by what I'm taking on. Conversely, I begin to wish I was in his shoes and had more time to enjoy a leisurely hike.

It's feels bizarre to hold a conversation with someone I don't know. As it's late in the Te Araroa season, I've rarely bumped into any other walkers since Dave in Paihia. *Do you even want to talk?* I strangely consider. Conversations usually come easily to me but today, it feels like any instinct for social situations has deserted me. Fortuitously, I navigate a clumsy conversation, whilst the impending pressure to get on my way builds to pull me out the door. I leave thinking how unnatural it feels to talk with someone, and concerned that a part of me didn't even want to talk.

The trail continues along the ridgeline through the thinning forest, allowing glimpses across the ranges. Although the views are slightly hindered by immense tree trunks, there's still enough of a gap to see the green mountains stretch on for miles into the hazy horizon.

There's something I can't quite put my finger on. I can't understand it. I've felt in awe many times on this trip, but this time it feels like something is missing, or as if something is holding it all back. There's no time to stop and think about it, I must drive and push on, but something doesn't feel right.

The descent from the ridgeline flicks a switch in my brain; I become ultra-focused again. Two huts are coming up, and my objective is to reach the furthest one, so it becomes a race against the light. My focus is solely on moving forward. As the light begins to drop, and the distance gets smaller, so my desire and aggravation increases. I've been on my feet for over ten hours, and it's all boiling down to this. *Can you get there before nightfall?*

Having dropped from the ridgeline's open heights into the dense forest valley, the light is getting lower by the minute. Passing the first hut, Brownings Hut, after a fast and tricky descent, leaves me confident that I can easily make it to Hacket Hut.

My confidence is high, but strange thoughts begin to occupy my mind during the last kilometre. *Will anyone be there? Do I even want anyone there?* Usually, my answers would be, *yes*, or, *it would be nice to speak with somebody*, but I don't know what I want. I'm anxious to see how many pairs of boots sit outside the door.

The sun has disappeared but there's enough twilight for me to strain and see sets of walking poles hanging outside the front door. *Is that a welcome sight?* I'm still not sure. *Do you want to be around people right now?* This is so uncharacteristic and such a new feeling that I can't identify or understand it. Something is eating away at me in my deepest thoughts and emotions.

I make my approach, throw my bag down and let out a great sigh of relief, *You can relax.* Or so I thought. The moment you stand still in the South Island, the sandflies get you. Not even five seconds and the little mites are nipping at any open skin they can find. Maori folklore has it that the sandfly was invented to stop people from being lazy, and they certainly get me moving. Shoes off, one last breath of fresh air and into the hut I go.

I'm greeted by the beautiful smiles of three Te Araroa hikers, which puts me at ease but, at the same time, I don't know the protocol. I'd only been in a hut once, and that was just Louis and me. *What bunk do I pick? Where do I put my stuff? Who starts the conversation?* My mind scrambles, but these worries are soon quashed as everyone is friendly and quick to ask questions, which relaxes me somewhat. It is great to have the opportunity to chat, hear other people's experiences but my mind is still unsettled and I'm finding conversation demanding. I'm happy to talk but, at the same time, all I want to do is eat and lie down with my own thoughts. This desire to shy away feels so new, and it really is getting the better of me. I'm conscious of my feelings but feel helpless in addressing them.

I lie on the plastic mattress, with my sweaty back sticking to its surface, being nipped at by the bastard sandflies. My choice is to be boiling hot in the sleeping bag, but relatively safe from the bites, or cooler out of the bag but exposed to the little beasts. Neither option is great, so I opt for half and half.

I stare at the ceiling and ponder. *You're a day's hike from anyone you know, and you're pretty much on your own. It's all on you, can you handle it?* My eyes begin to well. Never have I been in a situation like this before, and it's starting to feel more challenging than I'd ever imagined.

Distance: 47km
Elevation: 2072m.

Day 36 - Rocky Mountain Tops

I find myself waking to the sounds of other bunkmates scuttling to gather their things and be on their way. I appreciate their efforts to be as quiet as possible, but we all know that every sound made seems amplified when someone else is sleeping. Fair play to them, they're up and at it early and maybe I should be too, but I want my eight hours sleep. I know I'll be out on my feet until the last light.

Bags packed and freeze-dried Bolognese devoured, it's time to crack on. I know today will be a big day. I haven't shifted the funk from the previous night and wake up plagued by feelings of anger and sadness. If I want to take it, there's a quick route back to the van but, as much as that idea toils in my mind, in truth, it's never an option. I'm sad, angry, and struggling to focus, overwhelmed with a desire to cry, but I can't figure out why. *Why do you have to feel like this? Figure it out. Figure it out!*

The trail starts with a big march up through the forest to Starveall Hut and, with an overweight bag on my back and my mind far from settled, it's one of the most challenging climbs of this whole adventure. The ascent seems never-ending, and the seven kilometres take me just under two and a half hours. If this is to be my pace, we're in for a long day of not going very far.

Despite completing this first task, I'm still bewildered by anger and sadness, finding myself continuously on the verge of tears. I can't shake it, so descend into my bubble, keeping me even enough to at least keep moving. What else can I do? If my negativity wins, I'll end up sitting on a rock, going nowhere, in a puddle of my own sorrow. It's either that or push on. So, push on, I do.

Breaking from the treeline is magical, although I'm struggling to care. The tangled roots under the forest canopy have been displaced by rugged and dry alpine conditions. Countless rows of peaking giants stretch South as far as can be seen. Too magnificent to seem true as their jagged summits fight to be the tallest around. I've been amongst mountains before, but never anything quite like this.

Looking back over my shoulder serves up a reminder of my responsibilities. Out there – the team. In here, I'm continuing my lone journey deeper into the heart of these terrifyingly beautiful mountains, and that is precisely the paradox – the more beauty these mountains reveal, the more terrifying they become.

From under the moody Mt. Starveall, the trail grinds the ridgeline to Slaty Hut. With more wondrous views on offer, now is no time for debilitating sadness. It's taken me 4 hours and a 1,300 metre climb to get here, and it's precisely that effort and its reward that begins to shake me from such awful feelings of resentment and trepidation. Nature and my efforts are saving the day, and they must. The long morning climb is out of the way, but that doesn't mean the climbing is over. It's time to spend the afternoon tackling the three peaks between myself and the next hut. *It's time to focus.*

The sun's at its pinnacle, with the rays belting my neck and my t-shirt soaked to a dark green. The ridge gets leaner, and the drops on either side become more alarming. I'm now scrambling a deadly path. One misstep, and I'll be sent tumbling hundreds of meters to an ugly death. There's no space for the distractions that have been occupying my mind.

I reach the end of the line to find a sheer drop where I thought the path should go. First thought, *this can't be right.* Followed swiftly by, *well, it has been a crazy trail*, and I entertain outrageous thoughts of climbing down. Fortuitously, common sense kicks in and I ask myself, *maybe you missed a turn?*

Sanity prevails. I slink down the steep ridge side to join the path amongst the trees once again. Staring over that deadly drop, the old cliche of 'my heart's in my mouth,' comes to mind.

A small break in the trees reveals the first of the three peaks and, as I gaze up, the realisation sets in at just how much of a slog this will be. I've already bagged myself a massive climb, and now this steep 200-meter ascent stares down from above. It's not colossal but, wow, it looks near vertical.

Without hesitation, it's head down and get after it. Continuous small steps, poles thrusting into the ground, a fight for propulsion. No sound but that of my own breath and the clink of the poles as I wince and work my way up. Legs burning, sweat dripping, and the sun punishing every move. *Do not stop!*

If I think that was tough going, reaching the summit, and catching a glimpse of the next two mountains, tells me that was just the warm-up. Not only are they much higher and, by the looks of them, even steeper, but the path across is pretty much non-existent. Ahead lies a boulder field, scattered and smashed down the mountainside, with a line of orange poles displaying the general direction to move in. If I think my pace was slow coming up, trying to hop from boulder to boulder with a backpack throwing me around, slows me down even more. One misstep or a loose rock could be game over for the adventure, or worse. If you fall and break a leg out here, the only way out is to crawl, or be retrieved by helicopter. *Focus.*

Although the terrain is terrifying, the views are, of course, breathtaking. The higher I trek, the more expansive the scenes become. I look ahead to see more mountains than I can count, knowing that beyond them are even more to follow. In amongst this madness and gruelling effort, a daring smile slips through. *I am so lucky.* My redoubled efforts seem to have pushed this morning's demons to one side.

Thankfully, the second climb rejoins some semblance of a path. As with the first climb, it's head down and attack with everything I have. My mind has been so intensely concentrated for the past seven hours, I know it's only a matter of time before I'll be hit by weariness and exhaustion. Only 21 kilometres have been covered, but they were some of the most demanding I've ever faced. Eventually, after a 35-minute slog, peak number two is in the bag. One to go, and it looks the highest and meanest of the day.

The previous descent was pretty gnarly, but this next one, to Mt. Rintoul, takes it to the next level. There's a clear ridgeline between the two peaks but, with no path, the orange poles send you sharply off the mountainside to skirt below and across fallen boulders. The drop is so steep that one slip would be it. With fear-induced focus, every move matters, and each grip must hold as I pray and lower myself down. This trail has covered beaches, forests and cities. Now it's cascading off a mountainside along its shattered debris. *This is ridiculous!*

Although fearful, I'm focused. I know my capabilities, and I'm just wary of my confidence turning into arrogance. My trepidation is mixed with gratitude for being here, and joy from the experience. Here I am scaling across mountains with this beautiful backdrop on this insane adventure. *Life can be scary and good at the same time.*

The final climb. Up to Mt. Rintoul's summit at 1,731 meters. The boulders have been replaced by scree which makes for energy-sapping conditions underfoot. With every step forward, it feels like my foot slips back to its original position; true to Te Araroa form, it can't be too easy. Step by step, I inch my way forward, but it feels like I'm getting nowhere. I'm absolutely shattered, and the path gets so steep I have to meander my own line for fear of falling backwards. However, after a back-breaking 45 minutes, there I stand atop Mt. Rintoul.

Taking in a deep breath and looking up at the sky, an uncontrollable smile stretches across my face.

It feels miraculous to stand atop a summit and take in the immense landscape around you, knowing that it was by the power of your own two legs that you got to where you are. Two days of a continuous physical contest, two days of battling with my demons have brought me to this point, confirming to myself, *I am capable. I can do this!* However, the realisation dawns, I still have days ahead of me and many more summits to conquer. It doesn't tarnish the sense of achievement, but it does bring me quickly back to focus and the task at hand.

After another steep descent, I arrive at what is potentially my stop for the night, Rintoul Hut. A six-bunk hut, just off of the summit. It's around 6.30 p.m. and rather busy, with more northbound hikers still to come. That makes it an easy decision. It would be wrong to stop, especially with some daylight left. Everything is set for another race against the sun. Eight kilometres to Tarn Hut.

I cop a few surprised and confused looks, but they almost feel compulsory by now. One American says,

"Good luck, man," in a disbelieving tone, which only serves to spur me on. The fact I've labelled it a 'race' against the sun, and now this guy thinks I'm a loon, helps me summon the last bit of energy. *I will show him.* Show him? I'll never see this guy again, but it's enough to fuel the fire.

I'm well off the rocky mountain tops and have settled back into life below the treeline. As the sun gets low, and the day draws to an end, a sense of accomplishment and serenity flows. I can feel the hut getting closer, and I know it's nearby, but I can't see it. Any minute now, the humble abode in which I can rest my bones will come into view, allowing me to score a mark under the day. I run with my head held high, scouring the distance to catch the first glimpse of the sweet little hut. My heart rate builds, breathing becomes excitable, and my eyes widen.

Is that it? "Is it?" I repeat to myself as if having a conversation. *It is!* "It is!" I reply, shouting the now customary "Get the fuck in there!" A sense of relief is felt in every bone. My shoulders drop with a deep exhalation as I stare up into the sky. Another spontaneous smile crosses my face. That is all the confirmation I need to know that today was a good day.

I approach wishing for a quiet night. Low and behold, I'm in luck. The only other inhabitants are an elderly local hiker, Sarah, and her little terrier Milo. My first thought is, *how the hell did that dog make it all the way across those mountains?* Maybe New Zealand terriers are made of sterner stuff than their British counterparts. Even so, it baffles me to this day.

Sarah was born and raised in nearby Nelson, and she knows these mountains like the back of her hand. She's very slight, and there's a frailty to her, but she obviously still has enough energy and know-how to get herself up here. There's a smile too, but a little sadness in her eye.

After discussing my charity venture, Sarah shares a little about her own problems with alcohol addiction. Maybe this is the sadness I can see in her. She spends time in the mountains to escape the drama in her life, clear her head, and get away from her vice.

This chat with a complete stranger comes at the perfect time. To receive such support and gratitude from someone who can clearly understand the struggles that others might be going through, reminds me of why I'm here. At times my motivations can be clouded by my own negative thoughts. However, this conversation was a timely reminder to remain steadfast.

Distance: 35km
Elevation: 3135m.

Day 37 - A Mouse is Better Than a Rat

I wake to the sound of Milo scuttling around. Sarah is up sorting her morning coffee, and I lie there warm, cosy and well-rested. I'm happy. Yesterday, although gruelling work, was one of the most phenomenal days of my life. Add the range of emotions experienced to the range of mountains walked, mix with the sheer effort I'd dug deep to find, and you get one satisfied man.

I can also sense a shift in focus; reaching the end of these mountains seems fathomable. There's no chance I'll be out of here today, but I can get myself a good deal closer, leaving, hopefully, a shorter day tomorrow.

The first six kilometres are slow, a combination of the terrain underfoot, the steep descent and, of course, fatigue, but one positive is that my bag feels a whole lot lighter. With more freedom to move, I can enjoy the drop into the deep a little bit more.

Next, I ascend up through Wairoa Gorge, where I pass pristine pools, and waterfalls cascading down into the mesmerising river. Giant ferns hang overhead, the tall trees let just enough sun glint through, and the clear pools look so inviting. If only I wasn't racing time, I'd be straight in the water. Such beauty keeps me entertained for the relentless climb. I use it as a distraction from the pain.

After nine blissful kilometres, another contrast as things take a sudden and even steeper turn, up a slippery ascent. One misstep on this copper scree slope, and I could be sent tumbling.

Scree slope dealt with, the scenery changes again. Surrounding mountains are awash with an array of reds and coppers, creating a strange, other-worldly landscape. With my interest piqued, I can't wait to charge forward, but of course, my path is slowed by yet another boulder field. I'm enamoured by the environment but infuriated by it at the same time. *Would it be so beautiful if it wasn't so harsh?* Another conflict for the mind. However, just as it has for the past 37 days, one thing remains constant, *Just keep moving*. This mantra, alongside *One foot in front of the other,* does exactly that and keeps me on the move.

The Richmond Ranges continue to take my breath away, both literally and figuratively. This time it's crossing Mt Ellis that provides another moment of awe. It's been nothing but climbing up gorges and across boulder fields for four and a half hours, so far. This is today's peak and the prize for all that hard work. The trail cuts across the face of the mountain on a cascading scree slope. To my right, the rockfall gets steeper as it rises to the mountain ridge and, to my left, it falls away deep into the vast basin below, revealing views of what looks like the entire Richmond Ranges in one take. Rushing winds rise as I cross the narrow trail, adding an element of jeopardy to the beautiful yet rugged views, creating an exhilarating experience. This is the cherry on top of my Richmond Ranges. *Be Present.*

I leave Hunters Hut behind with enough time to make the ten extra kilometres to Porters Creek Hut, and it's a brilliant decision to do so. Although beginning to feel weak, I'm rewarded with the trail's Mars-like landscape. It's an arid, rocky land with chips of red amongst the silver and grey gravel as the trail winds from creek to creek. Each peak makes its case to be the day's most stunning view and, with every climb, the sun drops lower and the clouds spread thin, blanketing the sky. To the sounds of my heavy breath and shuffling feet, I take the last few steps to the final peak, rewarded with one last look at the land I've conquered, and the sight of my home for the night, Porters Creek Hut. *What a stunning hike.*

This day has been superb – its beauty, its challenges, and the hard work I've put in. Over the last three days, I've only taken two ten-minute breaks per day, and these mammoth sessions have instilled in me a level of self-belief that I can keep going, regardless. I'm comfortable pushing myself constantly for 12, 13, 14 hours at a time, and it's beginning to show in my performance. That, to me, is just as beautiful as the nature surrounding me.

I'm getting more used to spending the night with fellow hikers as well. This time with an American, a Canadian and a German, who didn't walk into a bar, and one other who, it seems, has made this his home. I didn't see much of him at first, and he didn't say much, barely a peep, but as we all lay in bed, he started to pipe up.

Rustling sounds scratch from the general direction of my bag. I shine my head torch towards my belongings but can't see anything there. I listen intently and begin to hear unsettling squeaks.

"Is that a mouse?" I ask the others.

"Yep" is the unfussed response. These guys are seasoned pros and have been on the trail for three or four months. They've encountered a mouse or two on their travels. Concerned that the scampering little thief is cashing in on my goods, I think it best to jump down and rescue my backpack. I'd separated my food to hang it out of reach, but there might be some remnants of a previous meal still in there. *It's a mouse – a mouse is better than a rat,* I tell myself. Such are the little victories we grant ourselves!

Distance: 35km
Elevation: 2296m.

Day 38 - Lessons, Achievements and Doubts

Scampering for the loo first thing in the morning is the one remaining constant from life at home. With eyes half shut, I tiptoe across the cold, wet grass to find the long drop, allowing myself to go about my business and gather my thoughts for the day ahead. *Today I will finally make it out of these astonishing mountains, only 23 kilometres to go.* However, from experience I know this could take anything from three to thirteen hours, depending on elevation and terrain. I'm hoping closer to three.

The plan is to break the day into three sections. Firstly, to complete the initial 12 kilometres to Red Hills Hut. Secondly, the last 11 kilometres of the Richmond Ranges to meet the van and, finally, a further ten kilometres into the picture-perfect St Arnaud. If I have the time and feel like it, I can make a go for the next hut along, but I can see myself calling it a day from the moment I reach civilisation.

Plan in place, I take a moment to soak in the surroundings. The quiet mountains are covered in the morning dew, and clouds sit low amongst the distant peaks. It's one of those rare moments to be truly present and take everything in. It's a moment to reflect on my own genuine personal achievements over the last few days, allowing another smile to break out. I know the task is far from done, and that the mountain ranges are far from finished, but I'm confident I'll make it out and be proud of what I will accomplish.

A snapped twig breaks my reverie. Time to focus. Bag packed, water supply filled, and my breakfast of spag bol wolfed down. It's time to go.

Porters Creek is slow going, with much of the trail climbing through boulders, along creek bottoms, or over steep broken banks. Although challenging and bothersome, I don't mind it one bit because I know I'm on my way out. The trail snakes alongside the chalky blue waters that tumble through a mass of copper boulders collected in the creek. Small tributaries cascade from all directions, creating a bright scene of vibrant, silky blues amongst the dusty red and rocky surroundings. The sun is already intense but I feel patient, not in any rush. I'll be out and back with the team before the end of the day, and that puts me at enough ease to not be aggravated by the slow pace.

Three and a half hours in, I reach Red Hill Hut, where I meet again with the Canadian lad I'd stayed with last night. Fair play to him, he was up and at it at the break of dawn. Fluffing up my own ego, I'm secretly chuffed that I've managed to catch him, forgetting that this guy isn't in any kind of race. I'm not missing the point. He's hiking for the sake of hiking and is probably disappointed to get out of the mountains. I'm hiking to get somewhere as quickly as possible – a much different experience!

He clearly knows his stuff. His bag is so neat, everything packed to perfection, and a small umbrella sticks up to protect his skin from the sun. Most importantly, he has the biggest smile on his face, genuine happiness. However, the biggest lesson he has for me is that he only carries a single water bottle with his filter nozzle on top, and there's me lugging around three litres.

"As long as you have the means to filter the water, you'll be fine, there might be a couple of sections where you have to drink sparingly, but for the most part, water is never really an issue here," the Canadian expert explains to the British ingenue.

Lesson learnt: stop carrying so much water and only pack the essentials.

I would love to say I've found my second wind, but it's more likely my sixth or seventh over the past four days. I rush off so quickly, raring to go, but soon realise I've left my precious poles behind. It's always a little embarrassing to walk back and explain you've forgotten your equipment. Especially when you've just demonstrated a propensity to carry too much.

I can tell I'm nearly at the end. The mountainous conditions have changed to a light forest, and there are more people around, plenty of cyclists and fake cyclists. That's right, you know the ones, the ones who ride E-bikes! I think my reaction is more of jealousy than disgust. Oh, how I would love to jump on a bike to get up and over this last peak, especially one with a little electric motor.

Unfortunately, I shall have to make my way through the sweatbox of a forest by the power of my own legs to make it through the sweatbox of a forest. *Just get this done!* My efforts do not waver. I'm tired, I'm hot and bothered, but my mind is singularly focused on getting to that van.

I thought reaching the peak would be a blessing and that I could coast downhill. I'm wrong. The farm track meanders down the steep hillside, but with days of fatigue in my legs, I can barely hold myself up. Corner after corner, I slap my way down, thinking to myself, *I wonder if I could just cut straight across*? No, is the answer, far too steep, and on I go.

I finally round the last corner.

"Get the fuck in there! You did it, Lewis. You did it!" I scream and shout, before I hear the delighted screams of Jill and Phil reverberating back. I can't control it; a beaming smile spreads across my face, a genuine feeling that you don't often get to experience in life. I can't possibly hide or contain the emotion. I've done it. I've completed the Richmond Ranges in three days and seven hours, and it's taken nearly everything from me physically, but more so, mentally.

I'd been on this trail for 34 days before encountering a multi-day epic alone. Of course, the Tararua Ranges were demanding, and madly complicated, but I was lucky to have Louis alongside. The first day way back on 90 Mile Beach was also a stretch but, again, the team and van were there. This journey was 12 to 14 hours of constant hard work, with only two short breaks a day, and gave me a real sense of accomplishment and self-reliance.

I sit with Phil and Jill, and their company is so precious. The conversation flows naturally, and it feels so good to be back in the company of two people I've come to know so well. Although I walked, ran and climbed my way through the Richmond Ranges alone, without the team setting me up, preparing me for it and being my safety net, it would have been impossible. To say I did this alone would be very egotistical and entirely not true.

The joy and relief are clear to see, but they aren't my only feelings; underneath it all, a discomfort still remains. I'm still anxious about what is to follow. Doubts linger. *Can you keep this going again and again? How will you cope on the next solo section?* I will need to face these worries head-on. They are legitimate questions that will need answering in the days to come. What is the best way to respond? By answering, *Let's go and find out.*

These questions are arising because I'm nervous, but the real question is, why? Is it because it's hard? Do I have safety concerns? I'm not sure, but one thing is certain – I'm struggling to remain objective.

The lengthy break is welcome, but one final task lies ahead, a 10-kilometre run into St Arnaud. My first few steps feel strangely consistent. All of a sudden, I feel light. I'll almost dare to say that, without the backpack on, there's nearly a spring in my step. My legs begin to pick up a little bit more momentum, and I soon find myself running, actually running – not shuffling, not speed hiking – running. I complete the section in an hour.

St Arnaud is spectacular. The pristine lake reflects the huge mountains surrounding it. The sun is beaming down and, after such a long, sweaty and hot four days, there's no better option than to dive straight in. The water is blissfully cold and reviving.

However, I have a decision to make. Carry on into the next multi-day section or rest up and attack it tomorrow. I have enough time to make it to the next hut or maybe even one more along, but the idea of resting in this paradise with Phil and Jill is too enticing.

It's been a challenging four days away, and the idea of heading through more mountains sits as a daunting prospect. I relied on myself to make it through the Richmond Ranges, but that responsibility weighs heavy, it would be down to me, on my own again, with no respite. Add into the mix the potential for bad weather, and my already bruised mental state is beginning to struggle. I want rest. I desire the comfort of the van and, more importantly, my friends.

Also, my body needs calories and fast. I'm burning up to 6,000 kcals a day, and there's no way I've been eating enough to compensate. With more time in the mountains still to come, I'll need to devour as much food as possible. After a swim in the lake, and a bit of a clean-up, we head to town for a recovery meal. However, a large pizza is far from enough sustenance. We venture straight over the road for an XL fish and chips, chased down with a refreshing L&P and an ice cream for dessert. Not forgetting, half a bar of Whittaker's Chocolate before bed. Whittaker's Chocolate? If you know, you know.

Through the Richmond Ranges, I've proven that I can rely on myself. The task was placed in front of me, and I took responsibility and ownership to pull through the other side. There was no one else to rely on. Only I could keep moving forward, keep putting one foot in front of the other, and remain focused to the last step.

This is just the first of multiple multi-day sections. Will I be able to continue pressing forward alone? One of the factors that plays on my mental state is the sheer amount of time I've spent on this adventure. If you told me we were heading into Nelson Lakes or Richmond Ranges for a three or four-day speed hike, it would be an exciting prospect, but when they are small parts of a more extraordinary adventure, it seems more daunting. I've been on this adventure for 38 days and still don't know how many are yet to come. Mini-adventure after mini-adventure pass by with barely a break in between, and it's starting to eat away at me. What has happened to the elation felt just a few hours before? I'm up and down like a yo-yo.

The first region of the South Island is complete with 1,946 kilometres behind me since leaving Cape Reinga. 1,060 kilometres to go.

Distance: 37km
Elevation: 1417m.

CANTERBURY

INTEGRITY

'If it is not right do not do it; If it is not true do not say it'

-

Marcus Aurelius

Day 39 - Alone With My Thoughts

I'd gone to bed the night before with a conflicted mind. Jubilant after my efforts of the past four days, but still daunted by the prospect of what is to follow.

We check the weather report and the sun that had blessed the Richmond Ranges is to be replaced with plenty of rainfall. I'm always wary of the weather warnings because they have to acknowledge the potential worst-case scenario, and it often turns out to be not that bad. It seems clear that today, it will rain for sure. The question is – how heavily?

It's the thought of a torrential downpour on the riverbeds which concerns me. I've heard horror stories of people being swept away in flash floods. To put me at ease, we will head over to the Department of Conservation (DOC) in the morning for some insight and advice.

I won't lie. Waking up to the sight of the descending grey clouds completely engulfing yesterday's spectacular scenery fills me with trepidation. So much so, I wish for the weather to be so bad I'll be advised not to go. What was I scared about? If we get the all-clear, what am I dreading? Maybe I'm just exhausted. Perhaps I'm getting to the point of simply having had enough. Is adventure after adventure getting to be too much?

For most of the questions we ask the DOC, we don't get a straight answer, and that's understandable. Unless conditions are so bad that they are going to close the trail, all they can do is give us the facts and let us make the judgement.

"Would you go in?" I ask the expert.

"I'd rather be sitting in the pub in this weather, but if I was going through, yeh, I'd be fine," he replies.

In essence, this is the answer we need. He doesn't directly tell me to 'stop being a wimp and get on with it', but that's how I receive his answer.

It's the answer we're looking for – and the one I was half-dreading. Ahead is a 115-kilometre trail over two harsh mountain passes, around stunning mountain lakes and alongside rushing rivers that can whip you away in a heartbeat. In perfect weather, this trail would be difficult enough but, in this weather, it's on another level. I've challenged myself to complete the 115 kilometres over two nights, which adds an extra edge. My most significant motivation is Keily's impending arrival. To know she'll be waiting to greet me on the other side is more than enough fuel to keep my head down and legs churning.

Keily has been the most incredible support from the moment I told her about this crazy idea. Her arrival has been the milestone I've been anticipating from the moment I hit that pole at Cape Reinga. *If I can make it to the day she arrives, I can make it all the way to the end.*

We've learnt our lesson from overpacking on the previous stint. I change from the big 48-litre bag, which was ridiculous, to go with the 28. To give you an idea of what I needed to carry, here is my little list: Food for the anticipated two and a half days. Waterproofs, worn or hung on the bag. A small sleeping bag and bivvy for emergencies. I've replaced my ridiculous 3 litre water bladder with two 500ml bottles, to be refilled and chlorinated on the go. A dry set of pants, socks and a T-shirt. A little first aid kit, one small battery pack, my GPS tracker, my trusty spork, and that's about it. I carry far less water, less food and less pointless stuff that won't get used. If it isn't a necessity, it's gone.

The weight-saving pays off. I'm able to actually run the first five kilometres alongside the now sinister-looking Lake Rotoiti. Yesterday it reflected a beautiful blue sky. Today, it reflects the black mountains and the thick grey rain clouds that I will eventually ascend into. What a difference a day makes.

I'm fortunate to have been lent a set of top-quality wet weather gear from a member of the British Army, who will remain nameless as I don't think he was meant to let me use it. Putting the kit on and slinging the backpack over my shoulders instils focus and determination. I'm staring into the eyes of the adversity still to come, and my former dread has transformed into a gritty focus. Eyebrows down, teeth gritting, I'm ready to be a savage again!

The trail alongside Travers River is difficult in places, and the undulating nature of riverside trails is all too familiar, but this time, the added element of pouring rain makes for even slower going. There's a constant threat of one bad slip, but I soon find a pattern of what I can trust and what I can't and, in some places, just a blind hope that my grip will hold. Dare I say it? My dread has gone. I'm loving it.

Initially, the elevation is slight, almost unnoticeable, but the scenery subtly changes every hour. The rain switches to clouds and fog, the mountain walls close in a little more, and the forest begins to thin. As the cold and wet kilometres tick by, the gradient increases. The further I go, the steeper it gets, and soon I find myself having climbed up to the 1400 metre mark at Upper Travers Hut. I've stuck to the same pattern as the Richmond Ranges, and on the 30-kilometre hike to get up here, I only stop to sign my name in the huts as I pass.

I pop my head in the hut to find a group of ten sitting together, playing cards, laughing and joking. They've put their poles away and called it a day. I feel a pang of jealousy, reminiscent of the jealousy felt when looking through a pub window on a cold winter's day.

"Has anyone gone over the saddle?" I tentatively ask.

"I did," a young American answers. He looks like he's been put through an industrial washing machine. "It was pretty cold, horrible, and windy, but not too bad."

Looking at the rest of the hikers, sitting in their delightfully dry and warm clothes as their wet gear hangs overhead, it's clear they're here for the long game and will hike when it suits them. Their eyes meet mine, and their look alone suggests they think the young American and I are madmen.

From the moment he said, "but not too bad," I knew I'd be heading over. To avoid succumbing to the lure of the log stove, I sit alone outside to nail one of my cheese and beetroot sarnies.

I imagine the Travers Saddle traverse is filled with breathtaking views of never-ending mountains and a view back to the beautiful lakes. However, for me, it's of sharp rocks driving up into the drenching rain clouds. It's always a little unnerving to see your path disappear as soon as it begins. *Who knows how high this trail goes? I suppose there is only one way to find out.*

The rain is smashing the side of my face, and the wind chills me to my core. The deluge leaves me damp to the bone; my wet weather gear is no match for these torrid conditions. Each step is an all-consuming physical effort as the wind attempts to send me tumbling and I can barely see, for every time I look up, rain blasts my eyes. It's a case of grit and determination. Head down, poles digging in and feet moving forward.

I'm still loving it. It is stunning. To some, it may sound horrible, and initially, it did to me, but once you grit your teeth and push your way through the continuous and unrelenting adversity, it becomes a thrill. It's intense and feels never-ending, but you feel like the savage you need to be. That's where the hidden beauty lies. *Take this all in, the challenge, the adversity, the beauty. This is what you are here for.*

I thought the peak would be a welcome sight, but the moment I cross the line onto the descent, I'm smashed by a blast of chilling wind rushing up the mountainside, almost sending me rolling back to where I'd just come from. One of the most dangerous weather conditions on these peaks is severe wind. It's powerful, but it's just about safe enough for me to carry on. *Now I see why they all stayed in playing cards.* Any stronger though, and I might have to head back down to the warm hut.

Not only are there gusts to contend with, but another stressful mountainous descent to manage. If dry, I'd be treading very carefully but, in this ceaseless rain, I have to remain on high alert. The path drops straight off the mountain, leaving no other choice but to accept the slips and slides. Each foot placement is a stab in the dark and, gingerly, I place my foot, searching for some traction. Slowly, I transfer my weight to the point of no return, hoping the grip will hold with nothing but blind faith. At times, the gradient is shallow enough to pick up some pace and intentionally slide my way down. Yet, at the steepest points, there's often an alarming drop onto sharp and jagged rocks. One slip, and it's a scramble on the hands and knees to find anything to stop the fall.

After 75 minutes, dropping nearly 1000 metres, I reach the foot of the valley, shaking from the concentrated effort. The fear of an untidy death will do that to any person. Yet, there is no time to waste, me and my brain must move on. A further three kilometres downriver is West Sabine Hut. It's here where I have a decision to make – stay or move on. I stand outside, cold and soaked to the bone, staring through the hut window to see it packed and full of joy. People conversing over their meals, sharing stories of their own adventures, and there I am, outside like a neglected, wet dog. I don't even bother to open the door as the blast of warmth would be torturous.

I know I'll be moving on, so perch on the seats outside, chewing on another soggy cheese and beetroot pickle sandwich while the rain taps at my hood and drips down my nose. As I sit, slumped and dejected, a woman pops her head out the door. She takes in my demeanour and an apologetic smile crosses her face. She quietly slips back inside. Her expression is enough to tell me that even she knows I have to move on.

Blue Lake Hut is a further ten kilometres on. *Can I blast my way there and make it before sundown?* I've got two hours.

I turn my dejected and sombre mood into one of determination and focus. These small challenges have been acting as another fantastic coping mechanism. A difficult but achievable task enables me to shift from negativity to a more productive and positive attitude, ready for the task at hand.

In this case, it's head down and push forward. I'm still wet and cold, but used to that by now, and all that's on my mind is finally getting into my warm and dry sleeping bag to call it a night. With two kilometres to go, the Te Araroa Trail throws me another surprise, and this time one of epic and monumental proportions.

The trail escapes the forest, revealing the wonders of this mountainous world. Up ahead, and high in the misty mountains, magical waterfalls crash down the cracked walls to join the white rushing river in the depths of this majestic valley. Looking back, I see the endless cliffs climbing high into the dense, low-lying clouds with yet more waterfalls cascading from their dark and jagged walls. Mesmerising. My blind focus halts and dejection disappears, replaced by genuine awe and relief. Everything that I'd put into this day is being rewarded by this single beautiful snapshot. Another image I hope to never forget.

It's now 8.45 p.m., with a significant 50 kilometres covered. Finally, in the autumnal darkness and absolutely soaked, I swing open the door at Blue Lake Hut. It's almost full, and although I'm amongst many hikers similar to myself, everyone is settled in their groups. Some are playing games, some are huddled around the log burner and others are resting on their bunks, ready for bed. I feel like I've disrupted the calm by bursting through the door. Everyone looks up, gives me a smile and a nod as if to say, *well done*, and then gets on with their own business.

I get in, hang up my wet kit and get my bunk sorted for the night. By the time I sit for dinner, everyone has gone off to their bunks, leaving me sitting by the dwindling fire in the darkness, feeling alone amongst all these happy hikers. It's my own fault; I made a judgment as soon as the door flew open. In my mind, everyone was already settled and most likely wouldn't want to be disturbed.

It's possible that, because my focus is so entrenched in the task at hand, I end up isolating myself. I've become so intense and my thoughts so singular, I barely let myself relax. Even in my sleep, I'm half-aware of getting back to a heightened state from the moment my eyes open. Hence, I have little capacity for making conversation. But, for some reason, I think it's everyone else's fault.

In all honesty, I've carried a feeling akin to an uncomfortable sadness for some time. I can't quite put my finger on it. Whatever it is, it's beginning to cause problems in my mind. There's one saving grace which keeps me moving. *Keily is up there somewhere, shooting across the sky at 500mph. I can't wait to see her smiling face.*

Distance: 49km
Elevation: 2141m.

Day 40 - You Shall Pass – Eventually

In the early hours, people bustle about to make an early start. *You go ahead, I'll catch you up.* By the time I'm properly awake, the hut is nearly empty and the warmth from the log burner has all but gone. Only my dripping kit still hangs above. Dejection is the only emotion felt at such a sight.

The first task for the day is to get out of the sleeping bag, and much like a plaster, there's only one way to do it today – rip it off. Having packed light, the only dry clothes I have are my t-shirt and a pair of pants.

I stand waiting for my water to boil, staring out at the expanse of grey nothingness through the rain-splattered window. There's only one way to sum up my mood: fed up. My clothes are still wet, the rain hasn't stopped, and I still have another night in these mountains. All I want to do is stand here in my dry pants and wait for it all to pass.

This brings me to the next dismal part of this altogether disheartening morning. Quite possibly, one of the most depressing actions is to remove your dry clothes, replacing them with soggy pants and socks, your soaked t-shirt and shorts, and the damp waterproofs. Why this insanity? Because I need the spare dry kit for the overnight stays in each hut. It's cold, everything stinks, and I instantly feel dreadful. There's nothing but scorn across my face as I stare out of the door, knowing I have to head back into this awful weather for another 12 hours.

Right! Come on! You have no other choice. Stop being dramatic and get on with it! I give myself a good talking to. *You've got those Frenchies to catch!* Another opportunity to instil a competitive edge to the day.

My target is to reach Anne Hut, some 46 kilometres away. A decent daily total, considering the mighty Waiau Pass stands in my way. If conditions are anything like yesterday, it will be a big ask to make it that far, but the only other alternative is to cover just 20 kilometres to Waiau Hut.

The day starts high amongst the cloud-covered mountains along the rocky inclines. Visibility is so poor I can barely see the orange poles marking the way, leaving me to trust the map's directions and, in some cases, instinct. Occasionally, the clouds mysteriously move, opening up vertigo-inducing views of the dark and eerie Lake Constance/ Rotopōhueroa below.

The inevitable happens. I wander off course, finding myself further down the mountainside than I need to be. With a near-vertical wall in my way. I should backtrack, but the idea of slogging up the shale sounds too physically demanding and a waste of time. *The track is just at the top of this wall. If I can just find a spot easy enough to climb, I'll be up there in no time*, I reason with myself.

I know what you're thinking. I'm thinking the same. That sounds like the choice of an idiot. However, when you are that fatigued, your mind doesn't always function as it should!

Stupidly, I decide to cut corners and begin climbing. I'm no longer walking or trekking; this is now a ten-metre rock climb with a heavy backpack and no ropes. The route isn't quite vertical, so I'm able to lean in and ascend with caution, spurred on by the time I'll be saving. About halfway up, when staring down at the threatening rocks below where my body will be impaled if I make just one mistake, my blatant idiocy becomes apparent. Unfortunately, at this point, there is no better, or safer, choice than to keep climbing.

How have I got myself in this ridiculous and dangerous situation? My heart is racing, and I scold myself with insults whilst clinging on to slippery, wet rocks, as sideways rain stabs at my face. One treacherous movement after another, one hopeful grip to dubious footing, I somehow work my way up the wall with my heart jumping through my chest. I don't know how, other than through a mix of naivety and stubbornness, but things start to level off to a point safe enough to turn and lie on my back. Staring up at the grey, I curse my stupidity. *Don't ever do anything like that again!* There's nothing like risking your own life to wake you up in the morning.

I press on, soon finding myself climbing down a crack in the mountainside just as steep as that which I just climbed. Hopefully, it will bring me to the shores of Rotopōhueroa. On a clear day, you can see the trail dramatically drop to join alongside the lake, but today it's a sheer drop into nothingness. *Surely there is a safer way than this?* I wonder aloud, but this is the direction those beautiful orange markers point.

Tentatively, with the odd slip and poo-your-pants moment, I manage to scale down and safely reach the shoreline, giving me a moment to breathe and glare up at the dark, mysterious mounts belittling the morose waters. Grey commands the scene as the rocky mountains rise into the angry clouds, and the lake reflects the aggressive setting. This may sound dismal and depressing, but to me, it's mesmerising, leaving me to feel fragile and fearful of its fierce and unforgiving nature. I feel alive.

I follow the poles to the lakehead and then into the immense valley, halted by the giant alpine walls. From here, the path takes the direct route up the scree coated mountainside to Waiau Pass, somewhere up in the shadows. This is the moment I've pinpointed. The biggest hurdle of the day, a 500m climb over the drenched and windswept Pass. Not a monstrous ascent but considering, it's short in distance at one and a half kilometres, it's incredibly steep. At times, the grade will be a staggering 50%. Not only that, but the loose scree adds to the thrill.

For every step forward, my foot slides back to where it started. Nerves get put to one side, and I attack with an aggression matching the mountains themselves. Poles jam and clink, feet stamp to keep pace, and bit by bit, I scramble up. My head's down following the footsteps that have gone before me and, with the occasional check for the next marker, I keep myself on the right track.

I'm relentless, but soon enough, the mountain starts to get the better of me. The wind chill thrashing icy rain across my face, the treadmill effect of the scree underfoot, and the never-nearing summit are taking their toll. The Te Araroa isn't going to stand aside that easily.

Eventually, doing what we all fear and know not to do, I look back, dreading that the lake might still be just a few feet away. To my shock and surprise, I see only my footsteps falling into the chasm of clouds below. I'm now well and truly in the shadows and, no matter which way I look, I'm greeted with a giddying grey vacuum. My only guide is the trodden trail beneath my feet, the faint outline of orange poles in the hazy distance, and the knowledge that the only way is up.

Step after step, my legs continue to tire. It's the most challenging climb of my life. Every time the ground begins to even up, and I believe I'm near the top, the clouds break to reveal another scree wall to scale. Not only are my legs losing power, but my breath is getting short, and the battering cold is bringing on a spiralling dizziness. The only thing I can do is get my head down and march on.

After one hour of marching in a trance-like state, I make it to the top of the Pass. I'm absolutely drenched and weighed down by the bag and sodden clothes. I can barely see where I'm going on a stupidly steep hill and I love it. It feels like the Te Araroa has thrown down a challenge, to which I've snarled back, *Bring it on!*

On a clear day at the Pass, I'd be able to look back at views of beautiful blue lakes surrounded by the giant white-topped mountains. Ahead would lie the lush green valley I'd soon follow all the way to Anne Hut. However, today my only views are of the dangerously steep and technical trail off this treacherous mountain. I say trail; it's more orange poles adjoining in a general direction downhill, as opposed to any formed path.

I'm hoping the rocks will hold, and guessing where I won't slip. I'm grabbing shrubs to control my weight and wishing they don't break. It's a repeat of yesterday's descent off Travers saddle.

I feel slow until realising I've caught up with the Frenchies, their luminous rain covers making them easy to spot amongst the mist below. They're locked in my sights, but luckily sense prevails, and I refrain from going full tilt. I maintain my composure and slowly reel them in as the path begins to settle. With a nod and a smile as I pass, my ego is suitably fluffed up. I'm moving well, but even better, I've made it off that outrageous mountain.

What a difference a few kilometres can make. From the dark and dangerous Nelson Lakes, I make it onto the sun-clad and placid farmlands below. I look over my shoulder to the astonishing rain battering the giant saddle and compare it to the yellow and green fields that lie ahead. I hope to be much quicker over the second half of the day, as the gentle path meanders alongside the Waiau River. It's a much-needed respite from the sharp ascents and descents contended with up in the clouds.

I'm hoping to break into a run. The terrain is ideal, the sun is out and the path is slightly downhill all the way. Everything required to run is there, except for two vital ingredients: my backpack is too heavy, and my energy is completely zapped. A fast hike is doable, but to actually run? I just don't have it in me. The 26 kilometres take a long 5 hours and 15 minutes.

The contrast and variety of the Te Araroa have been constantly on display. If I look all the way back to Cape Reinga, this trail has been through pretty much every biome on this planet. Similarly, today, everything changed instantly after descending from the mountains. The previous evening involved a frantic push in howling winds and torrential rain, beneath threatening mountain walls. Today is a relaxed and gentle finish as the sun sets its golden cast across the still, open valley. This contrast is not only found in the scenery but in my thoughts and emotions too. I no longer feel like an outsider. I no longer feel agitated and anxious. I'm warm, relaxed and looking forward to arriving at the marvellous Anne's Hut, standing in the centre of the surrounding mountains.

The presence of a hut, and a clear path to its door, always brings a smile to my face, especially after two tough and somewhat miserable days. Feeling the familiar buzz of knowing I'm nearly at my day's end, I'm content, and this is evident in how welcome I feel. There's not much different from last night other than my mood. I make an effort to talk, and people speak back. I don't feel alone, and I don't push to be. Maybe the weight of the Waiau Pass is off my shoulders, and I know with a good start in the morning, I'll be back at the van.

I go to bed with a smile across my face, excited for tomorrow when I will finally have my best friend with me again.

Distance: 47km
Elevation: 1201m.

Day 41 - Reunited

How quickly can I get out of here? I'm excited to be reunited with Keily, and be back with the team, but I'm also fighting against agitation. I'm just plain fed up. Fed up with walking and running all day, fed up with putting soaking wet clothes on each morning, and fed up with having conversations only with myself. Boyle Village is 30 kilometres away.

30 kilometres in 6 hours – you'll be out of here by 2 p.m. That means I could, and should, continue on the trail once out, but deep down, I know that I won't want to once back with everyone. I convince myself to deal with it later.

Feeling conflicted dulls my enjoyment of my surroundings today. It's not until passing Boyle Flat Hut and beginning to turn west that I start to think in earnest about what to do once out of this section. I feel like my mind is pretty much made up. *I will stop and call it a day as soon as I see them.* Yet, something nags at me. *That isn't good enough. If you have time, you should keep going and get as much of the trail done as possible, in the remaining time. You have to be a savage.*

One half of me is calling me out for wanting to stop, and the other is persuading me to call it a day. It's the classic, *angel on one shoulder, devil on the other* scenario – except, in this case, both arguments have real merits. My mind is a mad jumble, exacerbated by being alone. I need someone to speak to – the team are always my best sounding board.

I round the corner at Magdalen Hut, join Magdalen Valley and continue alongside Boyle River. Here, the valley floor has much more space. Farmland and yellow tussock dominate the scenery beneath the looming valley walls. I listen to my country music as I hike this rural landscape, transported to what I imagine it to be like in the American Deep South. Tyler Childers' guitar springs its tune, and his raspy voice belts juxtaposed rhymes full of despair and sorrow.

Dreaming of this country life leads me to think of Keily. When you haven't seen someone you love for such a long time, and when you've put yourself through such physical and mental torment, it builds up. It's this culmination that brings a tear to my eye and a smile across my face.

I plough on in this dreamlike and emotional state for 45 minutes, and it works. Not only have I covered a decent five kilometres, but my mind has become more settled. Maybe I just had to let out some emotion to get back to a five out of ten. I'm ready to get to the van, just a quick three kilometres away.

Then I see the team, and Keily, making their way back down the trail.

"Oh, hi," I say casually, caught off guard. I'd played this scenario out in my head numerous times, and it was always full of tears and joy. However, in the moment, my overwhelming feeling is one of relief. We hug and hold on, and I feel a comfort, one I haven't had for so long. Our reunion is completely different from how I had endlessly imagined, but better for it. Meeting Keily is an unexpected return to familiarity. Such a sweet memory that I still cherish today.

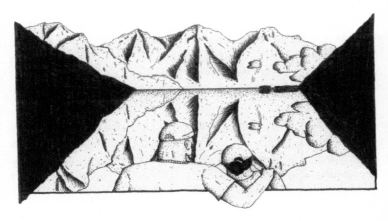

My mind is officially made up. I'm going nowhere. The relief I've felt and the comfort I've gained from Keily's arrival changes me from being so uptight and agitated. I've been all over the place over the last three days, and all I want is rest, more so mentally than anything. I want to stay in the familiarity of Keily's company, the team and the van, just for one night.

We reach Gerty and, in all honesty, we're feeling somewhat subdued. The campsite at Boyle Village isn't the most inspiring place to spend an afternoon. It would be perfect if I'd just rolled in at 9 p.m. to then be up and out again first thing in the morning, but it's the middle of the afternoon, and we don't want to spend it here with me stinking to high heaven and us all being bitten to death by sandflies. We scour the map for alternative sites but to no avail. There's nothing promising an improvement nearby. Get the bug spray out. It looks like we'll be staying put.

Despondent with the thought of staying here, we entertain the idea of heading further afield. In the end, we opt to drive the 55 kilometres over to Hanmer Springs. Don't get me wrong, I prefer the country and being outdoors, but my balance is out of whack. I want to be around people, I want to be around civilisation, I want a shower!

The nagging voice still sits on my shoulder, questioning my decision. I can either regret my choice and let it eat away at me or appreciate what is gained. If I'd carried on, I could have got another 20 kilometres under my belt, stayed in a beautiful hut amongst the ranging farmlands, and shared stories with other hikers on the trail. Still, I would have left Keily just as quick as we'd met, missed the companionship with Phil and Jill, and missed a moment to simply stop. In my decision to stop, I allowed myself the time I dearly want with my friends and Keily, and I have the time to stop and take a breath. Yet, of course, the nagging voices still chirp away. *Because I decided to stop, am I damaging my integrity?*

Distance: 31km
Elevation: 677m.

Day 42 - 'Jack.'

I wake with a sense of familiarity and comfort that I didn't know had been missing. It's not the comfort of the air bed or the cosiness of the tent. It's having Keily next to me.

I lie staring at the red walls from the warmth of my sleeping bag, noticing it's a little darker, and a few degrees cooler too. With each passing day the temperature is slowly dropping, and daylight gradually reducing. Lying here, comfortable and rested, there's still a conflict to battle with. *Soon, you have to step up and get on with it.*

This blissful morning moment has to end. The allure of an extra couple of minutes draw me in, but I know the day must start at some point. Luckily, I'm rejuvenated and, although a little sad I have to leave, I want to show Keily what it's like out here. She's been keeping up to speed from home, but it's different to being in on the action.

As we pull off the road to get back to the trail, my confidence grows. I'm walking tall with a spring in my step, determined to get on the move and prove to the team, and myself, that I will smash this next section.

I'm so assured that we only pack for one night away. Is it arrogance? Perhaps I'm beginning to peacock a little with Keily here. Yet, if that's the case, it doesn't matter. I now have self-belief and assuredness, feelings so opposed to my previous agitation and frustration which had haunted me before her arrival.

"See you tomorrow," I confidently shout whilst shuffling from the van and into the valley. The trail runs along the gentle Hope River that trickles and weaves through the golden tussock farmland covering the valley floor. To my right, the bush-clad mountains loom mysteriously in the low morning sun, and to my left, green and yellow-coated hills. The trail undulates from forest to farm, occasionally crossing the river, making it difficult to find a running rhythm. My established combination of run the downhill and flat sections, but speed hike even the slightest hill, will have to do.

The first stop is Hope Halfway Hut, there's no one here but I discover a shoe. Forgive the pun, but perhaps some poor soul has left it behind. I imagine an unlucky hiker getting towards the end of their day, confident they have everything they need. The weather turns, or the terrain gets tricky, so they decide to change their shoes, only to discover they are one short. It would be infuriating to realise the other one was sitting a day's hike back. Would you return or just press on? I can't decide whether to take it with me to Hope Kiwi Lodge or not. What if the hiker was going the other way? Thoughts about the man with one shoe keep me entertained for the rest of the morning, diverting my thoughts from my ever-draining energy.

The hut system in New Zealand is absolutely fantastic. More often than not, they're set in the most breathtaking scenery. Some are old and full of character. Others are brand new and feel closer to a hotel than a hut, hence they're called lodges, I assume. Still, no matter the state of the night's lodging – rodent-infested or not – the views are usually spectacular.

This brings to Hope Kiwi Lodge, unfortunately not my abode for the night but wow, what a setting. Tall golden grass surrounds the green-clad bungalow, with a backdrop of stacked mountains. People would pay a fortune to stay in a place like this anywhere in the world but, if you're in New Zealand and willing, it will only cost you $5 and a walk.

It would be a great spot to relax with friends on a weekend away but, alas, I can only stop for a cheese and beetroot sandwich and be on my way. I ask the hikers occupying the lodge if any of them had lost a shoe, but just get puzzled looks in reply. People often hike in groups, and so I often feel like the kid on the outside of the circle trying to find his spot to sit. Occasionally I try to strike up a conversation but, more often than not, the corner draws me in and I keep myself to myself. To most people, I must be a panting mess bursting through the door, wolfing down some food before they even have a chance to say "hello!" Gone again as quickly as I arrived. In reality, much like at Blue Lake Hut, I'm separating myself.

The trail continues for four kilometres across the farms before plunging into the forests above Lake Sumner. I swap the open valley floor for the enclosed twists and turns of the high woods. When the trail changes, you have to change too. I'd settled into my undulating rhythm and found myself day-dreaming amongst the open fields. Now I find myself developing a little intensity, a little bit of an edge, and focus on attacking the close and dark track. I'm so tuned in, I almost forget to notice the giant lake to my left. A sign points off-trail to a lookout point, but I'm in no mood to stop. I want to get as far as possible today, that means no stopping for pretty pictures.

This intensity can only last as long as the fuel from my cheese and pickle sarnie and, soon enough, my focus is broken. Naturally, when this happens, it comes out of nowhere and hits me like a ton of bricks. Not only does it affect me physically, but my decision-making too.

I'm sure you've felt it when it feels like your body has nothing left to give, no bursts of speed, not even a routine jog. It's like your car switching to limp mode, your eyes droop, and you don't have the energy to even close your mouth. Gormlessly, it takes everything you have just to put one foot in front of the other without falling over.

Clearly, I need calories and fast. What I should do is sit and have some food right away and then I'd be fine to carry on. However, for some reason, I push myself to reach the next hut, as if on some sort of heroic mission. I labour forward in a wobbling haze like some sort of wannabe hero. In reality, I'm just being an idiot.

I don't know if it's my dizzy and depleted state, or the trail becoming less clear, but it's soon apparent I've lost the path and any markers guiding the way. My phone's tiny blue dot and its trusty arrow still points to the next hut. Instead of spreading and scanning, looking for the route, I plough through as the crow flies, confident that I'd soon rejoin the marked passage. I flashback to the darkness along the Mangaokewa River. However, this time, I can at least see where I'm going.

Although in a trance-like state, my senses are alive for a brief moment. The leaves crackle underfoot, my hands scrape the coarse bark of fallen trees, my eyes squint as the sun pierces the cracks in the canopy, and my lips taste the salty sweat from the heat and hard work. This is a brief but vivid snapshot from a fractured and forgotten section. I can't tell you how long it took because I simply do not remember. I'd become so entangled in the forest I only managed to snap from my daze once back on the open farms. It's as if I've been released from the clutches of the encroaching trees, and the clear space gives me freedom from the maze and my own stupor.

It's an illuminating experience. The sun shines down and fills the sweeping fields with vibrant, natural colours as my mind opens from its dark and thoughtless tunnel vision. I'm awakened, much like the surrounding scene. My brain switches on. The next hut is just over yonder, only across the swing bridge and along the river. *Just make it to the lodge, and have some food.*

I arrive at Hurunui Hut at that time in the day when the sun starts to drop that little bit lower, and there's a strong urge to just stop and relax. With a couple of hours of sunlight left, sitting out on the hut's veranda would be a perfect end to a tough afternoon, and that's exactly what a handful of hikers are doing. They've settled down for the evening, with their bags off their backs and feet up to rest. No such luck for me.

"Are you Lewis, the guy running the trail?" asks one of the hikers. It really infuriates me that I can barely remember any of these kind and helpful people's names. I should have made more effort.

I'm stumped and don't know what to say. Basic communication and decency elude me. Someone is excited to see me, keen to hear about the adventure, and I can't find it in myself to have a conversation. I give one-word answers and ask no questions in return. In fact, I just sit as the group talks about my upcoming section. I have nothing to contribute.

I don't want to talk with these people right now.

Yes, but if you stay, you'll be able to have some great conversations, just don't be like you were at the other hut.

Too late, I've messed it up already. I can't stay.

To the lovely woman at Hurunui Hut, on the nineteenth of February, 2020. If you ever read this, I am sorry if I was boring and rude, but I hope you can understand. I hope you are still out in the world taking on more big adventures.

I crack on. There's plenty of sunlight left to cover the ten kilometres to Hurunui Hut No 3. Although the graph is sharp in places, there are no giant climbs. The only real obstacles are Hurunui's creeks and tributaries. I allow myself to trudge along, knowing that I'll eventually get there, something my mind and body can comfortably cope with, such a contrast to the previous section around Lake Sumner.

Hurunui Hut No 3 looks tired as it sits on the yellow tussock flats beneath the green valley walls. It's one of the earlier huts to be placed out in the wilds, and it's beginning to show. Nevertheless, if it keeps me dry and warm, I'll be happy. My fears of a depleted interior are soon thrown out the window. Swinging open the door reveals everything you could wish an old cabin to be. The centrepiece is a heavy-duty log burner. I can imagine frozen explorers huddling around the burning furnace, thawing out as the snow falls outside. At either end, two sets of triple bunks painted British Racing Green match perfectly with the dark brown floorboards and golden pine walls. It feels cosy, warm and welcoming like the lone man perching on the bench.

Jack's from California. He's an older gentleman – in his sixties to hazard a guess. He has small eyes and a strong brow beneath his weathered cap. A wiry grey beard takes up half his face, something he must have let grow freely in all his years on the world's hiking trails. They say an owner and their dog often resemble one another. If this man had a trusty companion, it would be a Scottish Terrier or Miniature Schnauzer.

Much like back at Tarn Hut, with Sarah and Milo, this turns out to be a fantastic opportunity to really talk with someone – to really get to know one another. I'm able to relax and be calm. Whether that's due to Jack's warm reception or me being finished for the day, I'm not sure – maybe both – but it was the type of conversation that really sticks in the mind. The kind I probably missed out on due to the nature of the adventure. Maybe if this was a hike instead, I would've had more opportunity to meet and share stories with other compelling and extraordinary people.

We learn about one another's lives, how we each ended up here in this hut together, and what drives us to be out in the wild. Jack tells me about his life as a teacher, and how he's spent years teaching English in China. He has spent the past five years on the world's great trails, from the Appalachian to the Pacific Crest and, for the second time, the Te Araroa. There's a sense of loneliness to his story – and demeanour. My suspicions are reinforced as he expresses his wishes to find a girlfriend who loves hiking just as much as him.

I think to myself, *with the amount of time you're spending alone out here, it's going to be tough to find one. Or maybe this is exactly where he might stumble across the outdoorswoman of his dreams.* I further wonder, *perhaps he loves hiking more than any woman he's ever met?* I can't help but feel that although Jack has a sense of sorrow, and a genuine desire to find a companion, he's almost given up the ghost. This is just a string he holds on to, something he wishes for but suspects he will never find.

A 50-kilometre day completed, getting me to the 2113-kilometre mark and ever closer to Bluff. Jack, I hope you have found your companion, and you're walking the world together.

Distance: 48km
Elevation: 1189m.

Day 43 - Churning Thoughts

Peering out of the small gap in my sleeping bag into the empty hut, I feel the cold chill on the end of my nose. The last rays of moonlight slip through the window, casting a cold stillness over what was once a vibrant and warming abode. Each morning is getting darker and colder, making it even more of a challenge to rise from my slumber.

I wander to the breakfast bench, barely able to open my eyes. Sitting alone, staring at the chunky floorboards, I think to myself, *I'm getting bored of this.* Most mornings, I either wake up preoccupied with physical pain, determination to push forward, or dread at what's to come. However, today I'm calm and comfortable, but bored, bored of waking up knowing that all I will do for the next twelve to fourteen hours is walk or run, eat freeze-dried meals, and be alone with my thoughts. I've done this, day in and day out, for 42 days. It's starting to become tedious.

I've felt bored many times on this adventure, but never first thing. Usually, I might listen to some music, play a game in my head, or stick on a podcast to keep me moving. Today, it feels like the best idea is to just start, just put one foot forward and see where it, and the day takes me. Action is better than stagnation and, at the moment, this statement applies to both the mind and body.

With a grimace I, again, reluctantly dress in my sodden clothes, compounding my doldrums. Getting on with the day hasn't got off to the best start. Some say sarcasm is the lowest form of wit, and I'm using it on myself.

Maybe things will get better once I get out? I doubt it. With the sun now rising above the valley silhouette, a wash of clouds paints the sky. Low strips of fog cling to forested walls and dance up creeks and streams in the distance. A freshness hits my body as the morning dew still sits at the tips of the long golden grass. In an instant, my boredom is subdued and replaced with gratitude. *I am in one of the most beautiful places in the world. Get over yourself.*

The morning is spent trying to wake up as I chip away kilometres across the tricky terrain.

The gradient gradually increases and, as I reach the Hurunui's headwaters at Harper's Pass, the forest disperses – replaced by alpine scrub and tussock. The ground becomes full of moisture, causing a couple of heart in mouth moments. Although slow going – 13 kilometres in almost three hours – I'm appreciative of the challenging conditions. My mind cannot be preoccupied by unproductive thoughts. One misstep could be a broken ankle or worse.

Concentration also has to be at its peak on the unexpected descent from Harper's Pass, a clamber down wet rocks and boulders as the trail joins the converging creeks forming the Taramakau River. At any moment, I could either slip into the rushing water, or a boulder could tumble from underfoot. It reminds me of the gnarly descent off the Waiau Pass. I'm certainly no longer bored.

The valley opens back up and it's here, on the wide Taramakau, where the path all but disappears, with only sporadic orange poles. The objective is straightforward, but the trail is nowhere to be seen. All that lies ahead is the spread of boulders and braided rivers that I seem to cross every ten minutes.

Although vast and open, I reach a dead end. I'd scuttled along the river's true left side before reaching a dense forest with no sign or clear path through. *Do I have to cross that bloody river again?* The current is rushing and smashing into the riverbank at terrifying speed, and has recently dragged a couple of giant trees, and half the bank, into its depths. This water is not messing about. S*urely I don't cross here?* I check the map, and the trail line goes smack bang through the middle. I recheck the forest, and there's nothing close to resembling a cut through. In my fatigued state I decide, *I have to cross that river.*

With my bag on my back and poles at the ready, I tentatively advance, instantly feeling the rivers full force as it tries to sweep my feet from under me. My mind is plagued by dark visions of being swept away, dragged over boulders, or getting stuck under the white water against a sunken tree trunk. After a couple more steps and jabs with the poles, I somehow begin to find my balance. Now, leaning into the flow of water, it's easier to traverse diagonally. The further I go, the higher the water creeps, and the more it wants to pull me under. By now, I'm one slip away from being hauled towards my worst fears.

Somehow, I reach halfway. My stupidity dawns on me, again. *If you keep going, and it gets deeper, or there are far worse braids still to cross, this could go terribly wrong.* Somehow, bent over and fighting against the flow, I have a moment of clarity and halt proceedings.

Turn back! Cursing my idiocy, I luckily reach the shore and take a moment to stop and take stock. *Yes, you're tired, but you must stop making stupid and risky choices. It may be slow, but you're going to have to hack and crawl through the forest.* Once again, fatigue has blurred my decision making. So much so, risks aren't being identified. Or even worse, they are, but I'm ignoring them.

Hacking through the forest isn't a great route either, but at least in here, there's no risk of drowning. However, there is a risk of falling. At times there might be some semblance of a recently trodden path, or possibly just a gap in the jungle. Yet, most of the time, I have to climb the near-vertical banks or traverse from tree to tree, putting all my faith in their tired and rotten roots, daring not to look down at the forest floor some five metres below.

It feels like this goes on forever; it's been like this all day. There's never, and I mean never, an opportunity to break into a run for more than ten metres. It's either up a stupidly steep bank, rock-hopping across giant riverbed boulders, or clambering through the non-existent forest floor. This goes on for hours – ten and a half hours in fact – just to cover 40 kilometres. Painstakingly slow.

After days like this, I dream of a straightforward approach to the finish line but rarely does one arise. Today is filled with 20-metre climbs on my hands and knees, through the forest's dying debris with perilous drops back over my shoulder. Followed by nerve-wracking descents back down said dangerous drops. Not for one moment is there a steady and straight path. Every step takes concentration and skill, and more often than not, a lot of luck.

Although one of the longest and slowest days of the adventure, upon reflection it has also been one of the most enjoyable. It's on days like this, when you think you have nothing left to give, that Te Araroa throws down a bigger challenge to you. One where you have to call on all your will to find whatever strength you have left, where you feel your legs burning and screaming at you to stop, but you snarl back and drive forward, knowing you will never give in. It's in these moments, when it is all on you, with only fumes left in the tank, you dig deep into your darkest demons and still demand more. It's in these moments that you feel most alive.

"Do you want the good news or the bad news?" Jill asks. *Not this again.*

"Come on, get it over with. What's the bad news?"

"You won't be heading over Arthur's Pass tomorrow. Severe weather warnings from the DOC. They are telling people not to go in and hoping those already up there have the sense to stay put," Jill explains sympathetically. Keily puts her arm around my shoulder.

Part of me feels this is the good news. More and more each day, my emotions are becoming heightened, and slowly, I'm struggling to deal with them. Not only are they beginning to overwhelm me, but I'm also struggling to understand them and starting to be genuinely scared. I'm scared of sections not dissimilar to ones I've previously conquered, and the next mountain pass always looks more daunting than the last. The thought of what is to come is often worse than the actual experience, but sometimes that is enough.

I'm back to a conflicted mind, with elated and gutted thoughts just split seconds apart. For a moment, the relief of an anticipated rest day tastes so sweet, but it's soon poisoned by self-doubt. *You're giving up!*

Now, I know this next section is a no go. The DOC doesn't take weather warnings lightly, but still the devil on my shoulder berates me, as if I'm quitting or taking the easy option.

Could I go in? Maybe, and perhaps I would be fine, but equally, it could end terribly. At this point, I'm no longer chasing a record, and my 100% trail completion is out the window. All I'm running for is the three strands left to hold onto: charity, inspiration, and personal integrity. If the 100% completion was still on, and if the record was still being fought for, then perhaps I'd have waited, maybe even have gambled but, today, there's no need. There's a fine line between bravery and stupidity.

In truth, my mind is a mess. I'm angry and demoralised, and it's not just because I can't go through Arthur's Pass, but because things haven't gone to plan, maybe even since Day 1. I sit questioning my own credibility and ability. *Who do you think you are, assuming you can actually do something like this? Did you really think you were going to break a record? You bottled it long ago back in Tongariro. This has been a write off since then. Pathetic.*

My head is full of these poisonous thoughts. I do all I can to hide them but, undoubtedly, they are clear to see. The night is as sleepless and filled with as much nightmarish despair as ever before, as my thoughts race and the rain batters our tin roof. *You're a failure Lewis.*

Distance: 41km
Elevation: 759m.

Day 44 - Rain, Rain – Go Away!

We awake to a morning where the weather is more than a match for my mood. The van sits in Arthur's Pass car park, being trounced by torrential rain beneath the darkening clouds that have consumed any sight of a mountain. Much the same, I lie staring into the void of the van's grey roof, after a sleepless night of toxic thoughts. I'm despondent and distraught – dangerously so. Everyone is awake, but no one says a word. Perhaps everyone else is feeling the same.

The deafening rain is enough to let us know the feared forecast has come true. Not only is Arthur's Pass a write-off, but the trail to Lake Coleridge is too. Someone has to break the silence.

"Right, What's the plan? One thing is for sure, let's get away from these mountains and out of this bloody rain," Jill expresses.

I don't respond, I can't respond, but I can begin to clamber from the top bunk to initiate our movement. Nothing needs to be said. We just need to get on with it, whatever 'it' is.

Not much else is said that morning. Each other's company is enough for now. We set our sights on Methven on the Canterbury flatlands, a point where we can make our move back into the mountains, according to the upcoming forecast. I sit, staring out at the clouded mountain walls, not taking anything in, just consumed by thoughts of failure. *You have bottled it, Lewis. You've gone soft.* Savage Mode is long gone now, left behind somewhere in Nelson Lakes, I'm sure.

It's not until we scamper to the range's outskirts, stopping in Springfield for some breakfast, that I can think with some sort of clarity. Is it having something to eat? Getting away from the threatening peaks? Or breaking into a small conversation? No idea, but whatever happens, it works, as some rationality comes back to us all.

"What are our options?" I ask. "Most of the Canterbury Mountains are underwater. We can't even go to the next rain-free section. It's just too far away. We can't skip that much of the trail."

"We could wait it out and go back in at Arthur's Pass, but we don't know when that will be, and to be honest, Lewis, we are running out of days," Jill responds. She's right. We've got sixteen days left in the country, before our flights home, so realistically fourteen days left for the trail – fifteen tops. The buffer we'd allowed for delays and injuries is completely gone. We're cutting it close.

"Maybe things will clear up tomorrow, and you can go back in a little further down. Wherever might be possible," Phill adds.

His response burns the most. The thought of skipping more of this trail feels fraudulent, but deep down I know it's the most sensible course, and the most likely thing to happen, but it's a struggle to accept it. I feel like a failure.

Phil and Jill have watched me run off into the distance at Cape Reinga, and now they are desperate to see me arrive in Bluff. To them, it doesn't matter if we miss a few sections. They just want to see the adventure being finished off. It's probably easier for them to accept the failures, to concentrate on the successes that have still been achieved. Arrive at Bluff or not, the attempt, the money raised for charity, the potential inspiration should all be more than enough. I can't see it. I cannot get my head past failing.

It's also Keily's birthday so, to cheer ourselves up, we spend a wet morning in Methven's eclectic Primo e Secundo, a madhouse of a coffee shop. The only way I can describe it is a well-organised hoard of old and interesting artefacts, collected over decades, with a coffee shop somewhere in the middle.

Maybe the time away from the trail will enable me to start contextualising our 'failure' and, more importantly, better value the objectives we're still fighting for. Yet, a constant struggle persists, a battle rages in my internal dialogue. *We can always push forward. Raising money is continually at stake, and there's still hope,* I dream. *You're a failure, Lewis, nothing but a wimp.* I scold.

Five minutes of personal berating pass before some compassion eventually shines through, a reminder to remove my ego and remain logical kicks in. *You did the right thing. You can't do anything about the weather.* I tell myself. Yet, the harsh self-inflicted insults flip back. *You never stood a chance. Who do you think you are?*

I'm stuck in a pattern of polarised thoughts, reasoning on events that have passed and now cannot be changed. I know this, even as all these thoughts happen, but it's a demanding fight to remain steadfast and remind myself of my typically strong philosophy. *Do not dwell on what has happened. Learn and move on,* I remind myself. Yet even knowing this, I'm still stuck, still contemplating past actions.

To compound the negativity, a look at tomorrow's forecast doesn't make things any better. A large section of the North Canterbury mountains is still to be buried under a veil of rain.

"Well, there is no way we're waiting for another day. Let's just go in tomorrow where the rain doesn't look as bad and just keep this thing moving," I declare out loud with frustration. "We can't do anything about what we have missed. We can't change the weather, we can only do what we can do," I remark in the late afternoon. I'm pretty sure the team had said much the same long ago. I just didn't hear it in my angry haze, signs of a Stoic mind coming back to life.

My mind is put slightly at ease after a conversation with the gentleman who runs the Alps 2 Ocean shuttle service, the bus that takes hikers in and out of different parts of the trail to Methven.

"I gave a young man a lift just a few weeks ago doing something just like you," he says.

"His name wasn't George by any chance?"

"Yeah, that was the fella!"

"What was the weather like?" *Please say it was brilliant.*

"Man, he was lucky. We didn't see a spot of rain for two weeks when he came through."

That's all I need. I have the card in my back pocket.

"Oh yeah, I got really unlucky with the weather," I might say to interested parties back home. Don't worry, whenever I pull the weather card out, I also mention that, even with good weather, I probably wouldn't have kept pace with George's 49 days. However, this conversation helps me realise that, while there are elements of this adventure where I maybe, just maybe, I could have continued, we should recognise we did get the shit end of the stick when it came to the battering rain. That's just part of the game.

So, what can we do? Painfully, the next place we feel I can rejoin is at Rangitata, where I'll then head over Stag Saddle, the Te Araroa's highest point, and drop down to Lake Tekapo. This is the painful part. That will mean missing 160 kilometres: three days of the trail. Mother Nature has got the better of us, again, but we have to make a decision.

There's no way we can spend a rest day in a funk. In the end, we eat cake and drink coffee. We play cards, try to laugh and eventually go out for a curry. Not an ideal birthday, but Keily, I hope you had some fun that day.

Distance: 0 km
Elevation: 0m.

Day 45 - Teeth Chattering and Unable to Speak

Time away from the trail has thrown me off course and out of rhythm, leading me down a terrible path of self-deprecation. The one thing I need most is to be out on the trail. Yet, it is the place I dread to be. That which I fear is what heals my fearful mind.

Across the flats and back into the mountains, we drive. The further into the South Island's spine we delve, the more rugged the terrain becomes and the more turbulent the roads, but Gerty takes it all in her stride.

I spend most of the journey staring out the window in awe of this astonishing place. The Rangitata river cuts through the centre of a sea of snowy peaks and ridgelines rising into the hanging clouds.

There seems to be an allure, a drawing presence felt when surrounded by mountains. It ignites some deep primal sensations within the human psyche, a sort of romance, maybe even the most organic feelings of awe and wonderment. Perhaps their overwhelming presence invokes a humbling reminder of our relative insignificance – temporal and physical – and encourages us to take stock and check our egos. *This isn't our world. We are just a part of it.*

Hit with some perspective, I'm now focused. It's as if someone has turned down the noise, or even hit the reset button on my mind. Any lingering negative thoughts have been forced to one side. Negativity will have to wait!

This doesn't mean I'm not a little nervous. I'm setting out to make it over Te Araroa's highest point, Stag Saddle, at 1925 metres. So, not only do I have two significant climbs to contend with, but I also have to cover 44 kilometres to make it to Lake Tekapo and the van. Otherwise, it will be a night in the mountains again, which isn't a problem other than falling 20 kilometres short. The nervousness stems from not only the physical challenge ahead, but also the possibility of rain. Looking up, the sky is clear but, as always in the mountains, you never know what's coming.

We arrive at Mesopotamia, the last stop for the van. Nothing but yellow farmland and imposing mountains stand ahead. From here I'll head into the belly of the beast.

The track runs up Bush Stream's rocky riverbed, and quickly the steep creek walls close in. A quick look back over my shoulder and the van is already out of sight. *It's time to trust yourself again. You've got this.*

Seven and a half kilometres in, the trail comes to an abrupt halt. The river runs deep as it corners through the ravine now blocked by vertical gorge walls. There's no route to continue upstream, so it's to be a straight scramble up. It seems as though the standard path has been washed away. A five-metre chunk has collapsed from the somewhat manageable slopes. As I start to rock climb, I remember my stupidity back on the Waiau Pass. *STOP! Go and find another way.* For once, sound judgement appears early, and I pile through the thorns and gorse until I find more of a goat track than a walking trail.

The sharp ascent rises high above the ravine, providing spectacular views back downstream to the beastly Rangitata and the frightening mountains further North. Climbing from the riverbed reveals the enormity of these ranges. What I couldn't see from the depths below was the sheer volume of peaks rising majestically from the maze of valleys. Immediately ahead lie the low grassy mountains, but in the distance are the giant lunarscape elevations, those that will soon have to be dealt with. *There it is again, that unequalled awe.*

With the elevation I'm facing today, I know I'll be slow but, once at these heights, I can't deny myself the opportunity to let it rip. The compelling combination of a thin, loose trail, meandering at vertigo-inducing heights, calls for an attack. *This is not the time to cower away and hide. You may never get to run a trail like this again in your life. Let loose and enjoy!*

Much like the diving mountainsides, I quickly descend to the stream down the thrilling goat track. From here, the day's first big ascent begins, an 800-metre climb over the next four kilometres, leaving behind the lush totara and mountain beech, up into the shrubs and tussock ridgelines, and beyond onto the baron rocky mountain passes. I've had my fun, now the hard graft really starts. *Dark clouds in the distance looks a bit ominous.*

These long steep climbs have become routine now. They are no longer that much of a challenge. My body and mind are more than capable of dealing with them. Ever since the scree slope up the Waiau Pass, most of these climbs pale in comparison. Every time one is set in my path, I'm able to hike with power and, if I do get tired, I have so much faith in my body I can just keep going through the pain. As was the case with this first climb up to Crooked Spur Hut and then beyond.

Those looming clouds are now not so distant, and the bright blue is being enveloped by the thick grey mass. Is it the decline in temperature or the dramatic drop in lighting? Can you smell it coming? I don't know, maybe all three, but it's clear, the rain is on its way. This isn't going to be a little shower. I'm doing just fine with the ascent, but now there is a new element to contend with. *I hope it doesn't pelt it down. I haven't packed my waterproof trousers.*

Up I go, always keeping one eye on the activity in the sky. *Don't get your hopes up. You know how this story goes.* I make it onto the lunar saddle, clear of any tussock and trees, and I'd love to describe the remarkable views from such a vantage point but, of course, the inevitable happens. The rain comes crashing down. In an instant, water tumbles down the rocky slopes, and clouds consume the land. Any chance of a panoramic shot has gone. Immediately, I'm being battered in the face, the all too familiar sharp sting of raindrops crashing on my cheeks. There's only one response. *Bring it on, Motherfucker!* It might be a bad idea to insult Mother Nature. This all happens at 12 kilometres in. *If I can just get past this rain, I can still make it to Tekapo!*

Now, much like when with Louis, just after we'd scaled the Tararuas, things take a strange turn. I've smashed my way to the day's first saddle, not quite Stag Saddle but still a good 1735 metres up. With no time, and certainly no point in hanging around, I race down, descending into the clouds below. It's at this point that I spot a man climbing northbound, and I have to do a double-take. There I am, freezing and soaked to the bone, and here he is in his short shorts, and thin raincoat not even zipped up, and that's it. No t-shirt, not even a pair of shoes. Now, as we know, I am a proponent of barefoot training and barefoot shoes, but to cross these jagged mountains with nothing to protect your feet, all I can say is, *fair play to the man*. It's not an easy surface to contend with, even with shoes on. The soles of his feet must be like leather. It's not just that he is so scantily clad, but that he has a massive smile on his face, compared to my grimace. That's not to say I'm not enjoying myself, but he does serve as a reminder to laugh in the face of adversity. I'm not certain this happened, it might have been an hallucination, but Barefootman, if you're out there, thank you. You gave me perspective and helped me push on that day.

From the saddle to Stoney Hut, the trail is made up of high-country tussock and scree, before Stoney Hut comes into view. I rush down and burst through its doors in an escape from the incessant torrent.

It's here where I find the lonely and despondent figure of a young American man. He very much resembles the state of the hut; tired, damp and fed up. We make pleasant conversation, although you can tell neither of us is really in the mood to talk. I'm still shell shocked from the battering rain, and he has an air of dejection. He's contemplating heading on to the next hut, but I don't think he even believes this himself. I certainly don't. A pleasant guy, but the whole drab setting is enough to let me wolf down my soggy sarnie and get on my way.

Torrential rain welcomes me back. These are the conditions that had brought us to a standstill but now, out here, I'm more than happy to carry on. In my defence, I'm out on the high country, and the Bush Stream will never create too many problems, other than a pair of wet socks. I guess at Arthur's Pass, and the further sections missed, there might have been rivers and streams that swell dangerously in such bucketing rain, hence the severe weather warnings. But, let's face it, I don't know, I never made it in. The demons resurface. *You were being a bit of a wuss, weren't you?*

With the bit between my teeth, I press on for the next hour, making my way upstream to Royal Hut, and, with time on my side, there's a chance I can make it up and over Stag Saddle before nightfall. *It's only 3 p.m. Plenty of time to meet the van, it's only 20 kilometres away.*

The adrenaline begins to wear off, and the closer I get to Royal Hut, the colder I become. My waterproof trousers would have been an absolute blessing as the freezing tussock grass brushes at my now numb legs. All I have are my long leggings and shorts, t-shirt, undertop and waterproof coat. In the bag, my spare socks, pants and a t-shirt, nothing much to help me in the cold. I can't afford to waste dry clothing, just in case I have to bail out and stay in a hut. I just have to plough on, despite the chattering teeth, numb limbs and frigid fingertips.

To make matters worse, I pop my head into the charming stone hut to a blast of heat from the raging fire. A beautiful German couple sit, warming their bones and drying their clothes.

"Oh, wow!" I exclaimed. "Oh, I am so jealous!"

"You're not staying?" Hans replies, surprised.

"Have you come over the saddle today?" I ask.

"Yes, this morning, but we are staying here now!" He responds, looking at me as if I'm crazy. "You do know it is snowing up there?"

"Snowing!" Now I'm the one surprised.

How bad can it be? If I stop here, I've only covered 24 kilometres. It's only 3 p.m. I have to at least give it a go.

"I have to go have a look, see if I can make it over. If not, keep that fire warm for me."

I go outside and stare up to Stag Saddle and, sure enough, the darkest of dark clouds has consumed it all. Not only is it snowing up there, but it's also beginning to fall down here at the hut. Before heading in, I'd read that today's freezing point was at 2000 metres. I acknowledged it but didn't actually think I'd end up having to deal with snow. I was trying to be smart; I was trying to pack light and be quick, and now it was biting me in the ass.

No sooner than five minutes in, not even at the gorge, the blizzard falls upon me. *I thought the freezing point was at 2000 metres. I'm only at 1300... snow falls, you idiot. I must at least try.* As soon as someone says, 'I must at least try,' that's basically them giving themselves an easy out. I know I will most likely turn around, but it wouldn't be a valiant effort if I don't go have a look. Although, there's a flicker of determination to make it through.

I press forward, crossing the icy stream and worming my way through the thick tussock. I'm both drenched and now chilled to my core. Once again, visibility is no more than a few meters. I'm barely able to identify the orange poles. *Just keep going. Maybe it will pass, and you might make it through.*

Onwards I go, a further two kilometres. I'm now shaking uncontrollably, teeth chattering and unable to speak, legs numb and hands almost frozen. I can't see for the blizzard, which is disorientating and, obviously, dangerous. Somehow, in the jumble of such scrambled thoughts, my mind has the all too critical moment of clarity, the involuntary check of your ego that slaps you in the face with sensible advice. *Just go back*, I tell myself. I've never been so cold.

Rationality wins. Who knows what might have happened if I'd continued? With incorrect gear, feeling dangerously cold and heading into the unknown, I would've been putting myself at serious risk. Perhaps with the correct equipment, I could have made a go at the saddle. Even still, would that have been wise in a blizzard? *At least I'll have the company of Hans and Sofia and that sweet burning wood. Get me back to that fire!*

Sitting in front of a fiery blaze in just my dry pants and t-shirt, still shivering and shaking some two hours later, I realise, *perhaps we did make the right choice back at Arthur's Pass!*

Distance: 32km
Elevation: 1671m.

Day 46 - Transcendence

For two hours, Hans, Sofia and I sit huddled together by the fire. I look on with jealousy at them, warm and toasty in their many layers, compared to myself – the fool beside them – shivering in just a t-shirt, a pair of boxers and socks.

Much to my dismay, the dwindling fire can only do so much to thaw my frozen bones before our small supply of firewood runs out. Yes, I'm cold, and yes, I've only covered 24 kilometres, but at least I'm not out in the blizzard anymore.

By 7 p.m., there's nothing else to do but hit the hay. Why not take this glorious opportunity to really get some rest? Bag liner, sleeping bag and bivvy bag all set up, I zip myself in, leaving a hole just big enough to breathe, and pray I will stay warm.

Oh, no, really? Now? I'm woken by the alarming midnight burden we're all too familiar with, the sudden need to pee. Combined with the freezing temperatures, it's a rude awakening. Thoughts of breaking from my dwindling warmth, tiptoeing over the cold stones, and bursting out to the wind and snow are dreadful contemplations. Yet, I must go. Swiftly, I do what needs to be done and dive back into my sanctuary, dreading my morning trip to the throne. *I knew I should have taken an empty bottle to bed.*

In the morning I'm in no rush as I wait for the snow to melt. A now clear and beautiful sky should see to that. I sit and enjoy a leisurely Beef Teriyaki breakfast whilst watching the snow retreat up the mountain, giving me ample time to reflect upon yesterday's madness.

I feel content. I can look back with reflective joy something, to this point, I have experienced in abundance. By reflective joy, I mean deferred enjoyment and happiness. For instance, the gruelling 24 hours on 90 Mile Beach was horrendous in the moment, but I can now regard it as inspiration. The unforgiving day-long ascent with Louis in the Tararuas was far from pleasant physically, but again I can look back at the finer moments and smile. Now, even the next day, I can look back at the madness in the blizzard and feel invigorated.

My contentment derives not only from my recollection of yesterday's events, but also because they feel like justification for the decisions we've made. Decisions that have plagued me, I now deem warranted.

For the first time in weeks, I set off with a smile on my face, starting the day with positive feelings. Despite having to wear the clothes still sodden from last night's blizzard, I'm ready to attack.

The saddle that seemed such a daunting prospect, now offers the prospect of postcard panoramas. I march up along the icy Bush Stream, snaking beneath the snow-coated valley. A quick look back to last night's humble abode fills me with comfort. The charming hut sits strong beneath the towering mountains from ranges gone by, unmoved by last night's tempest, a suitable metaphor for the unwavering character required on an adventure such as this.

Forward, as they must, move my feet, and, as the tussock and stream begin to thin, the trail ascends onto the scree slopes of Stag Saddle, where the proper climbing begins. Most of the snow has melted but, as I gain elevation, there is more to contend with, but I don't care. The sun is up, the wind is fresh, and I'm absolutely loving being in the mountains.

I reach the saddle with my mind in quite possibly the calmest and purest state it has been in for months, maybe even ever. To say I feel transcendent would be wrong, but close! This isn't anything beyond human experience, but I would say it's undoubtedly close to its peak. It's the rare moment that we all wish and hope to experience, the rush that people chase but rarely encounter. Maybe chasing such an experience is precisely what makes it elude us. It has to be organic. You can't create it.

From the crunch of the snow beneath my feet and the chilling air filling my lungs, to the pinnacle of Earth's beauty and the intense and gruesome effort expended to get there, everything feels perfect. The most essential ingredient is my mind; it has to be in the right place to accept it. Yes, all these external factors are perfectly in place but it's the interpretation of them, in the moment, that delivers this pure experience.

Maybe the saying, 'you can only control two things; what you think and what you do,' isn't entirely true. I certainly don't have complete control to create and manifest this moment. Without yesterday's snowstorm and today's beautiful sunshine, this moment would likely never have happened. Without endless days of success and many days of failure, this moment would likely never have happened. Without everyone's cooperation, all their support or the original idea in the first place, this moment would likely never have happened. It's the amalgamation of so much, just for this one memory of the purest bliss.

I make it to the top of Stag Saddle, Te Araroa's poster picture and the view is indeed spectacular. Off into the distance runs the mass of snowy peaks, down the spine of this jagged land, with Mount Cook pushing highest in the centre. At their feet sits the immaculate chalky blue of Lake Tekapo, a colour so mesmerising you have to look twice to believe it's real. To the left, the trail drops into the cavernous creek, and to the right, a tantalising ridgeline tracks high and long with everchanging and incredible views. *There's no way I'm heading down to that creek, not when running this ridgeline is an option.*

It is another moment of pure running pleasure. As the ridgeline slowly descends, the views morph and change, revealing different perspectives of this awe-inspiring land. The near transcendent state that carried me up the mountain is closely matched by that which takes me down.

Like all beautiful moments, this one must end, but I'm sure such a rich memory will live on in my daydreams for many years to come.

Ordinarily, the trail continues along the shelf above Lake Tekapo, but instead, I run down Ski Hill Road to meet the van. I need a rest, some food, and a complete change from these dank and disgusting clothes. I'll take a detour.

Upon meeting the team, I'm intrigued by their thoughts and feelings from last night. I know they trust my ability and decision-making, but I wonder what it must be like to look up to the surrounding mountains and see the dense clouds and snowfall, if they could see anything at all.

"Well, having seen the weather up there, we just assumed you'd be staying in," Jill says.

"Yes, and your SPOT tracker sent the message saying you'd stopped anyway, so we assumed you'd found a hut," Keily adds.

I was, almost hoping they were worried sick about me but, rightly so, they had everything in perspective. There it is again, a flash of ego – wanting people to feel uptight, wanting people to be anxious. How obnoxious! Maybe I want to feel like some sort of hero. For what? Not being an idiot and sheltering from the snow. *Get over yourself.*

After a rest, I'm off and trundling along the razorlike gravel to Lake Tekapo. A few podcasts pass the time, almost turning this into a pleasant evening run. The scenery isn't half bad, either.

We make it into town a little later than anticipated, so we drive into the country, pull off the roadside and call it home for the night. We soon discover we've pulled up near the University of Canterbury, Mt John Observatory. I can assure you; they have definitely put it in the right place. Although frozen stiff, we all stare into the sky, captivated by the angelic display overhead. Never in my life have I seen such a clear night and such a mass of stars. The more I look, and the more my eyes adjust, the more stars appear, and the more vibrant the scene becomes.

As I look up and out at space and think back upon the last few days, I'm once again hit with a humbling perspective. *Lewis, you're doing ok.*

Distance: 44km
Elevation: 1128m.

Day 47 - Integrity

Anticipation and excitement dominate my emotions. Mum and Dad have touched down in Christchurch and will soon join the team to help us over the line to Bluff.

I remember the day they told me they'd be coming out. Initially, it didn't look like it would happen. I mean, it's not exactly spare change to make it over here. But once we got the funding together, and the realisation kicked in that this was happening, they got excited and soon felt they couldn't miss out. It's and not every day you get the chance, and a reason, to fly to the other side of the world.

Today is also an excellent opportunity to get some miles in the bag. The sun is shining, and the trail is flat. The van will be close by, and I don't have to carry everything on my back. It'll be like being back in the Northland.

13 kilometres in, and clear of the tourist hotspot, the trail runs the canals connecting the turquoise beauties – Tekapo and Pukaki.

As a counterbalance, I'm back on immaculate tarmac roads, as flat as a pancake and as straight as an arrow, seemingly going on into eternity. My body rebels immediately, pains I'd almost forgotten resurface, and my energy dips to once lost lows.

Time moves on, and so do I, just painfully slowly. I'm hoping to run off into the distance, covering ten kilometres per hour but, understandably, I settle into my 1.20 pace. There's actually a corner in the road some six kilometres in, thrilling to behold! But then the immaculate tarmac turns into that bloody bastard gravel. *You have got to be kidding me.*

47 kilometres of serial boredom. A break at 22 kilometres does little to motivate, and the snow-capped mountains do little to stir inspiration. It's a stunning and beautiful scene, naturally, but it can only provide so much distraction from the monotonous, uncomfortable run. Although the salmon fisheries do bring mild

entertainment as I pass them by – their waters calm one moment and thrashing with life the next.

Yes, this sucks, you're going slow, and I know you don't care that it's beautiful, but you've fought this battle many times before. Just keep moving.

Eventually, and thankfully, my self-talk pays off, and Lake Pukaki comes into view. *Somewhere on its shores will be my sanctuary.* I dream of the van.

Well, this is new, and I'm surprised it hasn't happened earlier.

What happens when you mix heat, sweat, and a thigh-rubbing 80,000 steps? Yes, you guessed it. I run the last kilometres along the shores of Lake Pukaki as if I'd had a very unfortunate accident. Although that was close, it wasn't the case. The dreaded chaff has settled in, and I need some Vaseline relief. The last thing I want is a blistered bum.

"Don't worry, you three. I think I can apply this one myself," I declare, whilst walking along the road with a finger up my arse. Tourists on a road trip didn't expect to see that. *Needs must.*

As the pains return, so does the tight left hip and quadriceps from the early days. Come to think of it, I haven't really done much running at all in the South Island. I've speed hiked, run when I could, but it hasn't been for long. One full day of running, and it's like I've started all over again. The fix stays the same, a pummelling at the hands of Jill and Phil. Again, I don't imagine tourists expect to see two people aggressively pressing against a man's buttock at the side of a van.

'Vassed up,' and well massaged, it's time to hobble the last ten to Twizel. This really is reminiscent of the North Island. We've covered 66 kilometres, I've been bored out of my brain under the baking sun, and I've been reduced to a walk. I'd say it was a nice break from the mountain pass, but I'm not so sure.

Thankfully, Mum and Dad finally arrive after their extended cross-country drive. I find it strange to reach such a busy camp and it strikes an unfamiliar chord. Of course, I'm delighted to see my parents. One of the most significant driving forces in my life is to make them proud. So, to see their beaming smiles as we pull in is enough to let me know that, in their eyes, I'm doing a "bloody brilliant job," as my old man would later put it.

As I say, it's an unfamiliar chord because the dynamic has shifted. I'm aware that things feel different, but I'm just too happy to pay much attention to it. No longer is this just our little rogue group of three attempting the outrageous. It sounds sad to say, but everything feels as though it's beginning to come to an end, despite Bluff still being 600 kilometres away.

I felt a change when Keily first arrived. It was both joy that she was here and a desire to seek her comfort, something that hadn't been available to that point – something I hadn't needed until it was there. It was welcome, of course, but alas unsettling – a distraction. Adding in the emotional draw of close family means things will be different again. Is this good or bad? I'm not sure.

This whole adventure has tested my integrity, but the Canterbury region has asked the most questions. In the face of dread and fear, I remind myself that the obstacle is the way, and step forward again to where I must go. In the face of difficult decisions, we have consistently remained objective and taken what we thought was the right action, and not necessarily the easiest. Despite our failures, we've kept our mission at the front of our thoughts and pushed on in service of our worthy cause.

Integrity is defined as 'the quality of a person being honest and having strong moral principles,' and through our lives, such qualities are continually tested. The world throws challenges, grievances and questions our way to see if our integrity can withstand them. The world throws uncontrollables at us to see how we respond. It tempts us to stop, to cheat or give in, and at times we will waiver. But this is part of the ongoing test. It takes honesty and strong moral principles to acknowledge when we have lost those exact qualities. Upon reflection, through the decisions we made and the actions we took, perhaps my integrity was upheld.

Yet that evening, as I lie in bed, I'm consumed by self-deprecation. In my mind, I have failed and don't deserve the pride my parents are displaying. Canterbury was all about integrity, and to me, mine has been lost.

Distance: 64km
Elevation: 303m

OTAGO

ACCEPTANCE

'Most of death is already gone. Whatever time has passed is owned by death.'

-

Seneca

Day 48 - Breaking Point

How can they actually be proud of me? I'm a failure. I should never have skipped Tongariro or Arthur's Pass. So what If I'd never made it to the end? At least I would have given it my all, unbroken. I feel like a fraud. Yet, I can't let anyone know. I don't know why or how, but I have to keep moving.

I set off along the bank of Lake Ruataniwha. Rarely does a person feel physically strong when their emotions are so fragile. Still, I carry on, with something stirring inside, keeping me going.

I'm not managing to come to terms with, or accept, our failure – my failure in fact. It's a strange feeling to know you've lost, but you still must carry on. I say 'must' because that is what I said I would do from the get-go. I may well have missed sections, but one thing is for sure, I have to keep moving.

Since Day 19, Tongariro, I've pushed these thoughts to the back of my mind. I knew they were there, but I never gave them the breathing space to conflict me. There was still too much to do. However, now my family is here and the end is in sight, these thoughts of failure have come to the fore. Seeing my proud Mum and Dad leaves me thinking, *proud of what?*

As the mental battle continues, so does the physical, and I'm beginning to lose this one too. I can barely muster a jog. The first ten kilometres takes 90 minutes. It feels close to walking pace. By the time I reach the team at 15 kilometres, a moment I usually cherish, I can only look on in despair. There they stand, every one of them has helped me get to this point, and I just feel that I've let them down. Not even the idyllic Lake Ohau, and its mesmerising mountains, can do enough to rouse me.

Dad is so excited, and absolutely loving life. He can't help but explore the trail, hoping to bump into me on his forays, and always wearing a heartfelt smile. Mum, so often the one to keep things steady, looks peaceful and calm, happy to be here, taking it all in. They're both genuinely happy. Jill, Phil and Keily have seen me like this before. I can see it in their eyes. They know I'm struggling, even more so than usual.

For the first time on this adventure, I'm near my breaking point, and I don't know how to recover. I'm all too aware that a challenging 25-kilometre mountain pass is imminent. I can plod around the lakes in safety, however, the thought of tackling the unknown, the mystery of a mountain pass creates unease, even fear. I've successfully dealt with mountain ranges but, for some reason, the thought of being up there soon almost cripples me with anxiety, and I don't use that word lightly.

I struggle around Lake Ohau and arrive at my last checkpoint until the Ahuriri River – 25 kilometres away. This is a distance I know I can comfortably cover before nightfall. Yet, staring up at that giant rock wall, I'm feeling sick to the pit of my stomach.

I leave camp and, if anyone had been unsure about how I was coping, it must be as clear as the sky by now. I think Mum and Dad realise just how tough this really is, and the impact it's having on their son. Their smiles of joy have turned to expressions of concern.

I go into the mountains. It's 3 p.m., so I have six hours to make it out the other side. Instantly I'm struggling, but this time not just physically. I'm shaking, my heart rate is through the roof, and I can barely control my breathing. My mind is a muddle, full of conflicting and confusing thoughts. *You must carry on. No, just turn back. You can't! You have to go forward!*

This overwhelming feeling that has been nagging me is now crippling me. A feeling first experienced at the summit of Raetea Forest, on Day 3. A feeling I've felt every morning away from the team. A feeling which persists whenever I'm out in the wilderness alone.

This horrible feeling, that has plagued me for weeks on end, is an emotionally crushing loneliness. It didn't click when I took my first steps along 90 Mile Beach, or when Keily arrived. Yet now, with all these people who matter so much to me in proximity, I realise just how alone I feel when I leave them. Finally, it has all become too much.

It's the first time I have truly felt the ruin of loneliness. It is, by far, the most mentally challenging and debilitating place my mind has ever been. Up until this point, I'd either not recognised it, or it wasn't strong enough to cause such anxiety and fear. I think it's been brought forward by a combination of fatigue at levels I've never felt before, the challenge of dealing with perceived 'failures', and the arrival of Keily, Mum and Dad.

Maybe, if we'd continued as a three right until the last kilometres, I wouldn't have reached this emotional barrier. Perhaps I would have been worse, I don't know. However, I don't doubt that their arrival had an effect, though I don't regret their arrival. In the end, some of my happiest memories came from them joining us on this journey. However, for the sake of performance, maybe it wasn't the best. As strange as this may sound, I'm glad this all happened. I wanted to push my physical and mental limits, and that is precisely what I did. Loneliness broke me but from that, I learn so much.

Three kilometres into the forest, it all becomes too much. I slump onto a log and sob. Mentally I cannot take this. I sit and cry, not knowing why, other than because I really don't want to do this anymore.

It's a pathetic sob. How I wish I could say it was a proper cry, but in reality, I whimper, and a mere tear or two drops as I moan as if it were more. I sit for five minutes, letting my emotions out before realising I can't turn back, the team would have moved on, and I won't be able to contact them.

Sometimes, all you need is a little cry. It acts as a release. It's as if I was at boiling point, and someone opened the lid to reduce the pressure. Feelings of sorrow and despair change to anger, and this emotion becomes the driving force for the charge up the mountainside. The forested ascent soon changes to a boulder field, but nothing will stop my furious march. I'm driven by anger, and I'm further driven by my desperation to get back with the team, anything to cure the loneliness.

It is a gorgeous climb. The sun shines high on another clear afternoon, and the trail escapes the canopy cover onto the boulder fields and tricky tussock. Either side, giant walls of rock and scree ascend to neck aching heights and, ahead, a set of peaks stand menacingly where the grass disappears, and the terrain resembles a lunar expanse.

Turning back, I'm treated to a view I rarely get tired of – the lake I've just left, sitting at the bottom of the valley I've just climbed. I turn. *Wow, that's beautiful.* Step forward again and carry on. I'm in no mood to think pretty thoughts.

It's a tricky ascent matched by a similarly rocky, and at times boggy, descent through a sharp valley. I hot-foot my way down the scree slopes to the stream that will carry me the last 15 kilometres to the van.

As the terrain levels out, so do my heightened emotions. The day's end is in sight, and I know I'll easily make it out of what was worrying me so much. My anger dissolves into a mixture of contentment and sadness. Let's face it, I have completely lost management of my mind and am duly being ruled by my emotions. 'Controlling what I think and what I do,' is a battle clearly being lost at the moment.

The trail continues through the tussock and shrub along the Ahuriri River East Branch. Once again, it's stunning scenery in the late hours of the day as the sun lies low behind the golden valley walls, and the silhouettes of the team stand waving on the opposite ridge.

I've covered 60 kilometres, but a sense of failure is still tearing me to pieces. *I have to confide in someone,* and ahead stands my confidant. I cross the rushing Ahuriri, and there Keily stands on the other side, having waited hours for me to appear. I cross, we embrace, and she knows my mind is a mess. However, being in her company at that moment is everything I want.

"Keily, I don't know how I can do this. I know I have to continue, I know why, but I've failed, as simple as that," I confide. "Keily... this is so hard."

"Lewis, you have to tell the others, you can't keep this all to yourself. We need to know," she responds. She knows that sharing this with the team is the right thing to do, we all need to be on the same page, and their input can undoubtedly help.

Keily and I walk alongside Jill and Dad, and I express my thoughts and feelings. Dad responds with vigour,

"Lew, you won't realise this, but so many people asked me, 'How's Lew getting on?' or they tell me, 'He's doing so well!' I don't think you realise the positive impact this is having back home. The impact this adventure is creating."

Dad, Jill and Keily are all correct. This is about the charity now. It's more important than beating a record, and I must share how I'm feeling with the team. Everything they say is correct, but I cannot shake the feelings of failure and it certainly won't fix my loneliness.

I sit at the dinner table, hood up and quiet. Tomorrow is said to be a highlight of the Te Araroa, a challenging 50-kilometre route with some of the most stunning views on this earth. I should be filled with excitement, but instead, I'm brimming with fear; fear of the weather turning, fear of having to spend the night in the mountains, and mostly, the fear of being alone.

Distance: 60km
Elevation: 1286m.

Day 49 - Retreat

A cold and dark morning does little to help my faulting thoughts.

Not much is said. I sit, staring into space, trying to find peace of mind. One thing is for sure, the last place I want to be right now is back on the trail, it looks a sad and lonely place.

Reluctantly, I slip on my shoes and sling on my backpack. My hood hasn't come down all morning, and it's not going to shift until the sun rises above the dark valley.

Eyes brimming with tears, I set off. Once again, my heart is racing before I've even taken a step. The anticipation of the unknown, or more likely of being alone, leaves me feeling sick. Yesterday's triumph over adversity has failed to alleviate my fears. I'm no longer being objective. My emotions have well and truly taken control.

Autopilot carries me six kilometres along the Avon Burn. I climb broken banks and cross the chilling river multiple times, but it's the first drop of rain that snaps me from my daze. *That's it. You don't have the correct kit for rain. You must go back.* I think we all know that's just me looking for any reason to turn around.

I decide as quickly as that, without even a pause. *Just head back down and get out of here!* The chance of the van still being there is very slim. I mean, it has taken me 45 minutes to get six kilometres in, so there's no way they'll still be there in another 45 minutes. I don't care. I just want to turn back. I'm desperate.

Frantically, I scramble, praying that the team have decided to stick around, knowing that they won't have. I rise from the creek, knowing I'll have a view back to the road and, with one kilometre to go, my heart sinks. They've gone.

Although I might be off the trail, it doesn't mean I have an easy way out. Without a phone signal, I can't give the team a call, and who knows when I might see that glorious bar in the top corner of my screen. My only choice is to walk until I reach the highway – roughly 12 kilometres away. *Hopefully, I might get enough signal and give them a call.*

Sunlight creeps through the overcast sky to illuminate the golden tussock clad mountains standing tall above the arid farmland, cut by the deep Ahuriri River Creek. I feel like an ant on a sand dune amongst this vast and wild space, giving me the space and time to finally think about the decision I just made. I settle into the long walk to the highway and acknowledge my disappointment. *You made a mistake today, Lewis.*

My thoughts are disrupted by the beautiful rumble of tyre on gravel. Quickly I turn and, with my best smile, stick out my thumb, hoping for the best. It's my lucky day, well – lucky moment. The hurtling Audi pulls over and offers me my first ever hitchhike. Her name is Alice, if memory serves me, and our two worlds couldn't seem further apart. Alice works at the luxury lodges in the heart of the Ahuriri Valley. Then there's me, stinking to high heaven after not having showered for five days. If only we had known those luxury lodges were up the road, we might have got ourselves a night of indulgence. I'm sure Jill could have twisted their arm.

"Where are ya headin'?' Alice asks.

"Lake Hawea, if you're going that way?" I reply with hope.

"I'm headin' to Queenstown. I can drop you at Tarras."

"No idea where that is, but getting to the end of this road would help!"

I don't know where Tarras is, I don't know where the team are so, instead of gambling, I ask to be dropped at the highway. Alice suggests that the Hostel just over the road might let me use their Wi-Fi to make a call.

I find the owners and, in my most polite manner, explain the situation. Gratefully, they oblige.

"Lewis?" answers Keily with confusion.

"Sorry, I have to be quick. I walked back out, hitchhiked down the road and am in the backpackers using their Wi-Fi. Can someone come and pick me up?" I can feel my throat constricting. "I just couldn't do it."

"Ok... Well, Phil and I will come and get you. At the bottom of the valley road, yeah?" Keily asks, making sure we are on the same page.

"Yes, please," I respond. My only thought, w*hat have I done?*

Sitting at the end of that road, there's nothing else to do but think. I cannot wait to 'stop' for a moment, to actually be present with everyone as opposed to being my usual vacant self at the end of each day. Yet equally, I know this decision will haunt me. I knew it as soon as I turned, but the desire to be with everyone was stronger than my will to push on. At what price?

Keily and Phil arrive, and I tumble into the front seat. The three of us sit together.

"We were just having a coffee when you called. Want to stop there on the way back? What was it called Keily?" Phil asks.

"The Country Shop, wasn't it?"

"Where is it?" I ask.

"Began with a 'T', didn't it?" Phil wonders.

"Don't tell me, it's not Tarras, is it?"

"That's the one!" Keily replies with a beaming smile. I think you can guess the tone of my response.

The rest of the day is spent at camp on Lake Hawea, providing an opportunity to spend time with the team, my family and catch up with our good friends Tash and Gaz, who are over from Australia. It's almost perfect. Yet I'm still threatened by my questioning thoughts. *How can we possibly carry on now?*

This time, I don't keep my thoughts to myself. Credit goes to Phil. He puts the camera in my face and asks me to be open about the last few days. It's this honest and open conversation that helps me unravel my confusion, identifying that the true block to my progress has been that sense of loneliness. I feel that common relief we often encounter when sharing our emotions, or even when we untangle the mysteries locked within our minds. It's out in the open. We all have clarity on the situation, and the weight of the unknown is removed from my shoulders. I can now think again.

We have to be objective. There's nothing I can do to rectify the decisions I've made. All we can do is look forward, not neglecting to learn from our mistakes.

By no means have I suddenly removed my fears of loneliness and the anger that still simmers, but some management of my thoughts and feelings has returned. *Have I got it in me to go again?*

There's a long way still to go. Realistically, we only have 11 days left to run the last 452 kilometres. A manageable distance, even with a few mountains in the way. *Just go again tomorrow, that is all you can do.*

Distance: 0 km
Elevation: 0 m.

Day 50 - Back in the North Island Groove

The bright and warm mornings of the Northland are now a distant memory. Now we rise in the darkness, hoping that the swirling winds don't bring any downpours. The last few days, my mood has reciprocated such weather, but today I awake with less fret and angst over my mind. No obstacles lie in my way, and no serious time away from the van. All that's ahead is a flat route from lake to lake and over to Glendhu Bay. *No mountain, no trouble.*

Phil and I drive back to where my path would have reached and, although still annoyed with myself, I do not dwell on my decision. There's work to do. Today is lining up to be more comfortable, yet our rattling van and the threatening skies suggest otherwise. What looked such an idyllic and pristine lake yesterday, has turned into one of threat and danger. A mass of clouds lines the sky above the aggressive, encroaching mounts that cast their ominous shadow over the now dark and thrashing lake. *Looks a bit nasty out there.*

The first thing I notice is that a day's rest hasn't help me recover anywhere near as much as I was hoping. With the number of miles in these legs, they need a month off, not just a day. Secondly, I'm hit by some of the strongest winds I've ever experienced –I'm nearly knocked clean off my feet. It's a strange sensation to run with all of your might and find yourself getting next to nowhere. It's like having a bungee tied around my waist. Is this the Te Araroa giving me a clip round the ear for not treating her with the fullest respect? Still, I crack on until clear of the lakeshore.

Today, it will mainly be my mammoth levels of fatigue that stand in my way. To be frank, I'm spent. All I have left is my sad little shuffle. If you ask me to sprint, my face might grimace and my effort might skyrocket, but it's unlikely my speed will change at all. This is to be my pace from now until the end, nothing special. If anything, onlookers might think I'm in all sorts of trouble. I try not to care, even as the fresh-faced young man goes hurtling past, looking at me with his smug features. My imagination, I'm sure. *Who cares? Just like back in Auckland, they don't know what you're going through.* At least that's what I tell myself.

A move from one lake to another down here can be enough to change climates. Now clear of the looming mountains, and their angry clouds, I have the sun beaming down on my neck just as at the beginning of my run. I think what I've missed is the sense of a common adventure that we had back in the North Island. Up there, I could share every experience with the team, either during the day or later that evening. Yet, down here, most of the highs and lows have been experienced alone. We'd lost some of the feeling of this being a team effort.

But now I have the van back as a frequent target. I push on past Albert Town to Lake Wanaka's shoreline, meeting the team just out of town. Although physically challenging, my mind is comforted by the familiar routine – a 10 or 20-kilometre stint, followed by a short rest. It feels like we're back in the North Island groove!

There will be obstacles still to face, just not today. Yet, on the run from Wanaka to Glendhu Bay, as I stare at the clouds devouring the mountains and lake all in one, the nerves start to return. The thought of heading into the peaks again is enough to flip me back to my fearful and anxious self. I focus on self-talk as a coping mechanism. *You are worried about it, it is going to be tough, and it will test you, but it's nothing you haven't dealt with before.* Some objectivity has been restored.

However, with severe weather warnings for tomorrow, I'm again confronted with a decision to make. Questions come flooding back – about integrity, ability, and safety. *You're overthinking things. You must do it. Don't forget the last time you ignored the weather warnings.* My mindset is being challenged as soon as it finds a minute of calm. Again, that is why this is such a challenge!

Distance: 49km
Elevation: 718m.

Day 51 - Golf and Seneca

I decide not to go into the mountains today. I use the weather as a workaround, and maybe I'm right too, but in all honesty, I'm wondering if cowardice is at the root of it. It could be awful up there, or it could be a breeze, *but you won't ever know because you were too afraid to go and look!* Clearly, I'm not over the loneliness.

As the rain obscures the usually heavenly views at Lake Wanaka, my mind scrambles for an acceptable alternative. *You've got to claw back some integrity. You don't want to skip anything. You'll have to run the road.*

"Maybe I could run the Cardrona Valley Road?"

The team aren't convinced but it's settled.

"Let's get ready for a road run to Queenstown," says Jill cheerily, making the best of it. As we leave Wanaka behind, the team craft a makeshift, 'CAUTION – RUNNER IN ROAD' sign. I tell myself, *it's OK, there's a severe weather warning, and you're not in the race anymore.* I know I'm making excuses.

Yes, well, it wasn't such a good idea after all. The cars whizz by inches from my side as I jump to the grass verge. I'm in fear for my life where the cars can see me coming, let alone the undulating and winding roads still to come. We quickly realise this is a stupid idea; potentially getting hit by a car no way to save a bit of face. On to Plan C. We skip again, this time to Arrowtown.

Despite the stunning drive, I am exhausted by disappointment when we resume. My pace is the slowest it has been to date, and as I run the water's edge from Frankton, I'm frequently being passed by joggers. I'm going so slow I half expect a couple on a romantic walk to stride past.

I even stumble through the middle of the New Zealand Open Golf Tournament. Not accidentally, in a haze of fatigue. The trail does actually wind through The Hills Golf Club. With spectators everywhere and camera rigs following the action closely, I do have one amusing daydream. I can imagine Viv, Jill's uncle, who took us in with his wife Jenny to get over our jetlag, sat at home watching the golf and suddenly seeing me bob along in the background, looking like a hot mess. It's a small compensation on another disappointing day.

I run into Queenstown with one thought on my mind. *I've fucked it all up. I have absolutely ruined everything.* The previous three days stand out like a grim stain on what has been such an incredible journey. All the integrity I'd worked so hard to maintain through Canterbury now feels lost. Because the record and race have gone, I'm taking the easy option.

Something has to give, something has to change, and it can only come from within. The situation must be flipped, I need to change my perception of it all.

That night I go to bed experiencing a moment of decisiveness that comes from nowhere, a moment that will be integral to saving something from this adventure. *You have to complete a full line all the way to the end; whatever it takes, just get there. You don't owe it to anyone, only yourself. Get back some faith and self-respect. Stand tall in the face of the adversity to come, and finish strong.* I need to stop feeling sorry for myself and get on with what I said I would do.

If anything, this chapter is more about highlighting failure, mostly the failure garnered from losing objective judgement. I suppose the minor moment of acceptance that occurred that night in Queenstown may be what gave me the title of this book. The acceptance occurred when I realised, I couldn't keep looking back. All that I could change was what was happening right then and there. So that's what I did. I no longer played victim to my disappointment, and I decided to make an actionable change.

Yes, it's a plan as to how I will conduct myself in the future, but it is very much a positive action in the present. I can no longer live in a time that is now dead, no longer project forward anxiously in my imagination about what is to come. I have to remove it and be in the present moment. That's the moment of acceptance.

Perhaps today I should take my own advice. Writing the above chapter reminds me of the quote at its beginning. 'Most of death is already gone. Whatever time has passed is owned by death.' I should listen to Seneca and accept that what is done is done. I can't do anything about it now except learn and move on.

Distance: 24km
Elevation: 341m.

SOUTHLAND

REDEMPTION

'The impediment to action advances action. What stands in the way becomes the way.'

-

Marcus Aurelius

Day 52 - All I Needed Was A Burger

It's as if a switch has been flicked. Lying there, staring at the carpet canvas in my top bunk, I feel a renewed sense of determination and drive.

Waking up, something that had been such a feared chore, is now bright and full of energy. I'm awake again, and properly so this time. *Get up and get on with it, no fucking about today!*

Everyone else can feel it too, or I like to think they can. The focus and drive radiate from me like an enthused aura. We're all smiling, we're all a little happier – we all seem ready for this last chapter. Last night's Fergburger, the world's greatest burger in my opinion, might have something to do with it.

Today's section will start on the other side of Lake Wakatipu at the Greenstone River. That means an early departure to make our way around.

Sights that would've seemed terrifying just yesterday, now entice me. The cold mist sitting atop the dark, still lake aids my determination rather than filling me with fret and worry. The snow-capped mountains fuel me with wonder instead of fear. Everything feels different, our smiles have grown since leaving Queenstown, and the switch in energy is undeniable as we get the day set and ready. Previously, our faces were permeated with sadness and dejection, but now we are ready and raring to go.

In truth, that might just be me seeing what I want to see. When sad, do we project and see the same on those around us, and much the same when happy? Nonetheless, I feel strong and determined, perhaps for the first time since Wellington, and the team matches my energy.

It's clear what needs to be done. Get to Bluff in one complete line! It's a charge full of grit and desire for the first four hours. A 20-kilometre, undulating, rocky, rooted stream-side trail ascending from the lakeshore. The most perfect conditions you could ask for at the beginning of a run of redemption. *Don't give me long, flat roads. Give me more of this.*

By mid-afternoon, the trail splits away from the Greenstone River to follow the Mararoa, across the sludgy and soggy tussock flats towards the Mavora Lakes. Despite the slow pace, and no discernible route to follow, all is OK. The five kilometres per hour I'm clocking will be enough to get me to camp before nightfall.

Oh, my fickle mind. Now in the mountains, the idea of staying in a hut feels more appealing, either alone or with others. It is true, as Seneca put it, 'we suffer more in imagination than reality.' Yet, it can be hard to remind yourself of this when stuck in the deep doldrums.

I can now see the appeal of a hut because my mind is more receptive to doing so. Previously, the thought of being alone was devastating. I'd look on at others in a group and be overwhelmed with crippling jealousy. However, today, I watch a group of mates pull up to Cerys Hut from a day's fishing, I look on with a smile, and maybe a little jealousy – but a healthy amount. Perhaps it's because I know that *my* mates are waiting for me at the other end of this lake.

The clock pushes close to 7 p.m., and the van is only ten kilometres away. This run from Cerys Hut is the last chapter of the day. Daylight fades and the sky turns a deep purple. The only audible sounds left in the valley are my footsteps across the dusty 4x4 track and the patter of a fisherman's motor out on the lake. The serenity is paralleled in my peaceful mind.

The slow shuffle continues as it always does, even when meeting Keily, Jill and Dad, with three kilometres to go. They'd been told by the fisherman I was close by. Stopping isn't an option. I can't break my stride, if you can even call it that! My eyes are fixed on the end of this little black beach, and nothing is going to distract me from that goal.

After 11 hours covering 50 kilometres, the HiAce glows beside the darkened lake, looking as welcoming as ever.

"Get the fuck in there!" I shout again. My confidence is restored. *That's more like it, I'm back!*

Distance: 52km
Elevation: 1336m.

Day 53 - And Then There Were Three

Smoke, from a neighbouring campfire, drifts over the eerily still North Mavora Lake. The imposing mountains don't quite have their colour yet. The hiding sun still illuminates the bright sky, with not a cloud in sight.

The scene is not dissimilar to that at Ahuriri River on Day 49. It's a crisp, cold morning and a promising day lies ahead. We're all a little sleepy. However, today my thoughts and feelings could barely be more of a contrast to that dreadful day. Sitting at the breakfast table, staring out at this peaceful scene, my mind is at ease. The thought of a morning run actually appeals. Dare I say it, I'm happy!

It can't all be pleasure with no price to pay. You would have thought, after 53 days, enough tribute had been paid, yet the Te Araroa asks for more. The trail is perfect, the temperature is just right, and I'm raring to go. What could possibly be the issue? My legs – they're cooked and drained of all energy. These first ten kilometres are going to feel like the final ten of each day. This is annoying but, importantly, I know my mind is not going to stop me today. I know I can do this now.

The 13-kilometre forest run finishes at a swing bridge, where I chow down on more of Jill's Magic Porridge, and swig back some sweet, sweet coffee. *Oh, how I miss decent beans.* Having the van available to fall back on is ever so welcome, a luxury so sorely missed. However, I have to remind myself that it's there when I need it, not when I want it.

And how I so desperately want that van on the next stint. The trail runner's wonderland has transformed into a runner's tussock-filled nightmare.

"This is just shit!" I scream, throwing a tantrum.

The orange triangles are sparse when they're not hidden by the tangles of gorse and shrub. It's a battle to hack and whack in the general direction of the route. For all I know, the trail might be just a few metres to the left or right, but in the roasting heat, with my frustration boiling over, I'm never going to find it.

I'm doing all this, and getting myself cut to shit, and there's a bloody road just over there – go and run along that. Is it the right decision? You'd think so, unless faced with your old nemesis. *Gravel roads, we meet again.*

A second stop with the team breaks up a monotonous afternoon. If boredom is to be my only adversary over these last few days, I will gladly take it. By the blank look on my face, the team can see I'm hot, bothered and mostly bored. As she's dressed for it, Keily volunteers to accompany me and assuage the boredom.

Now, I'm sure she won't mind me saying this, but Keily is not a runner. She could be decent if she wanted to be, but she doesn't – so she isn't. So, credit where credit is due, she sticks in there for the last 15 kilometres and we treat it as an interval run – three lampposts run, one lamppost walk, and so on. It turns into a training run for Keily, and a desperate attempt to get to the end for me.

Having someone there to talk to helps ease the pain and boredom, but there's no way 53 days of mental and physical turmoil will be eradicated by one conversation – not with anyone, even Seneca. Still, it's enough to get me over the line and complete another day on the trail.

Looking to the next section, I have a decision to make. Ahead lie 72 kilometres across forest and tussock-clad mountains. Simply put, there's no way I'll make it through in one stint. I have to plan where I will get to – Aparima Hut, 25 kilometres in, or the less inviting Lower Wairakei Hut at 37. Straight away, unsettling feelings start to rear their ugly heads. *Just yesterday, out on the mountains, staying out for the night looked so appealing, and now, you are anxious again.* I haven't felt lonely the last few days because I knew the team were there through the day, and waiting at the end. Now with the prospect of being away and alone again, worrisome thoughts begin to prosper.

I'll be going in, that's for sure. That doesn't mean I'm looking forward to it. We identify a link road, just six kilometres from

Aparima Hut and, as Phil wants to film hut life, he volunteers to hike in along it. Keily, Jill and Dad throw their hats in the mix too, and soon enough, everyone wants to go. That's when Dad poses his suggestion.

"Son, I'd love to hike with you."

This takes me aback. Yes, I should probably push to Lower Wairakei, but I can't turn down the chance to hike with my dad in New Zealand.

"Dad, I'd love it," I tell him, feeling quite emotional.

"I want to come to," says Keily, who, having had a taste of the action, wants to keep it going. To my mind, it's a case of the more the merrier.

As long as I reach Bluff in time, who cares if there's a 25-kilometre day in there? Especially if it's a day's hike with Keily and Dad!

Distance: 45km
Elevation: 256m.

Day 54 - "There's always a little bit left in the tank."

With only 25 kilometres to cover, we're not heading in until midday. Eight hours of sunlight should surely be enough. Alone, I'd fancy my chances of covering the distance in four or five hours, but who knows with Keily and Dad alongside.

Although I'm excited by the prospect of hiking with them through some beautiful, rugged country, part of me is still questioning the decision. *Should I have gone in alone? Should I have left in the early hours to make it as far along the trail as possible?* Most probably, but by now, my mind is solely focused on finishing, not necessarily quickly, but getting there before missing the flight home. I'm determined to enjoy this special day.

There the three of us stand proud at the beginning of our little adventure, with the day's obstacle towering behind us. No time to hang about, a couple of quick pictures, and we turn to face our adversary. Beautiful, wild and natural, but with that comes rugged and brutal terrain. There's the concern again, *Do these two know what they're in for? Have we left enough time?*

Our first objective is completed quickly, a swift five-kilometre hike to Lower Princhester Hut. We are all smiles now, but our first test for the day is imminent, a 500-metre ascent through the forested mountainside, full of tricky slips, sharp steeps and dizzying creeks. Now the real action begins.

Dad goes flying out of the traps. All that time spent mountain biking in the Mendip Hills is paying dividends. I can't believe it; he's powering up the hill as if it's nothing. *Yes! Go on, Dad!*

Keily really has to dig deep to maintain some pace. As mentioned, she's not a runner, and she doesn't hike regularly either. We've climbed a few mountains together in our time but it's been a while. Yet, on she goes, fighting with every step to climb the collapsed trails and drag her way up the near-vertical root walls.

It's tough going, and I can see they're both pushing hard. I think Dad set his sights to conquer this first and most significant ascent of the day as quickly as possible, and then hopefully bring it down a notch when things descend or level off. Keily, although struggling with her fitness, has found a zone – a horrible zone at that – but one that will keep her moving, even if she's slightly regretting her decision to come along.

I stay at the back, doing my best to provide calm support, and to keep us moving while keeping a concerned eye on my watch. Knowing Keily, the aggressive motivation that serves me well will not work for her. A much calmer, positive and quieter word will be more impactful. To be fair, most of the time, just being there is enough for most people, and not much needs to be said. Something I'd learnt from my time with Louis in the Tararuas.

On we trek, high into the heart of this twisted and tangled land, and slowly we conquer the teetering creeks and slipping roots before reaching the day's summit. There's no vast, panoramic view for us, just more of the sweaty dense forest enclosing us from the rest of the world.

We'd covered eight kilometres in two hours, not too bad considering the elevation and conditions underfoot. Keily and Dad hope that things might get a little more comfortable with the day's big ascent behind us, but looking ahead, I'm not so hopeful. The dense and boggy trail sprawls beyond. If anything, we're going to be moving slower.

You'd think the tussock knobs and crests would bring some brief forgiveness from the grappling bog, but you'd be wrong. If anything, the spongy surface, and a non-existent route almost bring progress to a standstill. Every step is a blind gamble, hoping to find some stable surface. More often than not, you get sucked to its depths, sinking into the mud to your knees and, at times, hips.

Fortunately for me, I'm more than used to the perpetual shit being doled out, but Keily and Dad are both fatigued and at their wits' end. Fatigue will do that to the best of us, break us down to muttering swears and blood boiling bursts of emotions. Yet, like the troopers they are, like the savages they have to be, they press on with steely determination.

The more you push on, the more tired you get, and the more mistakes you make. The further across this land we travel, the more frequent the shouts from someone being pulled under, and the more I turn back to see one of them hilariously disappear. That may sound a little harsh, but you have to giggle when someone switches off for just a second, and suddenly vanishes from sight. Don't doubt it, it certainly happened to me a couple of times, and those two duly laughed.

Six hours of this laboured work goes by as we cover 22 kilometres. With just two to go, our path looks clear of tussocks, which we have christened the Devil's Grass. As we continue forward, we're greeted by the sight of a cow's arse.

"Shoo!" we shout, "run along, girl," we holler. The cow doesn't budge.

We edge closer, now just a few feet away. Soon, up her head pops, annoyed to be interrupted from her grazing.

Christ, that's one pissed off cow; look at the size of its brow. Hang on...

"Shit, that's a bull." I express calmly, with what I hope sounds like a hint of authority. Keily, who's at the front of the line, turns to run back. I grab her by the backpack, bringing her to a sudden stop. "Do. Not. Run."

Carefully and slowly, with adrenaline coursing through our veins, we remove ourselves from the scene. We keep glancing over our shoulders for the sight of a head-down, charging slab of beef, but now the way ahead is blocked by more of the Devil's Bastard Grass. It's a lose-lose situation – the kind that nearly always occurs at the end of a long and knackering day.

Pushing on ahead and clear of the bull, we're treated to majestic views of the mountain range we've just conquered. Distant peaks, seemingly further than I can comprehend, occupy the horizon as whipped clouds begin to menacingly collect around their summits. The low sun descends out west, and the golden hour begins across this tranquil land. It's a perfect snapshot memory, perfected by the sight of my two companions tackling this last hurdle. Keily and Dad are both cooked, on limp mode for the duration, but they know it will soon be over.

9.00 p.m. We burst through the hut doors.

"Phil! You made it!" I yell, unable to contain my joy.

"Shhh," comes the response from the less than amused occupants, trying to get some kip.

"Phil, you made it," I whisper. Dad comes bursting through.

"Is there a shower?" he pleads in desperation.

"Dad, a shower? Out here? You're kidding, right?"

The despair across his face is answer enough as he collapses on the bench.

"Shut the door!" The disgruntled occupants shout, "the sandflies!"

We sheepishly shut the door behind us. We try to be as quiet as possible as darkness descends on the little hut, but the inevitable clanging and banging will unavoidably disturb some.

That said, one of our crew is awfully quiet. As I cook, Phil shoots video, and Keily sorts her kit for the night. But Dad just sits there, head in hands, barely making a sound, looking like he's been driven to his limits.

"You okay, Dad?"

"Son, if I ever tell you there's a little bit left in the tank, you can tell me to fuck off!"

His response is met with my rapturous laughter. Throughout my years spent playing junior football, Dad had been the team coach. There was only ever one thing he ever demanded, from us as children and, later, as young adults, and that was maximum effort and work rate.

"If you all work harder than your opposite man, we will win... When you're tired, so is your opponent, just remember," and here he would pause for effect, "there's always a little bit left in the tank."

That phrase had been etched into my brain after hearing it every Saturday for 15 years. It had been one of the motivating factors for this whole adventure. *How much is actually left in the tank? How far can I push it?* So, to hear Dad mumble those words, the man who is undoubtedly responsible for some of my madness, is just perfect.

Still, he's right, not that I could tell him to fuck off, but that there is always a little bit left. Even though he might feel he's at his limits, his body could still carry on. This isolated incident and the whole adventure act as a maxim for such a phrase. More often than not, the body will go on. It's our mind that gives in first. Just as mine had a few days ago.

Distance: 23km
Elevation: 990m.

Day 55 - 'Hard choices, easy life. Easy choices, hard life.'

Although a cold wind has descended upon these foothills, and the rain has come crashing in, it's still a sweltering night's kip; the mass of stinking sweaty bodies keeps the temperature at a sticky warmth, leaving us all terribly uncomfortable. A familiar choice: sweat inside the sleeping bag, with the lining sticking to any bare skin, or be free from its clammy grip, and cling to the horrid plastic mattress. Either way, we're in for a grim night, but at least we're not cold and wet.

We all wake with the air of unshakable tiredness that lingers after a restless and disturbed slumber. Your eyes struggle to open, and life is one endless yawn. All energy is exhausted. Phil sits rubbing his eyes, Dad stares into space, and Keily slowly potters around.

Everyone sighs simultaneously, almost in silent agreement. It's time to get on with it.

Yesterday's effort and the night with the team has almost been too perfect. I can't bring myself to leave them; the thought of going on alone fills me with a deep sadness. So much so, I'm adamant about finishing what we've started. I went into this section with them, I want to finish it with them. So I convince myself that it's OK to walk the link road out, and continue along an alternative route.

In truth, I can't bring myself to face another day alone after possibly the best section of the whole adventure. I tell myself I'm not breaking my rule. *I'll be getting there in one complete line, just along my own route.* But let's face it, I'm clearly running away from that which I fear most.

I know I've made the wrong decision, but I just do not care. In desperation, I'm taking the easy option, or rather creating an easier alternative.

'Hard choices, easy life. Easy choices, hard life.' Jerzy Gregorek's words ring true. I've created a choice: Take the easy option, and get out, or take the difficult option, and push forward. In that moment, I choose easy, and that will likely infuriate me more in the future than any amount of hardship I may face in carrying on. The pain of this failure is likely a greater burden than the temporary misery of a day's loneliness.

Once away from the foothills, it's as if I've been placed on the plains of Saskatchewan: a land so flat you can watch your dog run away for three days, or so they joke. It will be hours of laborious tarmac and gravel slapping, but at least I can meet the van at intervals. *At least I won't be alone.*

Our target is the little town of Nightcaps some 55 kilometres away, and the hours tick by with no drama, precisely what's needed to bring some calm to the early rumblings of inner turmoil. *You're not doing all this again. Just get on with it.*

We meet regularly, the team keeps me topped up, and I trundle along, happy to a certain degree, despite flickers of frustration because of my decision.

Our new route turns off the main road, along the backcountry tracks, and into Nightcaps. Keily and Jill tag along as we stroll with plenty of time left on the clock, and it's almost therapeutic.

The beloved and welcomed golden hour falls upon this boundless land, and with it comes its natural calmness, providing the perfect setting for a thoughtful and much-needed conversation. Although I'm content, this time spent walking with Keily and Jill offers the opportunity to open up a little, share my frustrations, and listen to their highly regarded counsel. Counsel that is honest and undeniably helpful to a confused and sad conscience.

I don't remember who said it, maybe my thoughts are an amalgamation of both their words, but it went a little something like this:

"Lewis, just keep going and get to Bluff. There have been good and bad choices along the way. Things will frustrate you, but look at the bigger picture, look at what you have done. No one is going to care about you missing this and that or creating your own route. What you have done and are doing is special."

I'm sure, in both a direct and roundabout way, they've all told me this many times before, but I haven't been in the right place to hear it. Now the environment, my mind, the group – everything is finally perfectly set for me to finally listen to what they have to say, without me getting in my own way. It's what I need to hear to remain focused on moving forward.

After the night in Nightcaps, there are only 180 kilometres to go!

Distance: 55km
Elevation: 248m.

Day 56 - Fairy-tale Forest

It feels as though we've been transported back to a brisk autumn day in the South West of England. It's complete darkness, not even the beginnings of a sunrise on the horizon and the clouds have moved in, delivering a drizzle to further dampen the mood.

I say the mood is damp. It's not dark and depressing, it's just another day, almost as if we're bored. With the end, hopefully, only a few days away, we feel the Groundhog Day effect. *Go and do what needs to be done.*

It was a poor night's sleep again. Now, in the darkness, it's time to knock back some porridge and don my many layers for a chilly run to rejoin the trail.

I'm used to temperatures ranging from 20 to 30 degrees Celsius, but this morning it's below five. Normal temperatures back home, but after two months of mostly warm weather, the rain and cold hit me for six.

In hindsight, I should have just braved it with shorts and a t-shirt, and maybe leggings underneath, but the desire to remain warm is too strong: under top, t-shirt, hoodie, waterproof coat, leggings, shorts and trousers, not forgetting the snood.

I head towards Wairo – another formerly bustling place which feels like a ghost town now, for some reason. From there, it's a westward turn to rejoin the trail at the foot of Woodlaw Forest. It's along these gently sloping gravel roads, after a battering from the morning drizzle, that the clouds are vapourised by the piercing the New Zealand sun. I have to strip away the layers, wearing them like a packhorse, seemingly just as hot as if I were wearing them normally.

Not only has the sweltering heat kicked in, but an abhorrent fatigue has reasserted itself. My eyes just cannot stay open. It's like that unsettling and dangerous situation you might find yourself in when driving tired, and your eyes keep slowly closing., I devise a plan to run with my eyes shut, occasionally peeking to check I'm still on the road and no farmer is hurtling towards me in their truck. I'm desperate to keep moving, and 'nap-running' seems the only choice. On Day 1, I'm pretty sure I hallucinated. Now I'm actually running while asleep!

I continue in this state until I reach the van, some 16 kilometres, and 2 hours 45 minutes, into the day. A new level of slow, but I suppose understandable, all things considered. The moment my head hits the pillow, I'm out of it, and I don't think the team even entertains the idea of waking me. Lights out.

Despite a gentle awakening, from the bleats of a thousand sheep surrounding the van, my mood is still melancholy. A change is needed to invigorate me today. What better than a stupidly steep climb? When a boost is required to obtain energy, the right amount of adversity brings it forward.

I charge up the 400-metre hill for well over an hour, listening to a podcast. Once again, lactic acid, heavy breathing and sweat are my saviours. So often it is the case, when lethargic or bored, that intense exercise is precisely the medicine needed to shake us from our funk.

The attack serves its purpose. I'm now energised and break into a run, across the tops of Twinlaw Hill and down through Woodlaw Forest, to the team waiting ten kilometres on at Scott's Gap.

We can afford for things to relax slightly. We have everything planned for the last days on the trail, - today we only have 15 kilometres to go – leaving plenty of time to reach the shorter than usual total of 45 kilometres. It's a short day because Longwood Forest looms, a 50-kilometre maze of tangled roots, overgrown bush and reputedly unidentifiable tracks. An adversary we decide deserves a full day's attention.

The relaxed and care-free atmosphere continues as Keily and Phil join me on a five-kilometre hike through a fantasy forest – the enchanting Island Bush. The dwindling afternoon sun sparkles amongst towering pines, and fairy-tale toadstools with red and white dotted caps. We share a sublime hour of friendship and conversation in this natural paradise. Again, I'm reminded that such scenes are so much better shared than experienced alone. *Part of the joy of being out here is sharing it with the people around me.*

With lifted spirits, the last of the day's kilometres are completed on a road run down to Merrivale; the starting point for tomorrow's forested maze. As I finish the last few kilometres, surrounded by magnificent deer farms below the evening sun, my mind is distracted. The stories of devastatingly slow terrain are a cause for concern. Yet, the thrill of this being my last forest, my last mini-adventure, draws out a previously deserted determination. *Get this dealt with, and the end is in sight, but it will be no easy task. You have to be on it tomorrow. I hope I make it through.*

Is the end in sight? Only 135 kilometres left to go.

Distance: 44km
Elevation: 983m.

Day 57 - Indiana Matthews

This morning Phil takes a single image that feels like it captures every aspect of what has happened, what is to come, and all that's felt, seen and heard in this exact moment. I stand facing the camera, my hood trying to hide my bedraggled face, yet my furrowed brow expresses sullenness, hiding the most jaded eyes. A terrible pre-pubescent goatee sprawls over my chin, and my pronounced monobrow tops jaded, reddened eyes. I look as though I've aged a decade as my weathered, sun-battered features reflect the extent of my fatigue and weariness. I look spent. Yet, there's a glint, a mere ounce of a grin, the slightest sparkle in my expression suggesting grit and determination and, dare I even say, joy.

It's no longer a surprise to be welcomed by a bitter chill. Of course, the rising sun will bring some warmth, just as it did yesterday, but I'm still going to run fully clad.

The trail ascends a 4x4 track that slowly deteriorates with every passing kilometre. The ruts sink deeper as the bush and trees converge, and the slips and bogs become more prevalent. The first few kilometres seem too good to be true, especially having heard what a nightmare these 50 clicks should soon become.

Promptly, I get my first taste. It's as if this giant forest is built upon a sponge. I'm faced with either sodden sinking grass, or boot-stealing bogs, wherever I run. Long gone is that beautiful 4x4 track. This is now a mad scramble. Still, as always, the adversity will keep me occupied. I'm almost finding an unlikely rhythm.

Hopscotching up the entangled gradient, I find myself in a zen and calm space. Ahead lies a tangle of moss-covered trees disappearing into the lingering fog. At my feet, the trail is scarcely identifiable, as it fades and disappears just as soon as it begins. One move in the wrong direction, and I could well be lost in this perpetual maze. Yet, it's this chaos that breeds focus, which in turn brings calmness and tranquillity.

My concentration is further heightened by the sight of three hunters up ahead. Ironically, they haven't spotted me. In my eyes-wide state, I make my approach, thoughts tumbling over each other.

What if they think I'm an animal?

I wonder how close I can get?

Isn't that a little stupid? You can see they have guns.

Don't shout. You'll spook any deer.

Shit, what do I do?

I jog forward, making enough noise that they might turn and see me, but I don't want to shout. I'll be honest, I don't hold much hope for these three hunting anything. It's not until I'm within ten metres that I simply say,

"Hello." Startled, they turn – guns down, fortunately.

"Oh, we didn't see you there," the lead hunter replies.

"I hope I haven't startled any deer on the way up. Having said that, I'm heading that way," I point along the trail, "I hope I don't scare them all off."

"Ah, no worries," the dejection on the hunter's face suggests he doesn't mean it.

With my tail between my legs, I don't hang around. I'm determined to quickly get to the meeting point, 15 kilometres in. *That's if the van has managed to get there.* Another punch from loneliness fighting for room in my brain. It has to be fought. *Someone will be there; think of all the places they've got to before. Have faith.*

Knowing, or hoping in this case, is enough to quash any rumblings of overriding loneliness. Just knowing that I will see a familiar face, just knowing that the solitude will be split by conversation and cherished company is enough to keep me moving, and more importantly, keep me sane. *They will be there, I'm sure of it.*

Now at the edges of the first knotting forest. A 200-metre tussock hillside stands ahead, and beyond that the forest road that, I hope, leads me to Phil and Jill. No Keily, or parents alas, as their bigger van just won't make it up the uneven track. With desperation, I charge, continually slipping and falling. I feel this isn't the time to carefully pick routes, it's time for head down, charge, and follow the orange poles, hoping to not lose half a leg to swamps.

My plan works, probably more by luck than design, and I'm free. With each corner I turn, I yearn for the team to be waiting. With every empty disappointment, my apprehension grows. *What if they couldn't make it? It will be another 12 kilometres to run, and still, they might not be there.*

It's a familiar mental pattern which, as ever, is only assuaged by the sight of Gerty – with Phil and Jill standing to either side of her. Despite my relief, I'm not allowed to hang around. Jill and Phil boot me out, something they've done numerous times, and are now pros at, with a mixture of authority and kindness. A potent combination and executed with such grace that it would motivate anyone to get a move on – especially with the promise of another break on the other side of the Longwood Range.

The routine continues, claustrophobic forested hillsides followed by open tussock heights, but with one slight difference. From atop Longwood Hill, I catch my first glimpse of this journey's end. The views cast far over the eastward flats and south to the Foveaux Strait. Finally, the ocean is within reach, and for the first time, I let myself genuinely accept it. *This is nearly over.*

It's an overwhelming mix of emotions, after 57 days of endless effort and pain, see where this journey will finally come to an end. I'm hit with all the highs and lows from all the way back to Cape Reinga, not knowing whether to smile or cry. My body shakes at the sight, and goosebumps coat my skin.

Bluff is still over 100 kilometres away, and there's still the matter of Longwood Forest to contend with, but the end is finally in sight. I do just enough to keep a lid on things. *Stay focused. You're not done yet.*

The trail dives to Martin's Hut. Stopping doesn't even cross my mind. The access road is just a kilometre away and, once again, I'm pleading aloud that the team will be there. When does a 'want' feel so strong that it becomes a 'need'? I'd argue never, but this is mighty close. I so deeply desire that one morsel of contact before heading into the final section, the maze-like lost world of the old gold mining water races down to Colac Bay.

Of course, they make it, this is Jill and Phil in the mighty HiAce. If anything resembles a road, they can deal with it, no trouble at all.

Now, I must admit, running around the corner to the sight of my two dear friends awaiting my arrival in the middle of nowhere, for what will likely be the last time, is enough to bring a lump to my throat. Memories from our early efforts that seem so long ago come flooding back, and I'm hit with a mix of pride and sadness. Sad that this adventure is coming to an end, but proud of the fact we've got this far.

We chat, reminisce, and I hang around for way too long, but none of us really cares. We're cherishing the moment, ignoring the familiar pressure of each minute lost. *This is the last time it will be just the three of us.*

Eventually, time dictates that I get a move on and, with my courage soaring, I rise and burst through the gap in the trees, determined to attack whatever lies ahead with vigour. *Come on, Lewis, come on! Make the most of this because soon, it will all be over.*

I've been thrust into the set of an Indiana Jones movie. Thick forest consumes any remnants of the old water races, and the meandering trenches have been reclaimed by ferns and moss and other flora. The trail criss-crosses with the channels, twisting down the hillside, providing challenging but engrossing terrain for this push to the coast. It's going to be a good old race against the sun again.

Matching the water that once flowed, the trail repeats its twists down the hillside. Despite the intensity demanded by such a route, the novelty quickly wears off. Dip, turn, run, climb, dip, turn, run, climb... and on it goes, kilometre after kilometre, hour after hour. Initially, it's fun. I feel as though I can attack. However, after an hour, and having only covered six kilometres of the 25, I succumb to the hypnotic charms of this mesmeric forest. I'm occupied by the woodland's demands, but all thought is lost to its never-ending cycle of *dip, turn, run, climb, dip, turn, run, climb...*

Old foes resurface. My watch tries to lure me to take a little peek, and my phone burns in my pocket, beckoning me to look at the map. However, I resist temptation. *You know you're on the right trail, and you know not to look.* Inevitably, the pull becomes too much, but at least I've stretched it out enough to not be dismayed by the unmoved tiny blue dot.

I conquer the Ports Water Race Track in a little over three hours, pretty good going in the end.

I sit and wait for pick up, and for once, I've stopped, not just in body but in mind. There are no rushed and worried thoughts, no planning for tomorrow, just peace and quiet. For the first time since tapping that pole back below the lighthouse, I feel peaceful. Perhaps a day of memories has served as closure for my frustrations, reminding me of what an outrageous and fantastic journey this has been. Yet, we're not done. There are still 85 kilometres to go down to Bluff, and my mind is made up.

It might be a double marathon, but I will end this tomorrow.

Distance: 48km
Elevation: 1317m.

Day 58 - Redemption

You've got this far. You're nearly at the end. There have been great moments, sad moments, and everything in between. You have failed and succeeded. But today, you redeem yourself, not to anyone else but yourself. The decision is made. *I will make it to Bluff before midnight.* Why? Redemption.

In truth, I'm still a little angry, still disappointed that we've failed. I'm left frustrated at our luck, and maybe our decisions, but mainly at the fact I'd turned back in Ahuriri Valley. The dark cloud from that day still hangs over my head, and it will be a very long time before it departs. It's important to note that, to me, it doesn't matter what other people think of our failures. What matters most is how I feel about my own conduct and, just maybe, I can find some solace in one last great effort. I can, at least, start making amends by doing my longest run to date, and getting this thing finished. I want to show myself that I can still be a savage!

I must add that this decision to do a double marathon is time-sensitive. We only have two days available, and I don't want to wake up the next day having to run 20 or 30 kilometres. I want us to have a full day off in Queenstown as a reward. *Time to get a move on.*

It's 8 a.m. The team drop me back at Longwood Forest car park, and everything feels a little strange. Running all day, and barely doing anything else, has become life, and now it's happening for the last time.

With a mixture of delight and despondency, I begin this mammoth day by running the road to Colac Bay. My nerves are piqued, and it shows as I set off at pace, making it back to camp before the team have even got themselves sorted. Not to worry, I'm moving fast and don't want to stop.

I have to laugh. The contrast with the start of our adventure is stark. On the Northland's tropical beaches, the hot sun shone brightly and the sea breeze gently floated in. Two months later, down here on Colac Bay, in the stern and rugged Southland, I'm getting battered by the biting Atlantic air, as the sun cowers behind the clouds, and barely a yard of firm sand presents itself. 90 Mile Beach doesn't seem so bad at this point.

Eventually, I leave the sluggish, soft sand behind, only to be buffeted by howling winds, over the undulating cliffs and bluffs. Te Araroa continues to test my resolve. Nevertheless, I am moving forward, and today that's all that matters.

I have decided, *que sera, sera - what will be, will be* - and my relaxed approach is matched by the team, as I bundle into the quiet and quaint harbour town of Riverton. We're all smiles, the pressure is off, and there's no rush to push on.

Mum personifies this calm and steady approach, as she looks out on the tranquil Riverton harbour. Despite all the action and, at times, frantic efforts going on around us, she's maintained the same beat and pattern since arriving. She's happy to be here, happy to be part of her son's adventure, and whether she knows it or not, her stillness seems to keep everyone ticking along. By being steady, everyone can get on with what needs to be done, safe in the knowledge that the things we often forget or neglect will be picked up by Mum.

But of course, the peace can only last so long. I say there's no pressure, but the trail has to be completed by midnight. Next up, a 22-kilometre beach run.

The soft sand, crosswind and unchanging scenes are enough to sap every ounce of energy from my dwindling reserves. *You're back in that familiar but horrible place, Lewis, and how could you forget? One foot in front of the other, it's got you this far.*

Three and a half hours! Three and a half hours to run – well run, walk and stumble the 22 kilometres. I finally arrive at the vans, dejected and beaten. Beaten by the relentless jabs pounding at my mind until it turned to mush. I can barely bring myself to talk, let alone move, as I sit on the step staring vacantly at the sand being blown across my feet. *I'm only halfway through.*

I've been in this position before, floating through the forest on the outskirts of Lake Sumner and, just as then, food is the answer.

It's coming up to 4 p.m. If I want any chance of covering the same distance again, I need to rejuvenate. If I don't, I won't even make it to the end of the road, let alone Bluff. Luckily, with the van comes Jill's Magic Porridge. That and some leftover pasta, plenty of trail mix, and some chocolate to top things off. Rejuvenated? Barely. Moving? Just, but that's enough.

From the beach, the Te Araroa heads inland and west towards Invercargill. There's nothing particularly exciting to tell about the next 20 kilometres, just an uninspiring plod, with all my classic mind games at play. A solitary shuffle along paved footpaths to reach my next destination, broken by a brief stop and more food, before heading on again for another ten kilometres. Each session takes me that little bit closer to Bluff.

Once clear of Invercargill, with the sun dipping to darkness at around 8.20 p.m., the mission is clear. Complete the last 20 kilometres in less than 3 hours and 40 minutes. The big question is whether I can make it.

Today's distance is a distance I've never run before, on the most tired legs I could ever imagine. The previous ten kilometres were spent in a continuous yawn. I can barely keep my eyes open. Yet, I have a saving grace to support me. Keily has donned her running gear and is ready to drag me down Bluff Highway. Whatever happens, no matter how shattered I might well be, this team will not let me fail. They will do what it takes to get me there.

With our fluorescent jackets on, and head torches to light the way, we begin our approach to Bluff, and most of our mental resources are occupied by not getting run over. If anything, it's probably best for the darkness to fall, we can see any vehicles approaching, and they can see our head torches shining brightly from a distance.

I'm cooked. We run for 50 metres before my tank is all but empty, bringing me back to a struggling walk. To be honest, we spend most of the time walking; it's all I can muster. Occasionally I rouse myself to push a little further, but that's it.

Keily plays her role perfectly, no whooping and hollering, no manic cheering, just an ear to listen, and a gentle push when required. A simple "come on," or "keep going," is enough. These last 20 kilometres could have been the loneliest of them all if it wasn't for Keily. In a moment of struggle, in a moment of fragility, she's by my side, keeping me moving forward.

Upon reaching the final town of Bluff and with only four kilometres to go, Keily's job is done. She wants to keep running, and maybe I should say yes, but I want to tackle this alone. The truth is, I want her to be at the end with the team, it's how I've dreamed it'll be.

I've thought about this moment many times. I've seen myself running through the town, as the locals go about their day, and the tourists flock to South Island's iconic southern tip. The sun is setting, beautiful colours dance across the sky, and I bound my final steps, ending this adventure to a chorus of rapturous applause.

In reality, the tourists are long gone, and the locals have gone to bed. The sun is set, and the beautiful colours are lost to the dark night's sky. My bounding steps look more like a shuffle, and it's only my lonely figure that plods through the silent streets. Quite a fitting end, perhaps. Yet, this solitude does give me the time to be alone with my thoughts and think back on this mad but wonderful adventure.

This was once just an idea said aloud in a coffee shop, and now here I am, running through the streets of Bluff about to finish it all.

This may not have gone anything like you planned, and you may not have had the success you were hoping for, but, Lewis, today you can stand with your head held high, knowing you gave it your all. Well done, Lewis, well bloody done.

Everything is silent. The claps and cheers have stopped. I take my last steps.

'Ping!' The sound of my hand hitting the pole sends a familiar shiver down my spine – except this time, it signals the end, not the beginning, of my monumental adventure.

Everything is paused. For a second, nothing happens.

I stand staring at the team as I try to collect my thoughts, but I'm frozen. I don't know what to think, and I don't know what to do. For 58 days, my life has been dictated by a single purpose, but now that has all moved on.

It feels like an age but, eventually, Keily steps forward, and Mum and Dad soon follow. That's when it all hits. The emotions of the last two years come flooding up, and I can't contain them. We hug for an age, and it's a hug I will never forget.

I turn to Phil and Jill, and a giant smile breaks across my face. We embrace. A year ago, Jill was just a client and Phil, I didn't even know. Yet, today, I can honestly say they are two of my dearest friends. An unbreakable bond has been forged between the three of us through this beautiful but brutal experience. If it wasn't for them, I simply would not have made it. I hope they know how grateful I really am.

So, have I redeemed myself? Well, no, because there's nothing to redeem. I was looking to save my integrity, but I'd never lost it. The actions and decisions of the past cannot be affected by the actions we take today. It's merely the act of continuing, of getting back up and going again, that upholds our integrity.

If you have got this far then, between you and me, we can change this chapter's title. It's less about redemption and more about learning, reacting and making progress. It is commonly said failure is an excellent opportunity to learn and improve, and I believe that to be true. Yet, it takes action on our part to identify our failure, take on the knowledge from it, and turn it into an actionable response.

Marcus Aurelius' words, 'The impediment to action advances action. What stands in the way becomes the way.' still rings true. That which stopped us within ourselves is the direction we must go, this time armed with the knowledge and experience gained from our last encounter. The fact that we are continuing to try, that we learn and move forward, and that we have the will to continue fighting the good fight, despite our own failures and any external influences, is what upholds our integrity.

Perhaps this chapter should be renamed 'Progression.' Whatever its title, I have learned so much on this adventure, gained so much and seen so much. I tried to run really far and, you know what? I did. I really did.

Distance: 82km
Elevation: 560m.

Epilogue

Thank you for picking up this book and reading this far. I hope you've found something of value in its pages.

In some of our endeavours, we failed. In others, I like to think we were successful. Clearly, we failed to set a new record time for completing the trail. In fact, we didn't even complete the trail to its fullest. Yet, when it comes to raising money and awareness for our chosen charity, we've had some success. Although, our efforts have been hampered by the pandemic. I would also like to think this story will inspire some, and maybe even elicit just a morsel of emotion in others.

This book attempts to share the experiences as I lived them and collates my thoughts upon reflection. I hope these final words can refine the lessons each wonderful region of the Te Araroa Trail taught me, and hopefully, they might help you too.

To me, the structure of this story and the lessons in each region are transferable to any challenges we might face. Hell, I'm writing this book during a pandemic. In fact, aiming to survive and hoping to thrive in these torrid times requires many of the characteristics I had to discover and draw on. More to the point, any challenge we face may be navigated with more success if we can utilise each lesson.

The defining characteristic of the Northland is perseverance. For adversity to be overcome, and for any challenge to be conquered, continued and consistent effort is a minimum requirement. No greatness has ever been achieved, nor innovation created, without comprehensive effort, regardless of the setbacks that inevitably come our way. Life is hard. It always has been, and so it should be. Through perseverance come the rewards of improvement, progression and finally reflective joy. Effort should not be something we dislike and avoid because, from it, we eventually find contentment and love. Through effort we make progress and grow.

Through perseverance, we find traction, which we use to settle into a routine and develop a process, just as we did through Auckland. Yet, it takes regular observations, and reflection upon our actions, to refine and further develop an optimal method for success. If we just blindly carry on, we might get lucky, but we give ourselves a much better chance to make progress through thoughtful discovery and planning.

We must try to remain objective and not be negatively influenced by our subjective input. How often do we get in the way of our own progress? By this, I mean it's us who apply the labels of good and bad. We add our emotions to events. Now, we cannot eliminate this, it's human nature to have an emotional reaction, but can we manage it? If we can acknowledge how the event makes us feel, accept it, but then use logic to observe and work with that which is in front of us, we stand a much better chance of making progress.

In this adventure, as in life, there were always things outside of our control. We are ultimately at nature's mercy. At times this can be a challenging idea to accept. Some of us are so consumed by our desire to control outcomes, we cannot accept this isn't always possible. From the storms that obstructed our path, to other people's thoughts and choices, these are things beyond our control.

In some instances, we might hold some influence but ultimately, no power. Though this can be a positive. By recognising that our control is limited to what we think and do, we eliminate many worries. Yet, it isn't always that easy. The process of knowing this and accepting it can take time, as is evident throughout this story. But it is a fight worth fighting.

Some of us may well be introverted and love to spend time alone, yet who we are today will have been affected by the social interactions we have experienced. The likelihood is that any success you own is not down to you alone. Maybe you had a great teacher who instilled self-belief and knowledge, helping an idea come to fruition ten or twenty years later. Perhaps your parents gave you guidance and encouragement, and inspired you through all of your endeavours. No matter what examples of success and progress we look at, we can always find support there, somewhere in the storyline. On this journey, I highlighted it down in Wellington, yet it was clearly in effect throughout. All the way back to the lessons learnt from my dad on the football field, many years ago. Support is inevitable in any successful endeavour. We should seek it, find it, give it and embrace it.

Even with the range of support we might gain over the years, the weight of responsibility still falls on our shoulders. If you're in a bad situation, even one not of your own making, it's still your responsibility to solve the problem. We have two choices; play victim to our position or step up to the plate and own it. I think it is clear which one will lead to progress and success. Some people may see this weight as a burden, as a negative. However, once you accept responsibility, you acquire the freedom to make choices. You are no longer shielded, nay shackled, by the veil of victimhood. It sounds like a scary weight to hold but, once on your shoulders, it's yours to take action upon.

In our endeavours, we will undoubtedly come across distractions which might veer us off course. These distractions may come from our own impulses, such as seeking comfort and pleasure or avoiding effort and discomfort. Yet, we know they will ultimately be to the detriment of our progression. Distractions pull us in. The allure of pleasure, and the temporary convenience of avoiding adversity, divert us from our goals. Deep down, we know these desires will ultimately hurt us. It is up to us to remain astute and robust in our morals. To stay the course and uphold our integrity. This isn't easy, and sometimes we fail. Yet our integrity grows stronger each time we get back from the grips of our impulses.

Part of this struggle with our integrity is to accept our failure. How often do we become consumed with our faults? How often does this fixation help? We can sit and stew all day long, lamenting our shortcomings and leaning into the vicious cycle that paralyses our progress. Or we can break from this carrousel by accepting that that which is in the past cannot be changed. It is not enough to just blindly accept that we messed up again and carry on with our lives. We have to acknowledge our mistakes, study them, analyse them, and learn from them to find the resolve not to fall prey to such distractions and impulses in the future.

As I ran through the Southland, I genuinely thought I was out to redeem myself. Even as I structured this book and wrote the last chapter, I still thought this to be true. It was only in the last few days, nearly a year after finishing the run, that I realised this was not the case. I might have used redemption as motivation, but in the grand scheme of this adventure, and on the bigger scale of my life, my journey through this stunning region was about learning from past failures and implementing an actionable response. It was about making progress. It's often said that 'knowledge is power,' but it would be more accurate to say, 'knowledge is potential power,' and that action unlocks it. We might know where we've gone wrong, but what's the point if we do nothing about it?

I think it is fair to say that progress is part of our human nature. Don't most of us want to do better, be better and help everyone else do the same? We can be grateful for where and who we are but still desire to improve and change. With that in mind, is life not one enduring challenge, one great game, full of big and small obstacles along the way, often simultaneously?

I've come to see these principles ever-present in all challenges I face. From the smallest difficulties each day, to the largest projects over the years to come, I'm somewhere along this cycle, reminding myself to use the principles described. In one aspect of my life, I may be in the process of accepting a failure. In another, I might be getting my head down as I begin to persevere. In a project, I might have developed a working process and now find myself having to avert from impulses and stay the course.

Multiple plates are spinning for all of us as many obstacles lie in our way. My final thoughts are for us to look at how we perceive such obstacles and the principles to overcome them. Do we view them as adverse problems or positive opportunities?

What about what it takes to overcome them? Life and its challenges often take grit, pain, and a whole host of discomforts to succeed, so should we view these requirements with fear and hatred, or with a grin across our face?

I propose we change our relationship with challenges and obstacles to one that sees the opportunity, for on the other side is progress. I suggest we view the price we have to pay, not as a negative sum, but as a positive vehicle, for it is this which carries us forward. We should seek discomfort, if necessary and useful, with a smile on our face, because as we know, ahead lies progress.

To say the team returned home to their normal lives would be wonderful to write, but as we all know, a global pandemic had other ideas. Much like the rest of the world we didn't really know what was in store. We landed back in the UK, expecting to return to work and some semblance of normality, but within two weeks we were confined to our homes. Keily and Jill - both key workers - had to carry on whilst the rest of us got to put our feet up. Perhaps that's exactly what I needed.

During the first four weeks of lockdown, I barely moved. Keily would leave for work and return to find me sitting exactly where she left me. I could barely stir myself to make a sandwich, let alone go for my allotted one hour walk. I was physically depleted but, quite shockingly, I didn't want to do anything but sit alone as the days passed by without me noticing. Eventually, I managed a walk around the block and held a conversation with a neighbour from a distance. My road to recovery had begun.

Despite the tumultuous 18 months that we have all lived through, it hasn't all been doom and gloom. Jill has become a grandmother again and has moved herself closer to the sea. I do wonder if our time spent on such glorious beaches has drawn her to such a wonderful move.

Exciting news for Phil - he has his first child on the way. So, it's straight from one mad adventure into probably life's greatest. I am truly delighted for Phil and Lauren – they will be fantastic parents. I think Lewis or Louise would be a fantastic name.

As for Keily and I, we've started our own little adventure. Earlier in the book I mentioned our favourite coffee shop, Strangers With Coffee. Well, we are no longer customers, but proud owners of the shop we love. So do pop your head in if you're ever in town. I won't lie, Keily is the boss, I just drink and eat my profits away!

What next? Is there another adventure on the horizon?

A few ideas tumble around my head, and daydreams burn a desire for more. I'm certain more challenges await, but what and when I do not know. One thing is for sure, when the time comes Phil and Jill will be the first people I call.

Lightning Source UK Ltd.
Milton Keynes UK
UKHW011302021221
394963UK00005B/249